Naturalism and Social
Philosophy

ESSEX STUDIES IN CONTEMPORARY CRITICAL THEORY

Series Editors: Peter Dews, Professor of Philosophy at the University of Essex; Lorna Finlayson, Lecturer in Philosophy at the University of Essex; Fabian Freyenhagen, Professor of Philosophy at the University of Essex; Steven Gormley, Lecturer in Philosophy at the University of Essex; Timo Jütten, Senior Lecturer in Philosophy at the University of Essex; and Jörg Schaub, Lecturer in Philosophy at the University of Essex.

The Essex Studies in Contemporary Critical Theory series aims to develop the critical analysis of contemporary societies. The series publishes both substantive critical analyses of recent and current developments in society and culture and studies dealing with methodological/conceptual problems in the Critical Theory tradition, and is intended to further enhance the ability to address the problems of contemporary society.

Naturalism and Social Philosophy

Contemporary Perspectives

Edited by
Martin Hartmann and Arvi Särkelä

ROWMAN & LITTLEFIELD
Lanham • Boulder • New York • London

Published by Rowman & Littlefield
An imprint of The Rowman & Littlefield Publishing Group, Inc.
4501 Forbes Boulevard, Suite 200, Lanham, Maryland 20706
www.rowman.com

86-90 Paul Street, London EC2A 4NE

British Library Cataloguing in Publication Information available

Library of Congress Cataloging-in-Publication Data is available

ISBN 9781538174920 (cloth) | ISBN 9781538174937 (epub)

♾™ The paper used in this publication meets the minimum requirements of American National Standard for Information Sciences—Permanence of Paper for Printed Library Materials, ANSI/NISO Z39.48-1992.

Contents

Chapter 1

Naturalism and Social Philosophy

An Introduction

Martin Hartmann and Arvi Särkelä

In everyday discourse, social science, and social philosophy, a "naturalistic" vocabulary of social critique is commonplace: social entities are critically characterized as "alienated," "petrified," "dead," or "ill." "Social pathology" seems to have taken on the role of an umbrella term for such social states. In addition to this, a peculiar feature of social philosophy is that, often, particularly in the attempts to distinguish it from moral and political philosophy, it articulates its method and subject matter in naturalistic terms: social philosophy "diagnoses" or even "cures" the "pathology," "anomie," or "alienation" of "the social organism," "social life," or "second nature" (Honneth 2007, 2009, 2014; see also Freyenhagen 2015; Hirvonen 2018; Laitinen 2015; Laitinen & Särkelä 2019; Neuhouser 2016; Särkelä 2018; Särkelä & Laitinen 2019). However, while in other philosophical disciplines, such as philosophy of science, ethics, and metaphysics, there are numerous debates about the meaning of "naturalism," in social philosophy it is not generally regarded as a position to be taken seriously.[1] While the "naturalistic" vocabulary plays such a crucial role in the practice of social criticism, it is surprising that social philosophers have not inquired so much into the naturalistic commitments of their discipline. After all, it might be that the naturalistic vocabulary of social criticism turns out to be not merely metaphorical; perhaps this vocabulary even carries part of social philosophy's critical weight. Is the social philosopher's evaluative approach to social reality dependent upon some conception of nature (including nature's relation to social life)? Philosophical social criticism would, then, turn out to be at least partly committed to naturalism in one way or another.

To tackle these questions, this volume sets for itself the task to introduce and discuss the naturalistic bearings of modern and contemporary social philosophy. The three main issues to be dealt with concern the general relation of social philosophy to various naturalistic perspectives implicitly present in the social-philosophical approaches themselves or taken up as external positions for (mostly critical) confrontation (a); analyzing the possibility of a refined progressive naturalistic vocabulary as a tool of social critique (b); and reemphasizing the relevance for recent Critical Theory to take up and confront the challenges posed by the naturalistic approaches in ethics and in the wider sciences as well as in current crises such as climate change (c). The contributions of this volume are briefly sketched in section (d).

(A)

The title of this book is *Naturalism and Social Philosophy*. We suggest that social philosophy is treated as a philosophical and social-theoretical discipline in its own right that should not be reduced to the perspective of moral or political philosophy. While moral philosophy, roughly, analyzes the conditions for claiming an act as right or wrong, political philosophy analyzes the conditions for claiming an act or an institutional arrangement as just or unjust, legitimate or illegitimate. As a helpful initial pragmatic hypothesis, open enough to encompass the diverse perspectives in this book, we follow Axel Honneth in defining social philosophy as the discipline analyzing social processes that either enhance or obstruct the possibility for the members of a society to lead a good life (Honneth 2007; see also Fischbach 2009).

Naturalism is not a rigid term and comes in many conceptual shapes (for a helpful overview see De Caro & Macarthur, eds., 2010). Instead of supplying one general definition to support the various approaches taken up in this volume, it will be better to leave the specification of naturalism to be developed from within these approaches themselves (see section d). Of course, on a very general plane, naturalistic social philosophies converge in treating human beings as part of nature but, as Bernard Williams has pointed out, it is not easy to stabilize which idea of nature is at work even on this general plane (1995, 102). What's more, in its capacity for non-genetic learning, human nature appears to essentially develop within cultural and social contexts that require their own specific methods and instruments of analysis.[2] While this outlaws a narrow physicalistic reductionism as relevant to social philosophy (accordingly, none of the approaches in this volume identifies naturalism with this sort of reductionism), it certainly raises the stakes of recognizing what is particularly natural in the various social arrangements under consideration in social philosophy. Put differently, the naturalizing talk will be put aside as merely metaphorical unless it can be shown to rest on a conceptual basis that allows one to develop an account of naturalism fully compatible with the fact of culture as essential to human beings.

One obvious way of doing so is to call certain cultural achievements *second natural*, but it is important to emphasize that the accounts of second nature are not absolved from clarifying in which ways what is the second natural is still natural. Habits, for example, may be called the second natural in appearing necessary or lacking a particular type of historicity (forgetting or ignoring the historicity of a recurring act is, as it were, essential for a psychological tendency to stabilize it as a habit). But is this felt necessity more than just analogous to the necessity ascribed by modern science to natural phenomena? Is it even analogous? After all, the impression of compulsion or even just normality generated by deep-seated habits is, if looked at from a critical perspective, illusory. Habits are contingent and have a history (sometimes a microhistory) of their own. What then makes them second *natural*? The simple answer is: that depends on what we understand nature to be and whether we are ready to *pluralize* our understanding of what it means for something to be natural. As will become obvious in this volume, social philosophers embrace this pluralization of nature and naturalism and thus do not only reject narrow physicalistic models of nature, whenever they are taken to be the only acceptable approach, but also find fault with evolutionary models of the Darwinian kind that come with their own variant of reductionism.

True, this means that the contours of naturalism at stake in social philosophy sometimes remain vague and imprecise. But vagueness need not mean weakness. Rather, it seems very much in place when inquiry not only confronts with a highly complex topic but with a phenomenon undergoing rapid and radical change, such as it is arguably the case with our relation to nature.

If we accept, then, that human beings are part of nature, there is no reason to assume that being part of nature will not have an impact on the social arrangements and institutions set up by them. Even Williams accepts that there may be some biological constraints on social arrangements and adds that some patterns of human behavior some of us seem capable of adopting or that others have actually adopted appear to be "biologically discouraged" in the long historical run (1995, 108). However, he is careful to emphasize that we need to read the historical record well to make such judgments and that there is no other way in order to derive simpler, more straightforward, and uncontroversial biological constraints on social arrangements. Put differently, whatever we take human nature to be is expressed through conventions with a history in need of careful analysis: categories such as *the* natural or *the* biological cannot be extricated or abstracted from this analysis. In a similar vein, Sally Haslanger has recently suggested (2012, 192) that when we classify or distinguish a phenomenon as "natural," say as a penis or as a (biological) sex, we articulate certain purposes or reflect social pressures that lead us to make the distinctions in the first place. In some contexts, it might be reasonable to define "penis" or "sex" in physical terms, in others it might be wrong or deeply problematic. In this sense, social philosophy is not inimi-cal to naturalism as such; it just calls for embedding accounts of nature and biology in historical or sociological narratives that absorb given complexities and shy away from easy and sweeping generalizations.

In this sense, it is one of the tasks of social philosophy to sensitize us to the many pitfalls attached to naturalistic accounts of human nature. To offer one last example, Tommie Shelby, in his *Dark Ghettos*, critically introduces what he calls the "medical model" as an analytic tool used in studying poverty and crime-ridden ghettos in North America. According to this model, the policy-oriented approach to studying the ghetto is this:

> Describe some salient and disconcerting features of ghettos (the prevalence of impoverished single-mother families and youth violence). Identify the linchpin that keeps ghettos in place (joblessness and segregation). And then propose a cost-effective solution that would remove this linchpin (a jobs program or an integration initiative). (2016, 2)

Shelby calls this model "medical" because it takes certain features of the ghetto as given and suggests local reforms that alleviate some of the bur-dens that allegedly keep the ghetto poor, as opposed to inquiring about more fundamental and structural problems of American society that lead to the existence of ghettos in the first place. In the same way, a physician diagnoses an illness by taking basic human functions as given and neglects the larger background of physical health. Even if it is correct, then, to treat the medical model as metaphorical, it is important to understand that the model produces its own cognitive biases and thus prevents some important questions from even being asked. Naturalistic vocabulary, one might say, discloses some aspects of reality as much as it forecloses some other aspects of reality; it serves as a potent critical tool as much as it discourages the use of certain critical stances.

(B)

The claim that a refined naturalistic vocabulary may carry some of the weight of social philosophy's critical stance is most openly embraced by ethical naturalists of an Aristotelian bent such as Philippa Foot or Sabina Lovibond. Non-Aristotelian approaches will find it more difficult to derive normative principles from naturalistic assumptions. Take the case of climate change: we obviously can and do emit excessive levels of carbon dioxide. But we seem to have reached a stage where biological reasons, among many others, begin to speak against further increasing or even just keeping the current emittance levels, reminding us, as it were, that our complex cultural practices have a natural base that enables and upholds them. Clearly, the way of life of most of the rich industrialized countries of the world is biologically unadvisable, to say the least. The decisive question for a naturalistically minded social philosophy is whether the natural sources or preconditions of these practices, arrangements, and institutions really generate the distinctive standards of evaluation that seem to be at work when we call a society or a social arrangement "sick," "ill," or "pathological." It might seem that, unless we can prove that it really makes sense to apply biological theory or language to human affairs in an attempt to vindicate the claim that societies are, among many other things, also organisms, it will be difficult if not impossible to develop a truly naturalistic normative language of more than metaphorical reach. Consequently, Honneth at times seems ready to endorse a full (functionalist) social organicism. When we call a society "ill" or label contradictions between institutionalized forms of material production and the values and norms fueling and backing them "pathological," the

> parallel to the living organism that comes to the surface in such formulations is not arbitrary and cannot be avoided. One can only eventually speak of "diseases of society" coherently and substantially enough if one represents the society as an organism in which the individual spheres or subsystems, thought of as organs, are cooperating so harmoniously that we can work out an idea of its unhindered, "free" development." (Honneth 2014, 701)

Of course, the fact that biological or organicist vocabulary seems unavoidable does not necessarily imply that societies really *are* organisms; Honneth, it appears, is reluctant to engage in deeper ontological commitments and settles with the apparent need of organicist images as we attempt to understand, say, the ruptures between evident functional social requirements and their accompanying normative frame (for a more literalist reading of Honneth, see Särkelä and Laitinen 2019). But even if we merely stay within the realm of analogy or "parallel," the powerful status that much naturalist vocabulary enjoys in critical social theory suggests that it could be fruitful to discuss, once more, the idea that "there is not one but many ways of being nature (e.g. physical, organic, mental, social)" (Laitinen and Särkelä 2018, 24) and conceptualize various forms of illness (with the quotation marks finally gone) as pertinent to some of these differing ways. Seen in this light, nature should no longer just be seen as a "'tap' to provide inputs to production and also as a 'sink' to absorb the latter's waste" (Fraser 2018, 35) but as a condition of possibility for all forms of economic, social, and cultural life; accepting this, in turn, might generate a more nuanced normative vocabulary beyond the well-established die-hard forms of biological racism, sexism, or ethnocentrism, or the typical forms of an industry- or market-driven forgetfulness of the limitations of natural resources. It might then make sense to allow societies to grow or stagnate, to flourish or wither, to be healthy or ill, to degenerate or transform by adapting to new environments.

(C)

As indicated, the term social philosophy is used in a very broad sense in this volume; however, part of the inspiration for the volume is also to reassess the relation of naturalism to the type of social philosophy developed within the Critical Theory tradition of the Frankfurt School. The relation of Critical Theory to variants of naturalism is fragile, to say the least. In other words, it might not be self-evident at all to speak of the social philosophy of the Frankfurt School tradition of Critical Theory and naturalism in one breath. It suffices to remind us that one of the starkest critiques the *Dialectic of Enlightenment* articulated was that "any attempt to break the compulsion of nature by breaking nature only succumbs more deeply to that compulsion" (Horkheimer and Adorno 2002, 9). To be sure, the compulsion generated by the enlightened attempt to break nature was not exactly the same compulsion the enlightened mind originally responded to. Mythical nature was not treated as the unified, disenchanted, and law-like nature Enlightenment had set up in its attempt to systematize its approach to the world at large. But whatever the difference in the respective notions of compulsion might have been, if the enlightened world was seen as unfree and governed by its own variant of a "fated necessity," it was because it had never managed to truly emancipate itself from the relentless system of natural bondage exerted in its own name, masquerading as the liberation of humankind from the thralls of nature. Given this, nature is anathema to the truly enlightened mind, and the critical theorist representing this mind will have to devise conceptual means to analyze the continuing spell of natural compulsion in order to loosen its grip. Thus, as aporetic and unfathomable as the project of the *Dialectic of Enlightenment* might be, it can be read as a critique of the naturalistic mind that does not recognize itself to be what it really is: unfree in having extended its stance toward outer nature to inner human nature, thereby totalizing nature's realm of unfreedom (see Honneth's reading of the *Dialectic of Enlightenment* in 1991, ch. 2).

The problem with this story is that it cannot be the whole story about the relation of Critical Theory to naturalistic approaches in philosophy and science. For one thing, though it might be correct to point out that the developments broached in the *Dialectic of Enlightenment* lack specifiable historical dates (Schnädelbach 1992), what is narrated is still a history of the different stances adopted toward nature by pre-enlightened and enlightened humanity. In a way, then, even this most somber work of Critical Theory contains a *plurality* of conceptions of nature guiding different approaches toward nature—from within and without. Just think of the one positive figure of speech mentioned in the book, the virtually untranslatable "remembrance of nature within the subject" (*Eingedenken der Natur im Subjekt*) (Horkheimer and Adorno 2002, 32). Obviously, this remembered nature (to be remembered in response to earlier oblivion) is not to be the nature brought to nomological order by the modern natural sciences. But what then does this remembered nature, opposed as such to the principle of domination and escaping, if taken up in thought, "the spell of nature by confessing itself to be nature's own dread of itself" really amount to? Is its dreadfulness truer than its conquerable law-like character? Truer in what sense? Whatever the answer to these questions is, early Critical Theory has always treated human beings as part of nature and conceptualized the catastrophe of the seemingly enlightened mind as resulting from forgetting, ignoring, or combatting this fact.

Later Critical Theory, in its many Kantian, Hegelian, or linguistic turns, has pushed this dimension far into the background of the research agenda—one of the many reasons for its virtual silence on the climate problematic. Part of the problem can be traced to Habermas's attempt to disentangle instrumental from communicative reason and push mankind's engagement with nature to the outer edges of social theory, by associating it with the need of any society to continuously reproduce itself in material terms. In a way, instrumental rationality took care of what was left of nature in Critical Theory's attempt to break the spell of historical materialism and introduce an independent sphere of symbolically structured communicative reason. Thus, even though Habermas, in *Truth and Justification*, endorsed what he termed a "weak naturalism" (Habermas 2003a, 32–40), it came as a surprise when he linked his reflections on genetic engineering in *The Future of Human Nature* to a full-blown "ethics of the species," stipulating that our moral consciousness as autonomous human beings rests on a background of "nature-like growth" so far not at our disposal (Habermas 2003b, 42). Habermas's idea was that the morally relevant notion of being the author of one's own life rests on the assumption that no other human force intervenes in shaping the basic parameters of our personality. Put differently, that something has naturally grown and is not made by humans (as in genetic programming) is decisive for our species' self-understanding, as it allows us to clearly demarcate the merely given natural sphere from the realm of human intervention, in which autonomy is defined as a space of reasons governing decisions that are autogenous and cannot be referred back to the will of others tampering with our biology. This volume takes up the cue supplied by Habermas in *The Future of Human Nature* in reemphasizing Critical Theory's need to better reflect its relation to the concept of nature and to the naturalistic approaches in ethics and other scientific disciplines. Thus, what this volume aspires to is to renew a twisted debate within older critical social philosophies and bring it into contact with contemporary standards of argumentation.

(D)

The book has three parts. The first part focuses on two promising historical strategies of naturalizing social philosophy: conceiving the social as "second nature" or in terms of "forms of life." The authors of these chapters look back at these historical attempts in order to draw valuable lessons for contemporary naturalism in social philosophy.

In the second chapter, "Second Nature: The Profound Depths of a Philosophical Key Term," Axel Honneth starts by giving a historical overview of the social-philosophical use of the concept of second nature. Starting with Aristotle's rather affirmative view of a liberating second nature and Augustine's negative view of a corrupting second nature, Honneth discusses Hegel, Marx, Lukács, Adorno, and Dewey as distinct social philosophers of second nature. From this overview, Honneth concludes that four valuable lessons can be drawn for naturalism in social philosophy: first, it is important to distinguish "second nature" in the sense of individual habitual practice from "second nature" in the sense of the societal reality itself taking on a natural character; both conceptions of second nature also depend on different conceptions of "first nature." Second, a historically informed philosophy of second nature today has to do justice both to Aristotle's affirmative and Augustine's negative view of second nature; this involves grasping our ethical socialization as a fallible process. Third, the Marxist suspicion of the fetish character of second nature is still significant today as a check on the motivation content of ethical practices. Finally, Dewey's more differentiated account of nature warns against the dangers of reproducing the dualism between nature and culture in the distinction between first and second nature; a processual view of nature aware of the reflexive character of natural sciences, Honneth argues, can help avoid the oscillation between the Aristotelian and the Newtonian conceptions of nature.

Thomas Khurana takes a deeper look at one of these traditions of second nature, the Kantian and Hegelian. His chapter "The Stage of Difference: On the Second Nature of Civil Society in Kant and Hegel," investigates Hegel's idea of ethical life as "second nature." For the Hegelian spirit to actualize itself as second nature does not mean for it to somehow regain the immediacy and simplicity of nature, but to find itself in a nature it has yet to exceed and to produce a nature of a different sort. While this general characterization pertains to all three spheres of ethical life—family, civil society, and the state—it is the "second nature" of civil society which brings out the radically modern character of Hegel's conception most clearly: it is, Khurana argues, rather post-Kantian than neo-Aristotelian. To bring this into view, he reconstructs the way in which Kant characterizes cultivation and civilization as the production of a second nature which is necessary but not yet sufficient for a free and moral appropriation of our natural capacities. The author then delineates how Hegel builds on this Kantian conception of culture and civil society. Civil society as second nature appears as a strategic regression of ethical life in its attempt to deepen the appropriation of our nature. It presents itself as a spiritual animal kingdom, in which ethical life realizes itself in the state of its own dissolution. Khurana argues that to supersede the limitations and to develop the liberating potential of this type of second nature a politics of second nature is needed.

Barbara Stiegler investigates a more literal use of the naturalizing notion of "forms of life": Nietzsche's debate with Social Darwinism. In her chapter "1880: First Philosophical Critique of Adaptationism: Nietzsche, Reader of Herbert Spencer," she offers a detailed reading of Nietzsche's look at the junction of biology (Darwin and Spencer) and politics (various liberalisms): the adaptation of individuals and populations to a new and open environment and to constant processes of acceleration. However, what is interesting about his social and political reflections on the absolute flux and on globalization is that they themselves rest on the evolution of the living to criticize the new imperative. Rejecting the dominant adaptationism, as much in the biology of evolution as in the social and political field, Nietzsche presents Darwin and Spencer with the heterochrony of evolutionary rhythms, the necessity of stasis and closure, and the virtues of untimeliness and maladaptation. Stiegler's Nietzsche thus presents a new and original understanding of biological and social evolution that is still not adequately recognized.

In "Experimentalism, Naturalism, and the Grounds of Social Critique," Steven Levine takes a closer look at the very strategy of naturalizing social philosophy, which Honneth recommended in the second chapter: the Deweyan. Dewey often claimed that we need a measure or standard for judging the worth of any given mode of social life. According to Dewey's experimentalism, this measure is found by examining norms that already partly govern the common self-understanding of agents in the social life-world. These norms are instituted experimentally in historical times in order to solve social problems, and they are subject to revision when they no longer "work," that is, when they fail to facilitate joint action and social cooperation. Levine argues that Dewey's philosophy contains two additional theoretical strategies to derive standards of judgment and social critique, a social-ontological and a perfectionist strategy. The latter two strategies are not based on a historical-experimental account of norm revision but on certain aspects of Dewey's naturalism. Levine is careful to ascertain the ways in which these strategies are compatible and the ways in which they conflict.

In the last chapter of the first part of the book, "From Naturalism to Social Vitalism: Revisiting the Durkheim-Bergson Debate on Moral Obligations," Louis Carré starts from the oscillation in social philosophy between "reductive naturalism" and "social constructivism." He suggests trying to escape this dilemma through a "genealogical" and "vitalist" account of the "nature of society." To do this, he revisits the debate that once opposed Émile Durkheim and Henri Bergson on the sources of moral obligations. Both authors sketched a non-dualist conception of the relations between nature and society while insisting at the same time on the specificity of human societies. Durkheim's and Bergson's original solutions to the problem of the "nature of society" and of "nature in society" derive from the shift they took from a too narrow concept of "nature" to an enlarged and transformative notion of "life." If "social vitalism" seems better suited to characterize Bergson's social philosophy, Carré also shows how Durkheim actually challenged the two main criticisms Bergson addressed to him for not paying attention to the biological bottom below the "closed society" and to the possibility of transformation toward an "open society." Unlike the duality of "closure" and "openness" in Bergson, Durkheim pretends that self-discipline is not opposed to social change but constitutes its very anthropological condition of possibility.

The second part of the book addresses one of the key issues of any attempt to naturalize social philosophy: the problem of embodiment. Instead of offering wholesale solutions to how social facts are embodied, this part offers three more concrete accounts on the axes of action, gender, and work.

First, Italo Testa presents a naturalistic understanding of social action based on the notion of habit that can be traced back to pragmatism and that could be helpful in developing social philosophy as a cross-disciplinary program. His chapter, "The Dual Mode of Social Interaction: Habit, Embodied Cognition, and Social Action," seeks to show how such a socio-ontological understanding of habit can overcome the dualism between routine behavior and skilled action, which has dominated action theory and psychology. Testa argues that such naturalization of social action also allows for a plurality of forms of automation and habituation and takes both their flexible and inertial sides and the dialectical interplay between them into account. Furthermore, he argues that habit ontology can account for the two-sided—receptive and spontaneous, passive and active—mode of operation of interaction, which is a crucial and underestimated phenomenon for developing a naturalized understanding of action within both cognitive and social sciences. Such a dual, two-sided way of interaction can be captured by the notion of habit as a social attractor, which could be particularly helpful to connect embodied and extended cognition models with critical approaches to social practices and institutions.

Second, in "Sex, Gender, and Ambiguity: Beauvoir on the Dilaceration of Lived Experience," Mariana Teixeira tackles the well-known critical implications of the distinction between gender as socially constructed and sex as biologically given: if women are not inclined by nature to certain social roles, spaces, and activities, that is, if these constraints are historically imposed, they can be historically transformed as well. As liberating as its effects might have been, this idea has also been challenged for its purported masculinist detraction of nature in favor of culture. Within women's movements, these opposing stances are represented by xeno- and ecofeminist strands: while the former sees emancipation as transcendence, as the mastery of nature, the latter strives rather for immanence, a harmonious connection with nature. In both cases, however, a rather unmediated sex/gender divide tends to be preserved in its seemingly unsurmountable dichotomy. To avoid the unilateral embracing of one of the poles—either nature or culture, immanence or transcendence—Teixeira suggests that a more compelling treatment of the relation between sex and gender (hence, nature and culture, body and mind) can be drawn from Simone de Beauvoir's writings. While decidedly criticizing women's centuries-old confinement to immanence, Beauvoir does not equate emancipation with the mere increase of women's control over their bodies and the natural world. As women become free to pursue their autonomously chosen projects, the realm of the given is not to be suppressed, but rather assumed and creatively integrated in its givenness, since immanence is not only a limit to transcendence but also its very condition of possibility. She argues that Beauvoir's intersubjective conception of selfhood, and her refusal of an ontological duality between nature and Geist, allows for a conception of the ambiguity of the human condition as, at once, subject and object. Moreover, in order to understand the different ways subjects might experience this tension, she proposes a distinction between existential ambiguity and contingent dilaceration: from a Beauvoirian perspective, emancipation would be conceived of not as the elimination of ambiguity between immanence and transcendence; rather, it would involve overcoming an unmediated dilaceration through the reciprocal movement of embodied subjectivities toward one another.

Third, Emmanuel Renault's chapter, "The Naturalist Presuppositions of the Focus on Work and Economy in Dewey's Social Philosophy," raises the following issue: In what respect could it be said that Dewey's *social philosophy* is naturalist? Indeed, Dewey's naturalism is less apparent in his social philosophy than in his metaphysics, and there is a tendency, in Deweyan scholarship, to understate the naturalist premises of his social philosophy. According to a dominant line of interpretation, his naturalism only plays a methodological role in his writings about society and politics. The only implication of what Dewey called the Darwinian revolution for philosophy would, with regard to social philosophy, consist in the fact that it is no longer possible to consider that scientific methods are relevant only in so far as nature is concerned. Renault contends that the central role played by work and economic processes in Dewey's social philosophy shows that he is a naturalist also in a much deeper sense. The author distinguishes three types of argumentation in Dewey's social philosophy: a socio-ontological one, an anthropological one, and a socio-theoretical one. He then analyzes the naturalist premises of Dewey's support of the definition of human being as "*homo faber*" or "tool making animal." Finally, he reconstructs Dewey's view of economic processes as the "substructure of social life" as deeply naturalist.

The final part of the book discusses the contemporarily influential idea that social philosophy could be understood as "diagnosis" and "therapy" of "social pathologies." All three contributions take, as it were, a step back from the intense contemporary debate and try to reformulate the idea by taking the perspective of classics of naturalistic social philosophy: Nietzsche, Wittgenstein, Marx, Horkheimer, and Adorno. But they also present positive alternatives.

Arvi Särkelä's chapter, "The Meta(Physician) of Culture: Early Nietzsche's Disclosing Critique of Forms of Life," excavates Nietzsche's social-critical claim expressed in the figure of the philosopher as a "physician of culture" (*Arzt der Kultur*). According to Särkelä, this figure is illuminating from the perspective of contemporary social philosophy. It gives an inspiring example of a widely neglected and misunderstood form of philosophical social criticism: the disclosing critique of society. Moreover, it intrudes into the discourse on "social pathologies" in an unexpected way. In early Nietzsche, Särkelä identifies both methodological and ontological reflections on a kind of inclusive perspective on our social life that is in many ways similar to the enterprises we today, following Axel Honneth and others, would call "social philosophy." On the one hand, we have Nietzsche's conception of the philosopher as a "physician of culture"; methodologically, then, the work of the philosopher can be described in analogy to that of the physician. On the other hand, there is his strongly naturalistic vocabulary of "malady" and "degeneration" as well as "health" and "growth" of entities we would call "social"; ontologically, then, the philosopher's object is the kind of entity that can either degenerate or grow, fall ill or get well. However, these affinities aside, Nietzsche importantly takes a further step unseen of in contemporary social philosophy, namely what Särkelä calls his "critical cosmology": Nietzsche stipulates a robust metaphysical reflection to support the practice of the physician of culture; he mobilizes a naturalistic metaphysics of "plastic power" for social-critical purposes. Särkelä argues that what is challenging for us today is not so much what Nietzsche's cosmology of plastic power claims (it is indeed rather poor of a metaphysical account), but *how* he sets up a naturalistic metaphysics for social criticism. If early Nietzsche's naturalistic metaphysics of plastic power is read in light of his perfectionism about culture as the sphere of self-transformation and his aestheticism about social criticism as a kind of art, it gives us an example of a sort of philosophical social criticism that is both immanent and disclosing.

In the following chapter, "'The Sickness of a Time': Social Pathology and Therapeutic Philosophy," Sabina Lovibond reformulates the problem of social pathology from the perspective of Wittgensteinian therapeutic philosophy. Wittgenstein's later philosophy of language, she argues, can be regarded as "naturalistic" in that it treats language use as one of the characteristic activities of the members of the human species. In other words, it is not a reductive naturalism but a "naturalism of second nature"—one that acknowledges human language games, with their various inbuilt normative constraints, as cultural (and therefore historical) phenomena. She asks, however, whether we could read Wittgenstein's later philosophy as naturalistic in a further sense, involving the idea of a "natural" (normal, healthy, sound) condition of human beings with respect to their own linguistic activity—and, in contrast to this, a troubled or pathological condition. The discussion of this question opens on to that of the uneasy relationship between Wittgenstein and (some varieties of) present-day cultural criticism—a relationship necessarily limited by certain points on which the Wittgensteinian source material remains muted or unresolved.

Finally, Fabian Freyenhagen's chapter, "Objective Reason, Ethical Naturalism, and Social Pathology: The case of Horkheimer and Adorno," elaborates further the relationship between Wittgenstein and Critical Theory. He asks if the later Wittgenstein and the early Frankfurt School might have adopted similar conceptions of language, and, relatedly, might share a certain kind of unrestrictive, ethical naturalism. Freyenhagen suggests that—surprising as it may seem—this is indeed the case, albeit this was not known to either of them. Other commentators have sought to bring the later Wittgenstein into conversation with the Frankfurt School. But instead of mobilizing insights from the later Wittgenstein to criticize Horkheimer and Adorno (as Wellmer and, indirectly, Habermas have done), Freyenhagen suggests that these insights have a more appropriate home in their own work. The key lesson from these insights is not a purely intersubjective account of language (and, connected to this, of moral validity), but that the human life-form and language are inseparable, which enables language to be a reservoir for what Horkheimer called "objective reason." Moreover, Freyenhagen also argues that paying attention to this inseparability can enable us to engage in disclosive social critique. In particular, by considering as an example the current debates around sustainability, he shows how becoming forgetful of this inseparability can blind us to dependency relations in meaning, and how this can have pernicious effects on how public debates are framed and conducted.

First and foremost we would like to thank all the contributors to this volume—Louis Carré, Fabian Freyenhagen, Axel Honneth, Thomas Khurana, Steven Levine, Sabina Lovibond, Barbara Stiegler, Emmanuel Renault, Italo Testa, and Mariana Teixeira. We would also like to thank Emanuele Martinelli for copy-editing and spell-checking the manuscript and Anastasija Bosshard for preparing it for submission.

NOTES

1. Notable exceptions are Sabina Lovibond (2002) and Italo Testa (2007).
2. For a recent and particularly illuminating version of this argument, see Kronfeldner (2018).

REFERENCES

De Caro, Mario, and Macarthur, David (eds.). 2010. *Naturalism and Normativity.* New York: Columbia University Press.

Freyenhagen, Fabian. 2015. "Honneth on Social Pathologies: A Critique," *Critical Horizons*, 16 (2): 131–52.

Habermas, Jürgen. 2003. *The Future of Human Nature.* Cambridge: Polity Press.

Haslanger, Sally. 2012. "Social Construction: Myth and Reality," in *Resisting Reality: Social Construction and Social Critique*, S. Haslanger (ed.). Oxford: Oxford University Press.

Hirvonen, Onni. 2018. "On the Ontology of Social Pathologies," *Studies in Social and Political Thought*, 28: 9–14.

Honneth, Axel. 2007. "Pathologies of the Social: The Past and Present of Social Philosophy," in *Disrespect: The Normative Foundations of Critical Theory*, A. Honneth (ed.), J. Ganahl (trans.). Cambridge: Polity Press.

Honneth, Axel. 2009. "A Social Pathology of Reason: On the Intellectual Legacy of Critical Theory," in *Pathologies of Reason: On the Legacy of Critical Theory*, A. Honneth (ed.), J. Hebbeler (trans.). New York: Columbia University Press.Honneth, Axel. 2014. "The Diseases of Society: Approaching a Nearly Impossible Concept," *Social Research*, Arvi Särkelä (trans.), 81 (3): 683–703.

Horkheimer, Max, and Adorno, Theodor W. 2002. *Dialectic of Enlightenment: Philosophical Fragments.* Stanford: Stanford University Press.

Kronfeldner, Maria. 2018. *What's Left of Human Nature?* Cambridge, MA: MIT Press.

Laitinen, Arto. 2015. "Social Pathologies, Reflexive Pathologies, and the Idea of Higher-Order Disorders," *Studies in Social and Political Thought*, 25: 44–65.

Laitinen, Arto, and Särkelä, Arvi. 2019. "Four Conceptions of Social Pathology," *European Journal of Social Theory*, 22 (1): 80–102.

Lovibond, Sabina. 2002. *Ethical Formation*. Cambridge, MA: Harvard University Press.

Neuhouser, Frederick. 2016. "Hegel on Social Ontology and the Possibility of Pathology," in *I that Is We, We that Is I. Perspectives on Contemporary Hegel*, I. Testa, Ruggiu, and Cortella (eds.). Leiden: Brill.

Särkelä, Arvi. 2018. *Immanente Kritik und soziales Leben: Selbsttransformative Praxis nach Hegel und Dewey*. Frankfurt: Klostermann.

Särkelä, Arvi, and Laitinen, Arto. 2019. "Between Normativism and Naturalism: Honneth on Social Pathology," *Constellations*, 26 (2): 286–300.

Shelby, Tommie. 2016. *Dark Ghettos: Injustice, Dissent, and Reform*. Cambridge, MA: Harvard University Press.

Testa, Italo. 2007. "Criticism from within Nature: The Dialectic between First and Second Nature from McDowell to Adorno," *Philosophy and Social Criticism*, 33 (4): 473–97.

Williams, Bernard. 1995. "Evolution, Ethics, and the Representation Problem," in *Making Sense of Humanity and Other Philosophical Papers*, W. Bernard (ed.). Cambridge: Cambridge University Press.

Part I

SECOND NATURE AND FORMS OF LIFE

NATURALISTIC KEY CONCEPTS IN SOCIAL PHILOSOPHY

Chapter 2

Second Nature

The Profound Depths of a Key Philosophical Concept

Axel Honneth, translated by Joseph Ganahl

In his *Philosophy of Right*, Hegel describes ethical customs as a "second nature" (1991). He was quite aware of the philosophical history of the concept, being familiar with the ancient Greek philosophers who held that our primordial, "first nature" may manifest itself in our everyday practices and attitudes, provided that we establish stable patterns of dealing with things and persons by means of practice and habituation. These thinkers conceived of the formation of habits, both in terms of our physical actions and of our moral dispositions, as a kind of natural organic process germane to the human form of life. Although they did not actually employ the term "second nature," they did address the concept it denotes (Waszink 1980). As far as I am aware, Aristotle himself never used the term, but he does quote its use—at least according to a number of translations—at a crucial point in his own argumentation. In Book VII, Chapter 10 of the *Nichomachean Ethics*, Aristotle recapitulates an argument he has already made in Book II (2009, 1152a). There he distinguishes between epistemological virtues (i.e., "practical wisdom" we possess by nature and need only be taught how to employ) and our goodness "in respect of character." We can only acquire the latter through education, that is, via the repetition of practices leading us to become "habituated" to finding pleasure in appropriate behavior, such that we eventually develop a permanent disposition for ethically appropriate behavior. Aristotle describes this disposition by referencing Evenus's claim that it becomes "men's nature in the end." We can then draw a clear connection from Aristotle to the Ancient Roman thought, where we repeatedly encounter the term "second nature." Cicero claims that stable dispositions can be formed by habituation and thus understood as another nature (*altera natura*). There is no doubt

19

that Hegel was aware of this philosophical history, either through his own reading or through that of his peers. Yet, it is unlikely that he was familiar with another, starkly different Roman conception of second nature—one that might have discouraged him from employing the concept in a so consistently positive manner.

Already in the work of Augustine, it becomes clear that the concept of second nature may also assume a negative connotation devoid of any ethical content. Augustine draws upon Aristotle's concept of habituation, though he employs a characteristically Christian formulation and argues that we have become accustomed culturally to vices of ignorance and egotism, thus leading to the emergence of a *"quasi secunda natura."* Like Aristotle, Augustine views this second nature as the product of habit, though he views its product as "evil," a morally deplorable disposition to neglect God in the effort to maximize our own utility (Müller 2005, 317ff). This negative connotation of the concept of second nature can also be found in the work of Rousseau, though he neither uses the term itself nor shares Augustine's Christian presuppositions, drawing instead on the work of the French moralists. In his *Discourse on Inequality*, he takes up Augustine's distinction by ascribing the *"amour de soi,"* which ensures that we behave in a morally appropriate fashion, to our first nature, while assigning the crave for recognition at the heart of the *"amour propre"*—which is a product of socialization and thus an element of our second nature (1994, 62).

Both the positively and the negatively connotated understandings offer different arguments for conceiving of the product of cultural habituation, that is, our "habits," as our second nature. Aristotle writes in the *Rhetoric* that "something habitual inevitably becomes second nature," going on to say that "habit does in a sense resemble nature, in that 'often' is close to 'always,' and nature is a matter of 'always' while habit is a matter of 'often'" (2018, 41). Aristotelian thought therefore justifies the concept of second nature with reference to temporal repetition. Both ethical habits and natural processes fall under the same category, because they both re-occur regularly; perhaps the former not with the same constancy as natural processes, but nevertheless often. Of even greater significance in this context is the fact that Aristotle immediately goes on to emphasize that neither habits nor natural processes are "compulsory"; just as "force is unnatural," our habits are not the result of "compulsion." He justifies this claim by arguing that once something initially difficult or necessitating effort has become an acquired habit, it loses its compulsory character and comes easily to us. This second characterization of the similarity between habits and natural processes is surprising, because it stands in direct contradiction to the justification provided by the tradition that applies a "negative" connotation to the term "second nature." This tradition argues that our vicious habits can be understood as a prolongation of our first nature, because both have the tendency to enslave us. Augustine believes that if we constantly behave unethically, we will entangle ourselves ever further in sin, such that we will eventually feel a compulsive drive to continue to sin, thus acquiring this as a second nature (Müller 2005). In his *Discourse on Inequality*, Rousseau employs a similar formulation when it comes to the effect of the *"amour propre,"* describing this passion as a "fervent activity" that is nearly impossible to tame or control (Rousseau 1994). Therefore, both traditional understandings of second nature find a reason to conceive of our culturally acquired habits as an extension of our first nature, and yet both traditions characterize this first nature in nearly opposite ways. For Aristotle, it is primarily the non-compulsive character of natural organic processes—alongside their constant recurrence—that justifies conceiving of our ethical habits as a second nature; for Augustine, it is the forceful, compulsory character of natural processes that justifies conceiving of our sinful habits as a second nature.

Hegel apparently saw no reason to discuss the second "negative" tradition of the use of the term "second nature" in any detail. He simply assumes, like Aristotle, that our habits can only be regarded in a positive, often ethical sense, and that their similarity to natural processes lies in the fact that they both occur regularly and without compulsion. His first premise is that the effect of the habituation of our behavior, thoughts, and moral action is generally beneficial. In his *Philosophy of Mind*, he offers the following justification: through our repeated practices we learn to express our ideal self—our "genius"—unconsciously in our physical, cognitive, and ethical behavior, thereby freeing ourselves from the accidental nature of our ideas and desires and gradually becoming representatives of a rational "universality" (1894, 40–44). According to Hegel, this process begins with the practice of basic physical techniques such as walking upright or developing a resistance to unpleasant sensations; it continues with learning crucial cultural techniques, such as writing and arithmetic, as well as becoming accustomed to logical thinking; and, finally, similarly to Aristotle's view, it culminates in the internalization of ethically appropriate behavior. At every stage of this process in which our "specific feelings" gain "bodily shape" (Hegel 1894, 42), the sway of our natural, accidental feelings over us disappears at some extent. Ultimately, therefore, once we have habitually acquired the ethical rules of rational coexistence, we will have shed any remainder of our determination by our external nature. By means of habituation, we will have attained complete freedom of being "in ourselves," in "this spontaneity of self-centered thought" (*Beisichselbstsein*). Hegel expresses the point almost laconically when he writes that this is due to the "the habit of right and goodness is an embodiment of liberty" (Hegel 1894, 41)—a notion that plays a prominent role in Hegel's *Philosophy of Right* (1991, 195). Hegel mentions the possibility of "bad habits" only once, as if he wanted to pay at least a brief tribute to the alternative view of second nature after all (1894, 42). Yet, he immediately dismisses the prospect of moral disobedience or evil becoming a habit, as this does not conform to the development of rational subjectivity, the reconstruction of which represents the sole focus of Hegel's philosophical system.

This means that Hegel will necessarily meet several difficulties with the second premise he appears to share with the Aristotelian view of second nature: we can refer to our habits as a second nature because they recur regularly and without coercion like in the case of natural processes. At first sight, it is not at all clear how Hegel can regard the fact that our habits are not forced upon us as a feature they share with nature, while also claiming at the same time that all our habits (with the exception of our ethical virtues) retain traces of an external force of nature. At this point, we may ask: why we should regard such pre-ethical habits as similar to our first nature just because they likewise recur without force or, as Aristotle would have said, compulsion? The answer Hegel gives in his *Philosophy of Mind* is relatively brief and refers only to pre-ethical, physical, or cognitive habits: "In habit the human being's mode of existence is 'natural,' and for that reason not free; but still free, so far as the merely natural phase of feeling is by habit reduced to a mere being of *his*, and he is no longer involuntarily attracted or repelled by it, and so no longer interested, occupied, or dependent in regard to it" (1894, 41).

Clearly Hegel wants to say that the concept of second nature can be applied to the habits by which we control our physical movements, impulses, and thoughts even though we are bounded by our habits to natural or physical conditions or laws. This is due to the process of habituation itself, enabling us to learn to control and no longer be enslaved by these laws. Therefore, the entirety of our second nature represents an amalgamation of natural processes that restrict our free will, whereby the former remains under the control of the latter at least to a degree that natural processes no longer compel or determine us externally. This interpretation also corresponds to what Hegel claims a few sentences later by using a rather Kantian formulation: the stages of habit formation follow a linear path of "liberation," for at each stage a further emotion that customarily "affects" and thus causally determines us becomes "impressed and moulded." Though this does not cause these emotions to disappear, they turn into something we can control. Summarizing these two determinations, we can say that, for Hegel, the formation of habits implies an intellectual shaping of our impulses and thus the cleansing of any compulsion by nature. Unlike Aristotle, he does not view our second nature merely as an extension or continuation of natural organic processes at the level of human practices, but rather as the sublimation of nature's compulsion in the shape of conditional freedom. This distinction derives from the fact that Hegel, viewing our first nature from the perspective of the subjective mind, does not see it as being non-compulsory at all. For humans, this nature represents first and foremost a space of causal dependence and influences that we can gradually mold into a rudimentary form of freedom that suits us: this we achieve by forming a second nature.

If we agree to such an interpretation, then we are faced with the problem that it remains unclear why Hegel does not grasp ethical customs as belonging to the domain of our second nature. After all, he claims that the formation of our second nature is supposed to have liberated us from nature's compulsion; that which we have acquired by habit is itself already an "embodiment of liberty" (Novakovic 2017). In the same vein, Hegel states in the Addition to §151 of the *Philosophy of Right* that education causes "this spirituality" (*das Geistige*) to become a habit in our ethical life. If we act accordingly, then we can claim to be "free" not merely in a conditional sense but in a substantial sense as well (1991, 195). This formulation in particular underscores the fact that, when it comes to ethical life, we can no longer define second nature as we have above. We lack that element which, in Hegel's mind, constitutes second nature as such in the first place: the molding of a natural dependency into a measure of mastered freedom. Perhaps we can find a way out of this conceptual dilemma if we remember that, whenever Hegel refers to the ethical as a second nature, he often adds a further qualification. For instance, he refers to a "spiritual, second nature,"[1] as if to make clear that what becomes habituated are not our natural impulses and feelings, but rather mental facts. This, however, only makes more urgent the question why Hegel employs the term "second nature" at all with reference to the ethical, since he has abandoned the very thing that was previously meant to justify this concept, that is, our entanglement in both our first nature and the spiritual nature of our freedom. Would it not have made much more sense to speak of "culture" rather than a "second nature," in order to remove once and for all any unclear ethical attachments to causal dependence? Hegel is somehow convinced that the different classes of ethical habits must always satisfy natural or nearly natural needs: family life should satisfy our need for care and physical well-being; civil society should satisfy our individual interest in economic prosperity and give us pride in our work; finally, the state should enable us to satisfy our individual desire for honor. However, these formations of habits apply solely to already spiritual matter, that is, the normative rules of institutionally objectified spirit and thus do not represent a process by which we mold our natural impulses and purify them of any element of external compulsion. There could be another reason why Hegel nevertheless speaks of a second, spiritual "nature" with reference to ethical life, as he appears to share the Aristotelian idea that our ethical habits represent "extensions" of our first nature; this is because such habits share, though in a weaker form, the non-compulsory teleology of all organic life. This idea, based on the model of an organism, could then explain Hegel's preference for the concept of "life" and his tendency to speak of a spiritual "life" free of coercion. This concept of "life" implies an entirely different conception of our first nature than in Hegel's description of our pre-ethical habits' second nature, in which there is nothing accommodating about nature at all.

These inconsistencies in Hegel's terminology—the fact that he presents two different, irreconcilable conceptions of *first* nature as a basis for his concept of second nature—shed light on the shaky ground upon which this entire account stands. Depending on which characteristics we ascribe to nature as a whole, we end up with completely different understandings of what constitutes second nature. If we emphasize the aspects of compulsion, blind regularity, and causal determination in natural processes, then we will find corresponding traces of this understanding of nature in the quasi-natural habits of our social practices and attitudes. If, by contrast, we grasp nature primarily as an organic and harmoniously unfolding process of life, then our concept of second nature will prominently feature aspects of non-compulsive harmony between mutually dependent elements. Hegel seemingly wants to employ both understandings in his own use of the concept of second nature. On the one hand, he follows Aristotle and describes our first nature as a non-compulsive, organic process of life; on the other hand, he follows Kant and describes our first nature as a domain of causal dependence ruled by natural law. When Hegel speaks of ethical life, he seems to claim that it represents a revival of natural freedom (*Zwanglosigkeit*) at the level of our mental operations; and, when he speaks of pre-ethical habits, he invokes the spirit of Kant once more and claims that these habits represent possibilities or forms of sublimating our dependency on natural forces and compulsions.

This tension within Hegel's theory of second nature is likely one of the reasons why his considerations would soon form both the point of departure and the battleground for a dispute over the meaning, content, and appropriate use of the concept of second nature. Shortly after Hegel's death, a debate about what it should mean to speak of a "second nature" in human history and society would emerge—partly in agreement, partly in disagreement with his work. Starting in the mid-nineteenth century, both the content and the methodological justification of this category would ignite a debate that continues even today.

In the tradition of Historical Materialism that arose as a result of a critical engagement with Hegel's theory, we see already in the works of Marx the emergence of a tendency to present human beings' social relations and their history as a form of "natural history," thus introducing a polemic element into the concept of second nature. Marx's references to nature have nothing to do with what Hegel understood by second nature; instead, he claims that the "spiritual" molding of our first nature has not at all taken place. Because human history, as Marx argues, proceeds without humans' conscious control of their economic affairs; first nature—a blind process as inexorable as the laws of nature—continues to assert itself into the present. Marx employs many variations of this thought, speaking either of the natural quality of social life, that is, its law-like character, deprived of any meaning, or that of the "material shell," as he does in the chapter on "commodity fetishism" in the first volume of the *Capital* (1976, 163–77). In these instances, Marx refers to mere extensions of natural processes in the sense of seemingly uncontrollable law-like processes, which is entirely in accordance with a modernist, positivist understanding; but in other parts of his works, particularly in his early writings, Marx also employs more Aristotelian conceptions of "nature." He writes that the "essential powers of man" are the product of a natural process of life and that the characteristics of the human species can be regarded as extensions of organic growth (Marx 1975, 352–55). Marx does not explicitly use the term "second nature," but he does implicitly express it in two different forms: first, as a critique of the unfortunate fact that natural laws continue to reign in civil society, and second, as a positive reference to the fact that "industry is the open book of the essential powers of man" (1975, 354) and thus as a historical indicator of the naturally emerging and gradually unfolding capacities of human beings. And in no way does Marx, similarly to Hegel, present any mediation between these two contrary concepts of what constitutes first nature.

Georg Lukàcs is the first to truly revive Hegel's idea of a second nature within Historical Materialism, infusing this concept with a polemical substance that would prove to have groundbreaking significance for Western Marxism as a whole. In his early study *The Theory of the Novel*, Lukàcs describes the world of bourgeois "conventions" and customs—the substance of what Hegel terms "second, spiritual nature"—as a "charnel-house of long-dead interiorities." And as if he wanted to push this ironic inversion of the concept of second nature to the extreme, Lukàcs then goes on to employ a Hegelian formulation, arguing that the "natural unity of the metaphysical spheres" of ethical life "has been destroyed forever" (1974, 64 and 37). Lukàcs's diagnosis that our cultural customs have become overly rigid lays the groundwork for his claim that modern ethical life serves as a "prison instead of as a parental home" for our mental relation to the world (1974, 64). The theory of "reification" that Lukàcs would develop three years later in *History and Class Consciousness* essentially represents a radicalized continuation of this early inversion of Hegel's idea of second nature. Lukàcs claims that what Hegel understands as second nature has in fact devolved into our first nature, nature itself resulting from the capitalist commodity exchange system. The longer we practice commodity exchange, the more we become accustomed to viewing our fellow humans, our surroundings, and even ourselves as marketable goods, and the more we will grasp our own lives within our own culture, that is, in Hegel's ethical world, as if it were a piece of first nature. First nature, here, is intended as a space of merely observable causal relations between elements that are or have come to resemble mere things (Lukàcs 1968); We should note that Lukàcs does not grasp first nature in the Aristotelian sense as an organic process—as a true Fichtean, the notion would have never even crossed his mind. When he speaks of "nature," he instead refers to the modernist-scientific understanding of first nature as a causal nexus of occurrences in space-time. What makes Lukàcs's analysis of reification such a venomous turn against Hegel is the fact that he reveals the German philosopher's notion of the "second, spiritual nature" of modern ethical life to be a mere chimera, representing nothing but a revival of the immutable laws of first nature.

Theodor W. Adorno would then push the conceptual inversions of the Marxist tradition to the extreme, adding yet another turn of the screw to Georg Lukàcs's analysis of reification. At first, Adorno's critique of capitalism seems to be identical to that of Lukàcs, as he likewise claims that capitalism imposes upon us social conditions forcing us to perceive and experience social relationships as if they were the expression of purely natural laws—and thus products of first nature in the modern sense. According to Adorno, what is fatal about such a reifying system of perception and experience is not primarily the fact that it makes ethical culture, intellectual life, and so on impossible, though he certainly regards this as true. His major concern is instead the fact that capitalist reification prevents us from experiencing that element of our first nature which cannot be exhausted by the positivist conception of nature. For Adorno, unlike Lukàcs, the concept of reification does not entail a return or revival of first nature within society, rather a more intense continuation of a long-problematic understanding of nature in general. Adorno not only fears that the ethical world of the present does not represent second nature in the Hegelian sense, that is, spiritually molded naturalness, but also that the capitalist reification that has come to replace this second nature does not represent first nature at all, as we cannot have an adequate conception of what that would mean. Adorno claims the entire opposition between "first" and "second" nature will continue to be problematic as long as we thereby conceive of "nature" as nothing but a space of natural laws or a chain of causal events (Adorno 2007, 266–72; Habermas 2008). Although I do not wish to claim that Adorno must thereby resort to Aristotle's view of "nature," my impression is that he is forced to employ a concept that entails at least the possibility that what we have termed "first nature" in fact comprises something more and something different than what is implied by the positivist understanding of nature. It is in this diagnosis, and only in this diagnosis, that Adorno's analysis of reification is tangential to the current philosophical debate, led by John McDowell, on the presuppositions of the concept of second nature (Testa 2007).

Although Hegel's idea of a second nature resonated critically with the best thinkers in the Marxist tradition, this has never been discussed in academic philosophy after German Idealism. This lack of attention was not, however, the result of a lack of knowledge or intellectual awareness; rather it reflected an often implicit rejection of Hegel's idea. Neither Neo-Kantianism nor the emerging discipline of sociology, which in its beginnings owed much to contemporary philosophy, could find anything of use in the notion that we should understand social habits or customs as a spiritual molding of natural drives. Nor did they accept Hegel's second, Aristotelian idea that ethical life should be viewed as a continuation of natural organic processes at the level of social institutions. The reason for this lack of interest, if not outright rejection, is the same in both cases. This idea is too caught up in Kant's two-worlds interpretation to be able to grasp nature in a non-positivistic manner, that is, not in terms of purely causal categories. Contemporary philosophers and sociologists therefore preferred to replace Hegel's concept of second nature with terms such as "culture" or "civilization," partly to sever any unclear ties to nature and partly to emphasize the ontological particularity of the matter at hand. Here we often hear the term "spheres of values," which is also seen as representing the result of cultural habituation, though without any ties to first nature. Even German and British Neo-Hegelians prefer to use the term "objective *spirit*" in an entirely purist fashion, devoiding Hegel's "ethical life" of any connection to "nature" (Schnädelbach 1983). Astoundingly enough, the situation remains unchanged even throughout the 1920s despite the emergence of philosophical anthropology, which must have placed a special emphasis on the natural quality of our social lives. Although Helmuth Plessner uses the term "second nature" in *Levels of Organic Life and the Human* in order to explain the "natural artifice" of human beings, he opts to ignore the diverse possibilities of this concept entirely (2019). Arnold Gehlen occasionally uses the term explicitly, yet he sees no distinction from the concept of the "cultural sphere" and denies any relation to nature (1987). The major exception to this tendency to make a strong division between "nature" and "culture" and treat them as two categorically distinct spheres is represented by American pragmatism. Particularly in the work of John Dewey, who does not use the term explicitly, though we find a number of impulses to revive the idea of a second nature in the spirit of Hegel.

The theoretical step that enables Dewey to pick up on Hegel's account is of course entirely different from that taken by thinkers in the Marxist tradition. It is their critique of society that brings Marx, Lukàcs, and Adorno into contact with this older concept; it is capitalism that moves them to harbor strong doubts about the promise of reconciliation entailed in Hegel's idea of second nature. This compelled them to consider anew the historical mediation between nature and society, natural processes, and mental activity. As a result, Adorno resorts to a non-instrumental concept of nature, one that would allow us to redefine completely the second nature of human beings. But unlike such highly indirect and tortuous attempts to make this Hegelian concept fruitful, John Dewey takes a much more direct path. Encouraged by what he perceives to be the result of modern, reflective natural science, he develops a notion of the creative and processual quality of nature that makes it seem entirely plausible to view the development of society as an intelligent or spiritual continuation of natural processes (Dewey 1929).

In no way does Dewey consider reviving the Aristotelian idea that nature develops teleologically, unfolding ever greater potential. This would entail projecting far too much predestination onto natural processes, thus excluding the possibility of unpredictable developments and creative production. Although Dewey claims that "potentials," a term he uses often, are an ever-present ontological element of nature, he claims they can only be unleashed or realized by coming into contact with each other—or as Dewey puts it, by virtue of the association of isolated individual phenomena. The more developed such communication between previously separated elements of nature becomes, the more complex the shapes reality can take becomes—due to the unleashing of previously unused potentials. On this basis Dewey arrives at the claim which lies at the heart of his entire philosophical worldview: the organic life of human society takes on spiritual form by virtue of meaningful interactions, thereby opening up vast possibilities of action. By virtue of being included in the sphere of verbal communication, the organic is transformed, entailing more possibilities for unlocking latent potentials than ever before in natural history. What is so crucial about this theoretical step for our purposes is that it allows Dewey to reject the dichotomy between nature and culture or spirit, while still allowing for a qualitative modification of the organic by means of meaningful interactions:

> The members of society are living human beings with the characteristics of living creatures; but as they enter into distinctively human associations strictly organic properties are modified and even transformed. [. . .] The social affords us an observable instance of a "realm of mind" objective to an individual, by entering into which, as a participating member, organic activities are transformed into acts having a mental quality. (Dewey 1931, 83 and 88)

This passage sounds quite Hegelian and that is almost certainly how Dewey intends it. But, unlike Hegel, he avoids any ambiguity about the concept of "natural reality" or "nature." He does not alternate between a nature that restricts or compels us and one that enables or accommodates us. Depending on the circumstances, nature can be one or the other; depending on our aims, nature can be either a tool or an obstacle (Dewey 1929, 369f). Yet, regardless of our aims and whether natural conditions prove useful or obstructive, Dewey insists that no matter how we act, we always do so as an intelligent continuation of natural processes. Therefore, we might even be justified in assuming that the idea of a second nature is no longer appropriate, given that this idea asserts a division where Dewey sees a continuum. Depending on how our natural drives, our considerations, and our physical conditions interact, the respective portions of nature and culture involved will differ greatly.

I have arrived at a point in my historical reconstruction of the concept of second nature which has become once again the focal point of intense philosophical discussion: to what extent, if at all, can we speak of human beings' second nature in an Aristotelian sense? John McDowell's proposal that we employ the ancient Greek term to describe the ethical virtues into which we have been socialized played a particularly important role in initiating this philosophical debate about twenty years ago (McDowell 1996). His proposal was especially explosive because of its implication that we can only interpret the whole of our ethical behavior as a capacity for perceiving moral facts, and therefore also as our second nature, if we are capable of bracketing the traditional, positivist concept of nature as a space of causal dependence in order to interpret natural processes as the continual development of our particularly human form of life. If we are not able to do so, if we merely retain a modernist, "demystified" idea of nature, then McDowell is right to point out that we cannot justify the notion that our moral perception represents the realization of our "natural" capacities. It will not be possible in this context to recapitulate the entire debate once launched by McDowell's proposal; it is enough to say that this debate focuses primarily on what it means to conceive of a continuity between natural processes and our ethical virtues in such a way that the latter somehow naturally emerges from the former. Here it is often objected that if we believe such a claim, we will have to either abandon positive naturalism completely or plead for peaceful coexistence between two views of nature, which would exclude the possibility of a unified worldview.[2] Instead of recapitulating the debate, therefore, I will conclude by briefly pointing out the insights I regard as most important in the history of the idea of second nature I have roughly outlined here.[3]

First, it is crucial that we recognize that Hegel's idea of second nature can refer to two starkly different phenomena of social life: on the one hand, it can refer to the possibility of learning, by means of repeating appropriate practices, to control our causal dependency on our natural drives, thus causing them to lose their arbitrary power over us and become useful potentials at our disposal in the pursuit of our own well-being. On the other hand, it can refer to the possibility for human societies to carry out their own particular, rationally determined functions in a cooperative, free, and playful fashion, thus enabling us to grasp our social life as an instance of organic life at the level of social evolution. Clearly, these two ideas employ distinct concepts of a first nature with which our *second* nature shares certain similar character- istics. In the first case, which corresponds to Hegel's description of our pre- ethical habits, first nature is conceived of as a space of causal dependence, whose inevitable force remains in our second nature, though we can now steer it to our own benefit. In the second case, which corresponds to Hegel's idea of ethical life, first nature is conceived of as a sphere of organic life, while the second nature of our social life, under the right conditions, can come to resemble the free and harmonious interaction between the individual members of society. If, therefore, we are to continue speaking of a "second nature," then we will have to define more clearly which understanding of this concept we have in mind.

Second, we should note that, alongside the positive, originally Aristote- lian description of our habits that has accompanied us since Ancient Rome, there is also a second tradition that takes a very negative view of the results of habit formation. In place of ethical virtues, this tradition points to bad, even evil, habits of human beings' second nature in order to emphasize the fact that the inculcation of social practices can reinforce harmful elements of a given culture. In my view, this ambiguity about the meaning of our second nature—in the first Hegelian sense—should not be forgotten, for it enables us to explain those unfortunate cases in which ethical socialization has clearly gone wrong. If, on the basis of a pre-determined conception, we become blind to the fact that the process of getting habituated to a society's social practices may also entail the acquisition of malicious or inhumane habits, we will hardly be able to understand why societies bearing such characteristics could ever have attained any kind of stability and internal cohesion.

Third, this leads us to what my brief overview has shown to be an elemental feature of Marxist conceptions of second nature. I do not find it entirely plausible that the capitalist society, beneath the surface of its cultural achievements, is in fact determined merely by natural laws, such that our supposed second nature merely consists in a continuation of a first, causally determined nature. Such images and descriptions necessarily resort to over-dramatizations of the capitalist society that are of little use when it comes to analyzing the constantly changing features of capitalism and con- tribute nothing to an explanation of what is meant by the concept of second nature. Nevertheless, at the heart of such diagnoses lies a suspicion which I regard as an indispensable element of any serious discussion of the state of our culture and society: a suspicion that our belief in the success of our moral efforts—a belief that is germane to the concept of second nature in both meanings of the term—could in fact be a mere illusion or deception. If we abandon this suspicion, that is, if we become accustomed to no longer examining our behavioral practices as to whether they offer any motivational purchase or they could crumble at the slightest sign of turbulence, then we will have disposed of a crucial instrument for our own cultural self-understanding. In that sense, I find it absolutely legitimate to follow the tradition of Western Marxism in insisting on socially critical reservations about the concept of second nature.

In conclusion, it is worth mentioning in the spirit of John Dewey that the current discussion on the concept of second nature might suffer from the fact that two entirely irreconcilable notions of first nature are in play. If we can only explain our ability to develop ethical behavioral practices and perceive moral facts in our environment by resorting to Aristotelian ideas of natural teleology, then this enterprise will not prove very successful in the long run. This would mean either to abandon any notion of a natural space of causal dependence or to live with two conceptions of nature which cannot be reconciled with each other, in spite of our deep-seated desire for a unified worldview. In the face of such gloomy prospects, why not recall Dewey's attempt to draw on the work of the natural sciences and develop a conception of natural processes which make room for the idea that our mental capacities represent a continuation of a kind of communication that has always been a part of nature? Incidentally, this is a notion that Theodor W. Adorno also experimented with in his philosophical writings; in odd-sounding and quite touching passages, he refers to "the modern natural sciences," whose theories of relativity and quantum mechanics "peer over the wall" and "snatch a snippet of what does not agree with [their] own ingrained categories" (Adorno 2014, 245–58).[4]

NOTES

1. In §151, *Addition*, Hegel writes: "Education is the art of making human beings ethical: it considers them as natural beings and shows them how they can be reborn, and how their original nature can be transformed into a second, spiritual nature so that this spirituality becomes *habitual* to them" (1991, 195).
2. On the discussion of McDowell's concept of second nature, see Willaschek (2000) and Smith (2002).
3. An interesting overview of the current discussion, which also includes the discipline of psychoanalysis, can be found in Hogh and König (2011).
4. See also Adorno (1998). On this extremely fascinating topic, see also Ming-Chen Lo (2020).

REFERENCES

Adorno, Theodor W. 1998. *Metaphysik: Begriff und Probleme, Vorlesung 1965, Nachgelassene Schriften*, Theodor W. Adorno Archiv (ed.), 14: 118ff. Frankfurt: Suhrkamp.

Adorno, Theodor W. 2007. *Negative Dialectics*. New York: Continuum.

Adorno, Theodor W. 2014. "On Subject and Object," in *Subject and Object: Frankfurt School Writings on Epistemology, Ontology, and Method*, R. Groff (ed.), 245–58. New York: Bloomsbury.

Aristotle. 2009. *The Nichomachean Ethics*. Oxford: Oxford University Press.

Aristotle. 2018. *The Art of Rhetoric*, R. Waterfield (trans.), 41. Oxford: Oxford University Press.

Dewey, John. 1929. *Experience and Nature*. London: George Allen & Unwin.

Dewey, John. 1931. "The Inclusive Philosophical Idea," in *Philosophy and Civilization*, 77–92. New York: Putnam.

Gehlen, Arnold. 1987. *Man: His Nature and Place in the World*. New York: Columbia University Press.

Habermas, Jürgen. 2008. "I Myself am Part of Nature—Adorno on the Intrication of Reason in Nature: Reflections on the Relation between Freedom and Unavailability," in *Between Naturalism and Religion: Philosophical Essays*, 181–208. Cambridge: Polity.

Hegel, George W. F. 1894. *Philosophy of Mind*, William Wallace (trans.). Oxford: Clarendon Press.

Hegel, Georg W. F. 1991. *Elements of the Philosophy of Right*. Cambridge: Cambridge University Press.

Hogh, Philip, and Julia König. 2011. "Bestimmte Unbestimmbarkeit: Über die zweite Natur in der ersten und die erste Natur in der zweiten." *Deutsche Zeitschrift für Philosophie*, 59(3): 419–38.

Lo, Ming-Chen. 2020. *Jenseits des Leidens: Adornos Beitrag zu einer Denkpsychologie* (ch. 4.5). Berlin: de Gruyter.

Lukàcs, Georg. 1968. "Reification and the Consciousness of the Proletariat," in *History and Class Consciousness*, 83–122. Cambridge, MA: MIT Press.

Lukàcs, Georg. 1974. *The Theory of the Novel*. Cambridge, MA: MIT Press.

Marx, Karl. 1975. "Economic and Philosophical Manuscripts," in *Early Writings*, 279–400. New York: Vintage Books.

Marx, Karl. 1976. *Capital, Vol. 1*. London: Penguin Books.

McDowell, John. 1996. *Mind and World*. Cambridge, MA: Harvard University Press.

Müller, Jörn. 2005. *Willensschwäche in Antike und Mittelalter* (317ff). Leuven: Leuven University Press.

Novakovic, Andreja. 2017. *Hegel on Second Nature in Ethical Life*. Cambridge: Cambridge University Press.

Plessner, Helmuth. 2019. *Levels of Organic Life and the Human*. New York: Fordham.

Rousseau, Jean-Jacques. 1994. *Discourse on Inequality*. Oxford: Oxford University Press.

Schnädelbach, Herbert. 1983. *Philosophie in Deutschland 1831–1833*. Frankfurt: Suhrkamp.

Smith, Nicholas H. (ed.). 2002. *Reading McDowell: On 'Mind and World'*. London and New York: Routledge.

Testa, Italo. 2007. "Criticism from within Nature: The Dialectic between First and Second Nature from McDowell to Adorno," *Philosophy & Social Criticism*, 33 (4): 473–97.

Waszink, Jan H. 1980. "Die Vorstellungen von der 'Ausdehnung der Natur' in der griechisch-römischen Antike und im frühen Christentum," in *Pietas*, Festschrift für Bernhard Kötting, E.

Willaschek, Marcus (ed.). 2000. *John McDowell: Reason and Nature: Lecture and Colloquium in Münster*. Münster: LIT Verlag.

Chapter 3

The Stage of Difference

On the Second Nature of Civil Society in Kant and Hegel

Thomas Khurana, translated by Nicholas Walker

It is widely known that for Hegel ethical life (*Sittlichkeit*) can be defined as a "realm of freedom made actual" and that this realm must be understood as a "second nature" that is "brought forth out of spirit itself" (Hegel 2008, §4, p. 26). Yet it is by no means obvious how exactly this assertion is to be understood. In characterizing the realm of ethical life as a "second nature," Hegel seems, at first glance, to take up an ancient *topos* that has continued to exercise an influence on practical philosophy ever since Aristotle's interpretation of the ethical virtues. According to Aristotle, ethical virtues determine us neither *by nature* nor *against nature*; rather, they have to become our *second nature* through a process of practice and habituation (2009, 1103a). Already for Aristotle, the realization of ethical life therefore depends upon the production of a second nature. Yet even the brief remarks of Hegel to which I have just alluded indicate a departure from the Aristotelian paradigm. For what the second nature in Hegel's specific formulation is supposed to actualize is not a set of *virtues* but rather the realm of *freedom*. This alters the demanding character of the problem. It seems much easier to understand that an appropriate kind of virtuous practice may be realized by the right kind of habituation than it is to grasp how freedom, of all things, could be realized as nature. The different conception of the underlying problem here raises the question as to how exactly freedom is to be understood in this passage, and how the *second* nature involved must be constituted, if freedom can indeed be actualized through it, instead of thereby simply reverting to its opposite.

Hegel's formulation also suggests a second modification inasmuch as the issue of "second nature" is not solely a question of *subjective* dispositions, namely the second nature that a subject acquires through repeated practice and habituation. Hegel's formulation—the claim that the system of right is the *"realm* of freedom made actual" and the *"world* of spirit brought forth out of itself as a second nature" (Hegel 2008, §4, p. 26; my emphasis)—seems intent on emphasizing the *objective* dimension of this second nature. For Hegel, therefore, "second nature" refers not only to the altered subjective nature of the ethically habituated human being but also encompasses the objectified forms (signs, objects, mechanisms) and the institutions (practices, organizations, functional systems) of ethical life. Thus the concept of second nature in Hegel characterizes what can be captured in a comparably broad manner by the concept of *culture*.[1] Culture encompasses both the subjective and the objective dimension of mind or "spirit" (*Geist*) and refers to both the processes of production—of "cultivation"—and the dispositions and institutions that result from them. What is more, the concept of culture connects both aspects—the process of formation and what is produced through this process—in an irreducible fashion: it defines the "minded" or "spiritual" world as the ongoing process of its own production. It is in precisely this sense that Hegel understands the *second* nature of objective spirit which is mentioned at the beginning of the *Philosophy of Right*: as a "spiritually" produced world that continues to produce the same ethical spirit (Hegel 2008, §4, p. 26). Consequently, this second nature manifests the irreducibly double character of the product and the process of production, of what is present-at-hand and what productively points beyond itself—of "being" and "positing"—and binds both together in an internal way: ethical life is the production of something given and the givenness of the process of production itself, that is, the positing of being and the being of positing.

A third difference of emphasis (one which is not yet explicitly marked in the quoted formulation) lies in the inner dialectical tension and ambiguity which attaches to the very concept of second nature in Hegel.[2] "Second nature" here does not refer to a state of perfection, as it does in the Aristotelian paradigm, namely a perfect art which becomes nature again.[3] Rather, second nature is an embodiment of the tensed relation that holds between nature and spirit. The development of second nature manifests a double movement that involves the spiritual transformation of nature and the naturalization of spirit, a movement in which second nature shows itself both to be a necessary means for the actualization of freedom and simultaneously as the threat of reverting to its opposite, namely to a state of unfreedom.[4] The appeal to "second nature" does not aim at eliminating the tension between spirit and nature, but rather at the internalization of this tension that allows spirit to develop a free relationship to it. When Hegel writes that spirit is "the very *movement of liberating* itself from nature" (Hegel 1968, 249; my emphasis),[5] this liberation can neither be identified with simply the departure from nature, nor with the complete naturalization of spirit itself. Rather than consisting in a result that is beyond nature or nature again, spirit depends on the movement itself differentiating and relating nature and freedom. This movement is internally complex: according to Hegel, the self-liberation of spirit from nature also involves a liberation *of nature* (Hegel 1970a, §246Z, p. 13) and the liberation of spirit *in nature*.[6] It is precisely through the development of a second nature that spirit accomplishes this threefold movement, thus moving beyond the givenness of first nature (the "self-liberation from nature") in such a way that spirit also takes it up and lets it go free (the "liberation *of* nature"), and finally enacts spirit itself as nature ("the liberation of itself *in* it"). In this sense, the "liberation from nature" does not signify the overcoming of nature, but rather the liberation *from a dualistic relationship to nature*, that is, a process of opening up or setting free the difference between spirit and nature.

In Hegel's theory of ethical life, we find such a form of liberation sustained through a complex arrangement of different spheres of ethical life in which various forms of second nature are developed and in turn superseded. The spheres of the family, civil society, and the state, as particular forms of ethical existence, each make their own specific contribution to the realization of freedom, and they do so producing in each case a second nature of a particular type. All three spheres, therefore, can be understood in terms of the way in which they take up subjective and objective nature in a certain sense and transform the latter in a characteristic manner. Whereas Hegel's interpretation of the family still remains very close to the Aristotelian framework, describing how its members are habituated into an organic form of ethical life, civil society, by contrast, appears to emerge specifically from the dissolution or supersession of that kind of organic second nature. It is this distinctive second nature of civil society that lends Hegel's conception its particularly modern character and sets the dialectic of second nature into sharp relief. For this reason, I would like to explore more closely the specific character of this second nature of civil society, which separates itself from the *organic* second nature of the family and makes the *political* second nature of the state possible. Civil society is a second nature—or, to put this in the language of the *Phenomenology of Spirit*, is "a spiritual animal kingdom"—*not* in the sense that the acquired capacities of its members belong to them so easily, effortlessly, and unquestioningly that they appear as something natural again. It is not second nature in the sense of a happy state of completion, a perfected culture reconciled with nature. Second nature here must be understood rather in the sense of a strategic regression. Civil society describes an artificial form of nature-like sociality, a dissolution of ethical life that is produced by and required by ethical life; this is a stage of difference where the members of the family leave the sphere of familial ethical life to which they are accustomed and now relate as individuals whose motivations are naturalized in the form of needs and interests. Thus, civil society is a *second* nature insofar as it is itself a socially produced sphere that does not immediately arise from our natural dispositions or potentialities but already presupposes the ethical education of the family and its socially organized supersession. At the same time, it is a second *nature* insofar as the individuals step out of a first form of ethical life embodied in the family, are thrown back upon the particularity of their needs, talents, and ends, and realize the ethical universal solely in the form of an anonymous chain of necessity. In civil society, the individuals who have been ethically formed by the family relate as "spiritual animals" that are led and guided by their own particular interests and the resources that appear in naturalized form. Civil society describes a structure of systemically concatenated and interconnected actions on the part of such spiritual animals, one in which they undergo a further process of formation and development that no longer transpires as a form of education for ethical life, but rather as a process of individualization and normalization that unfolds behind their backs. It is accomplished in and through them apparently without their own will or knowledge—although this process is still supposed to "form" them for a life of freedom as citizens, that is as *citoyens* and not merely as *bourgeois*.

Thus, the sense in which civil society can be understood as second nature cannot be grasped on the basis of Aristotle's conception of ethical virtue or interpreted in terms of a teleological consummation, as art that has once again become nature. The character of the second nature involved here can only really be disclosed on the basis of that modern understanding of civil society that is essentially prefigured in Kant's concept of culture (*Kultur*). According to Kant, civil society is a kind of human *art, albeit one extorted* from us (2007a, 8:25), and is grounded in a *cunning of nature* which makes possible something that also points beyond nature. Thus, Hegel's conception of civil society as a form of "second nature" is post-Kantian rather than neo-Aristotelian in character. This does not mean, of course, that Hegel limits himself to repeat Kant's conception of the culture of civil society. Hegel goes beyond Kant in that he does not present the developments of culture as the mere unfolding and development of our natural capacities and potentialities, and as an expression of "the intention of nature" (*Naturabsicht*) (however metaphorically this may be understood). Rather, he understands culture as a means for the self-actualization and the self-transgression of spirit: as a second, socially created nature that emerges by superseding the ethical second nature of the family. The nature-like form of this second nature can be revealed with particular clarity if we consider it in the context of Kant's conception of culture.

As a first step, the following discussion will therefore outline Kant's reflections on culture as the ultimate end of nature (2000, 5:431) and on the "social unsociability" (2007a, 8:20) of human beings as an essential means through which nature can unfold our human capacities and potentialities. As a second step, I shall turn to Hegel's characterization of civil society as a stage of difference, where he takes up Kant's own characterization and interprets it not as the culminating point of a natural teleology but as a way of appropriating nature through spirit. In a third and final step, I shall demarcate the limits of the second nature involved in civil society and reveal how civil society points us to the problematic character of second nature in Hegel.

KANT AND THE CULTURE OF CIVIL SOCIETY

According to the definition Kant provides in the third *Critique*, "culture" is "the production of the aptitude of a rational being for any ends in general" (2000, 5:431). Kant distinguishes two dimensions of culture as understood in this sense: on the one hand, there is the culture of skill (*Geschicklichkeit*), which concerns the capacities of the subject to realize potential ends; on the other hand, there is the culture of discipline (*Zucht*), which consists in "the liberation of the will from the despotism of desires" (2000, 5:432) and allows the subject to choose freely between possible courses of action. In this sense, to be cultured or cultivated just means to dispose over technical capacities that enable us to attain any end whatsoever and to develop a capacity for choice (*Willkür*) for us to choose between possible alternative ends, rather than merely operating under the compulsion of immediate desires, inclinations, or instincts. Human beings do not have such technical capacities or this ability for choice immediately "by nature," if what we mean by this is directly or immediately after birth or through some merely organic process of maturation. Rather, the actualization of these capacities requires a social process of formation: the deliberate acquisition and exercise of our skills and some training or discipline at the hands of others. In his *Lectures on Pedagogy*, Kant describes this as a process that "changes animal nature into human nature" (2008, 9:441). From Kant's perspective, however, this process of cultural formation does not yet radically lead us beyond nature but reveals itself to be merely a second level, as it were, in the actualization of our nature. In other words, it is the actualization of a potential that in a specific sense is itself harbored within nature, involving an end that is still immanent in the natural system of ends. It is part and parcel of the natural predisposition (*Anlage*) of human beings that this endowment can only be brought out "gradually by themselves through their own efforts" (2008, 9:441, 443, and 444) and can thus only be unfolded by means of "culture." And such culture remains an end in itself that is enclosed and bound up within the natural system of ends. It is quite true that the cultivation of the human being in this sense enjoys an emphatic status of its own: on Kant's understanding, it is the *ultimate* end (*letzter Zweck*) of nature, the end in view of which alone nature can be articulated and closed as a system of ends. But this is still not what Kant describes as the *final* end (*Endzweck*): an unconditional end, or an end that is not dependent on an encompassing natural system of means-end relationships, yet existing as an end through and for itself. It is possible to describe the human being *qua* natural thing—and more specifically human "culture" understood as the complete unfolding of our natural predispositions—as the "ultimate end" of nature. But, as a natural thing, the human being cannot be described as a "*final* end." The human being can be described as a *final* end only insofar as it is "a being under moral laws" (Kant 2000, 5:448; 1993, B425 and A840/B868), that is, as a being that is free and precisely in this sense stands under the autonomy of practical reason. As something *unconditioned* (Kant 2000, 5:443) with respect to all natural conditions, the final end itself must lie *outside* of nature and can only be grounded in itself.[7]   In this sense, the human being only becomes a final end by making itself this final end through the use of its freedom.[8] As far as the human being is concerned, therefore, it turns out that nature *qua nature* is not teleologically closed and unconditionally grounded. For nature only finds its final end where the human being *makes* itself the final end of creation.

Even the fact that the human being as a natural being is the *ultimate end* of nature is connected for Kant to the capacity of the human being to make itself the final end of nature. The human being is

> the ultimate end of the creation here on earth, because he is the only being on earth who forms a concept of ends for himself and who by means of his reason can make a system of ends out of an aggregate of purposively formed things. (2000, 5:426)

It is only from the perspective of the human being that nature reveals itself as a system and not merely an aggregate of ends, and the human being alone is capable of consciously organizing nature in a purposive fashion. That is precisely why the human being proves to be the ultimate end of this system of ends. From this perspective, it also becomes clear why it is not human happiness but culture that constitutes this ultimate end: for human culture, in contrast to the happiness of the individual, refers specifically to our human ability to set any end we choose and to realize those ends through our own powers and capacities. The ultimate end of nature therefore lies in *preparing* the human being for what "he himself must do in order to be a final end" (Kant 2000, 5:431).[9] The ultimate end of nature is therefore culture insofar as it enables human beings to make themselves into the final end of nature.

In this sense, culture precisely defines the threshold between the realm of nature and the realm of freedom. Through culture, nature is formed and developed in such a way that the latter becomes an enabling ground for the realm of freedom. In other places of his work, Kant undertakes to determine this threshold by distinguishing between the process of cultivation, civilization, and moralization (Kant 2007a, 8:26; 2007b, 9:451): we are *cultivated* to a high degree through art and science—that is, we are enabled to realize whatever end we choose to pursue; we are also *civilized* to an almost excessive degree through civil society—that is, we are enabled to suppress immediate impulses and formed through social conventions to attain our ends with the assistance of others. "But very much is still lacking before we can be held to be already moralized" (Kant 2007c, 8:26). We cannot become *moralized* simply by cultivating our capacities or civilizing our forms of behavior, for in this regard what is required is a good determination of the will, an ethical mindedness *(Gesinnung)*. The kind of capacities and self-restraint produced through the processes of training and *discipline (Disziplin)* is not sufficient to create the moralization in question, for this requires us to act on the basis of *maxims (Maximen)*. The reliable and predictable character of *habits (Gewohnheit)* does not suffice here, since what we need is rather a specific *mindedness (Denkungsart)*.[10] In other words, moralization for Kant requires more than simply the alteration and transformation of sensuous nature; it requires us to take a supersensible character as the ground of the transformation of sensuous nature, as well as to transform this sensuous nature not merely into some kind of means, but into the very expression of that supersensible nature. In view of the apparent gulf between the realm of nature and the realm of freedom, it is not immediately clear precisely how this is to be accomplished.[11] And it is also unclear how the success of this process of moralization can be guaranteed, since a moral disposition cannot, for essential reasons, be explained by reference to a causal mechanism and cannot come about as the result of external compulsion. It is true that some behavior that is externally in accordance with one's own freedom and the freedom of others can be compelled through some natural or artificial mechanism,[12] yet the right-mindedness *(Gesinnung)* depends on it being freely grounded in itself. To this extent any attempt to provide a seamless and compelling explanation for such mindedness reaches an inherent limit when directed at a good moral disposition *(Gesinnung)*, for this turns into a mere semblance of good disposition to the degree that it seems to arise through external necessity. From Kant's perspective, therefore, any explanatory account of moralization must restrict itself to that which prepares for it and makes it possible—namely the work of cultivation and civilization.

In this context, Kant is particularly interested in the various ways in which an inner dynamic tendency of nature itself assists in the process of creating the indispensable presuppositions for the actualization of freedom. In his essay *Toward Perpetual Peace*, Kant formulates this as the question of

> what nature does [. . .] with reference to the end that the human being's own reason makes a duty for him, hence to the favouring of his moral purpose, and how it affords the guarantee that what man ought to do in accordance with laws of freedom but does not do, *it is assured he will do, without prejudice to this freedom, even by a constraint of nature.* (1996, 8:365; my emphasis)

One decisive means through which nature works in the direction of freedom is the two-edged natural human propensity what Kant calls "unsocial sociability," a propensity which also constitutes the fundamental organizing principle of civil society. This double tendency leads human beings, on the one hand, to enter into social relations in order to accomplish their purposes with the help of others, while simultaneously leading, on the other hand, to greater separation between individuals, arranging everything in society in accordance with each one's individual will. This propensity facilitates a particularly extensive and far-reaching development of human abilities and capacities, while also exercising a "civilizing" effect in the sense that it necessitates a process of reciprocal limitation and adjustment with regard to our own undertakings, without thereby simply promoting overall uniformity. Rather, this two-sided propensity intensifies the process of *both* individualization and normalization. In this context the persistent social antagonism, the constant interplay between cooperation and competition, between solidarity and conflict, appears in Kant's eyes as ultimately productive, however high the cost might otherwise be:

> If one hinders the citizen who is seeking his own welfare in any way he pleases, as long as it can subsist along with the freedom of others, then we restrain the vitality of all enterprise, and with it, in turn, the powers of the whole. (2007a, 8:28)

Civil society, by contrast, aims to intensify this "enterprise" in order to release vital human potentialities ever more fully and effectively. To make this possible civil society has to create a sphere of "labour and discord" (2007c, 8:118), a relationship where individuals caught up in both conflict and cooperation are forced to work and engage with outer nature and with other individuals, thus contributing to a process of generalization and specialization at once for their own capacities and predispositions.

  The juridical constitution of civil society that is required to secure and uphold this sphere of work and conflict, on Kant's account, does not itself necessitate specifically moral dispositions. In *Toward Perpetual Peace*, Kant famously expresses this idea by saying that the problem of establishing a political state might even be resolved by a people of devils.

> But now *nature comes to the aid* of the general will grounded in reason, revered but impotent in practice, *and does so precisely through those self-seeking incli-nations*, so that it is a matter only of a good organization of a state (which is cer-tainly within the capacity of human beings), of arranging those forces of nature in opposition to one another in such a way that one checks the destructive effect of the other or cancels it, so that the result for reason turns out as if neither of them existed at all *and the human being is constrained to be a good citizen even if not a morally good human being.* (Kant 1996, 8:366; my emphasis)

The juridical constitution of civil society does not yet require "the moral improvement of man," but merely the suitable application or promotion of a "mechanism of nature" (Kant 1996, 8:366) allowing human beings to become good citizens.

For Kant, therefore, the sphere of culture and civil society remains bound to nature and, at the same time, oriented to the process which prepares for the supersession of the latter. This is true in four respects: the cultivation and civilization promoted by civil society involve (i) a form that unfolds the natu-ral predispositions of the human species and prepares their actualization in a specifically moral sense. As a means of attaining this, (ii) the process relies essentially on natural inclinations and compulsions (the proclivity to unsocial sociability, the natural restraint required in our behavior toward one another), driving a process of cultivation that ultimately leads beyond nature. Third (iii) all these processes accomplish in the first instance a transformation of physi-cal nature which only prepares the way for moralization. The term "culture," as Kant deploys it in his *Lectures on Pedagogy*, does not yet signify moral or spiritual education in the narrower sense, but rather what he calls "*physical education.*" Irrespective of whether we are talking about physical or intellec-tual capacities, the process of formation or *Bildung* here is still "physical" in the sense that this does not concern the issue of the appropriate supersensible disposition in relation to how we set our ends. It is simply a question about the natural power we possess to dispose over ends and means.[13] Thus culture and civil society promote the unfolding of our natural powers and capacities, make use of our natural driving forces, and thereby accomplish a certain transformation of nature. Finally, in accordance with what Kant describes as a necessary fiction, all this transpires (iv) on the basis of a supposed natural end that finds fulfillment in the history of the human species. This self-realizing process comes about neither accidentally nor through any deliberate intention on the part of human beings to develop and improve themselves, but rather, as it seems, through the wise providence of nature itself which has furnished us with a contradictory proclivity that releases our potentialities and ignites the dynamic process of a more than merely natural history. Nature thus pursues an aim which escapes the particular individual that acts under the pressure of nature and thereby makes use of natural means which stand in tension with what is supposed to be attained through these means. The culture of civil society is thus a mere *"prelude* to the unification in society" (Kant 2007c, 8:118; my emphasis), a prelude in which society is produced in a nature-like manner and nature works toward a higher "spiritual" condition in an essentially indirect way.

HEGEL AND THE SECOND NATURE OF CIVIL SOCIETY

The formation (*Bildung*) enacted by civil society in Hegel possesses the same two-edged character as the work of cultivation and civilization in Kant's account: we are confronted with a process of formation which is supposed to equip individuals with the capacities necessary for an ethical form of life, through a process, however, which is not a self-conscious form of ethical praxis per se. Rather, it promotes ethical life behind the backs of the relevant actors precisely in allowing them, as it seems, to individually pursue nothing but their own natural interests. Thus civil society—just like "nature" in Kant (1996, 8:366)—with these selfish inclinations comes to the aid of human beings and cultivates individuals on the basis of their naturally interpreted needs and interests, without them actually knowing or consenting to this cultivation. In his account of civil society, Hegel is thus not simply concerned with the familiar trope that the interest and advantage of all can best be promoted by the consistent pursuit of individual interests organized within the market order. As in Kant, here too the development of civil society is not directed to the maximization of happiness but to the process of cultivation: the unfolding and full realization of the particular capacities of individuals and the intensification of the civilizing social process itself. The ultimate end which is realized in civil society, according to Kant and Hegel alike, is not happiness but "culture": the increased development of "the aptitude of a rational being for any ends in general (thus those of his freedom)" (2000, 5:43). Civil society accomplishes the extensive realization of individual capacities and the concomitant socializing and civilizing process of human behavior by making the pursuit of individual interests dependent upon their incorporation within a *system* of needs. Here, according to a formulation we find in both Kant and Hegel, the individual finds himself as a "link in the chain": considered as a natural thing the human being is "always only a link in the chain of natural ends" (2000, 5:430) as Kant puts it; and the individuals who pursue their own interests as members of civil society have to "make themselves *links* in this chain of *social connections*" (2008, 184; my emphasis) as Hegel emphasizes. In this sense, the individual fits into civil society as if society were a natural system of ends. The ends of individuals in each particular case can only be pursued insofar as these individuals at the same time become means for other individuals in pursuit of their own particular ends.[14]

Whereas Kant still traces the form of civil society back in a basically anthropological way to a twofold natural proclivity of human beings, leading them both to enter into society and to pursue greater individuation, to cooperate with others and to compete with them, Hegel develops this twofold character specifically in terms of the underlying structure of this social system itself. For it is characteristic of this system that it structurally encourages an ever greater and more intense connection between the processes of individualization and normalization. The members of civil society act as individuals who, at the same time, through the division of labor and the process of exchange are dependent on the other members for the attainment of their own ends. In pursuing their own particular ends, individuals are unwittingly also intensely socialized within the structure of civil society, without ever directly intending to be. Since according to the logic of the system they can only constantly concern themselves with their own particular interests, they also stand in competition with other individuals with whom they are only connected in instrumental terms. Thus, the universal reveals itself here simply as a means for the attainment of particular ends, rather than being itself the explicit end either of individual action or of the whole social relationship. In the unfolding of this system the individuals come to depend so essentially upon one another and upon the whole social relationship that the system creates new "social needs" on the part of these individuals (Hegel 2008, §194, p. 189), needs which in turn overlay the immediate natural needs and interests. Since the satisfaction of one's particular needs and the advancement of one's own interests also depend upon the actions of others, the process of "being recognized" becomes central here (2008, §192, p. 189). This yields a specific source of new social needs for recognition and distinction which determine this system more and more: a "demand for equality" and a need for distinction (2008, § 193, p. 189). Thus the inner logic and dynamic of the system of civil society itself creates a double tendency toward socialization and individualization, a striving for equality (in "*emulation*, which is the equalizing of oneself with others"—2008, §193, p. 189) and for distinction.

In line with the Kantian account, the formative effect produced through participation in civil society is not in and of itself regarded by Hegel as the constitution of an ethical disposition, but rather as the preparation or enabling ground for ethical life through a process of cultivation and civilization. The member of civil society multiplies, diversifies, and refines its needs; it develops its aptitude for pursuing whatever ends it chooses to pursue and acquires the skills required to realize its ends in the sensible and material world; and it learns "not only how to direct civil society for its purposes, but also how to fit in with civil society" (Kant 2007b, 9:455). Thus, the member of civil society transforms its needs, extends its technical-practical and specifically social capacities, and learns to adapt its activities not only "in accordance with the nature of the material worked on" but also to limit its activities "in accordance with the arbitrary will of others" (Hegel 2008, §197, p. 191). The subject thereby acquires a nature and a range of abilities which it needs not only for civil society itself but also for an ethical social existence. But civil society does not already actualize a self-conscious and ethical social life in which the universal itself would be the end of the willing and knowing of each and of all. It only realizes the ethical in a form that still remains external to itself. In other words, it presents us with the ethical as a kind of natural happening.

This structure, however, reveals more than just a *cunning of reason* where the latter allows nature to work for the realization of reason's own ends. As Hegel describes it (and here he differs from Kant), civil society does not just serve to prepare the way for the ethical sphere in the strict sense. Civil society also appears as a process that surpasses an initial form of ethical life that is already given: it appears as a departure from the organic ethical life of the family. Thus, Hegel shows that he entrusts an even more essential and internal function to civil society than Kant does. Civil society reveals a mode in which ethical life is realized under conditions of self-externality, where the loss of ethical life and its return to nature is accomplished as a form of self-supersession and as a further new production of ethical life. What we find in civil society therefore is not merely a preparatory stage, but a kind of second attempt: a deepening of the liberation from nature. If this is correct, the decisive reason for this externalized realization of the ethical is that this is the only way for ethical life to fulfill the task of spirit, namely that of liberating itself from nature in the threefold sense that we have already indicated.[15] If this liberation is not to remain caught up in a dualism that would effectively chain spirit to nature, then spirit cannot yield to the illusion that it could simply become independent of its counterpart just like that. If freedom is not just a matter of *independence*, but rather a mode of *being-with-itself-in-the-other*, as Hegel shows in ever-new ways, then the freedom of spirit with regard to nature cannot lie in sheer independence. Rather, its self-liberation from nature requires the liberation *of* nature itself and the liberation of spirit *in* nature. The kind of ethical life that simply seeks to leave nature behind has not actually liberated itself deeply enough; it must appropriate *nature* itself as a mode of ethical life in order to become free from and in nature. Through this deeper liberation, ethical life reveals at one and the same time both its power and its limitation showing its power through its limit and its limit through its power.

It shows its capacity to reach out and extend itself even to its counterpart, to realize itself as its other; yet it thereby also shows itself to be bound to it—especially where it attempts to become or to remain free in relation to itself, or, in other words, to surpass itself.

Civil society is thus more than a merely preparatory instrument. For Hegel himself, it rather constitutes a moment that is essential to the actualization of a properly "spiritual" ethical life, and for that very reason constitutes a distinct sphere of its own within ethical life. Ethical life requires not only a process of adapting to and settling into a given ethical form but also a way of moving beyond the finite forms ethical life has already established. Ethical life surpasses itself in a process of revisiting the nature out of which and in relation to which spirit attempts to attain itself once again in a new way. For Hegel, spirit can and must be realized even in a condition where it loses or releases itself. It is only in this way that spirit attains a radical freedom in relation to its own limited and restricted forms, a freedom in the face of the ethical limitation to what it already knows and intends.

The deeper liberation that civil society is supposed to achieve thus requires another further liberation *of* nature and the liberation of spirit *in* nature: civil society represents the infinite right of the idea to "allow freedom to particularity" (Hegel 2008, § 185Z, p. 184) and is oriented to letting particularity "develop and launch forth in all directions" (2008, § 184, p. 181). In civil society "there is free play for every idiosyncrasy, every talent, every accident of birth and fortune" (2008, § 182Z, p. 181). Civil society consequently aims at unleashing the realm of natural particularity in a new way. It does not, however, thereby simply abandon the project to liberate spirit from nature, for it is also concerned with a further liberation in and with regard to the nature that has been set free in this way. In other words, the nature that has been employed and released here is seen by civil society itself as an expression of spirit in which a formal universality and a certain kind of spiritual life are supposed to arise spontaneously, one which points beyond merely given nature and produces a second nature that has then to be appropriated through a third sphere of ethical life.

In Hegel's account, therefore, the "nature" that constitutes the point of departure for civil society appears, in contrast to Kant, not as some pre-ethically or pre-socially given point, but rather as something that first emerges through the dissolution and supersession of an initial form of organic ethical life. In accordance with this perspective, Hegel does not, as Kant does, trace the structure of civil society back, by appeal to a speculative natural teleology, to a supposed aim on nature's part,[16] and thus no longer attempts to ground the driving forces of this process in an anthropological fashion. Unlike Kant, Hegel does not explain the emergence of civil society as the realization of a secret plan of nature which seeks in this way to achieve the full development of all the predispositions and potentialities with which it has equipped the human species.

Hegel acknowledges that this whole way of speaking, as Kant himself also suggests, may amount to no more than a novelistic and fictitious self-presentation of reason.[17] From Hegel's perspective, the notion that culture is the ultimate end of nature is the *Bildungsroman*, as it were, that reason tells of its own genesis. The emergence of civil society as an independent sphere as well as the way in which it needs to be limited and sublated through the ethical life of the state is something that for Hegel arises from the history of freedom rather than from that of nature (in this regard see also Kant 2007c, 8:115). This process does not result from an intrinsically natural development. It rather takes on a "spiritual" necessity of its own because civil society realizes an essential moment of freedom, albeit one that taken on its own is inadequate and even dangerous for the whole, namely the freedom of arbitrary choice (*Willkür*).[18] The essential means and motivations that shape and promote this moment of freedom in civil society do not arise on the basis of an anthropological propensity but through social mechanisms involving both the liberation and transformation of nature. Those mechanisms operate by means of constituting individuals as particular subjects with their own interests within the system of needs.

To understand the extent to which the second nature of civil society is not a simple pre-ethical given, but a way in which ethical life is superseded from within itself, it is helpful to remind ourselves that the *formation* of civil society rests upon and goes beyond the process of *education* and *upbringing* in the context of the family. Hegel describes the family as a "natural" form of ethical spirit (Hegel 2008, §157, p. 161). It appears as natural not only insofar as it realizes ethical life on the level of feeling, but also insofar as the family finds its point of departure in a "moment of *natural* life" (2008, §161, p. 163). The achievement of the family, generally speaking, lies in the transformation of the "life process of the species"—of the sexual relationship on the one side and the relationship between parents and offspring on the other—into a "spiritual" relationship (2008, §161, p. 163). This transformation reveals itself not least in the process of education and upbringing through which children are introduced to an initial form of ethical life in terms of their family life. In general terms, Hegel describes pedagogy as "the art of making people ethical: It considers them as natural beings and shows them the way to a second birth, the way to change their original nature into a second, spiritual, nature, and makes this spiritual level *habitual* to them" (2008, §151Z, p. 159). The perspective adopted in the process of education is twofold in character: on the one hand, it recognizes that the one to be raised and educated is a natural being and recognizes its nature as such, precisely in order; on the other hand, to transform this nature into something "spiritual" and to turn this spiritual character itself into something habitual. The living nature of the child, through its life in the family, is supposed to be transformed in such a way that the child does not merely become familiar or make itself at home in the organic ethical life of the family but at the same time develops the capacities and the self-relation that eventually enables it to leave the family and to exist as an ethical being in its own right: as an agent within civil society, as a member of the state, and as a potential founder of another family. In this context, education does not merely take the form of introducing and habituating the child into a common social life and enabling it to make its own contribution to such a life, but also places it in a position to move beyond this initial form of spiritual life that it leads in the ethical sphere of the family.

As Hegel sees it, this is essentially dependent upon the fact that the negative instrument of discipline through which the child is meant to be liberated from its immediate natural determinacy and be inducted into a shared life also provokes an inner resistance. The function of discipline is not simply to overcome the natural determinations of the individual and to break the mere willfulness of the child but also to awaken the child's own "wish to grow up and be an adult, through which children are themselves brought up" (Hegel 1970a, 327).[19] In other words, discipline also has the function of encouraging the child to leave this discipline behind and become independent in its own right. In this sense, the discipline inculcated within the family is meant not just to procure the capacities for ethical activity generally but also to provide the child with an impulse to move beyond this educational relationship itself and thereby leave the sphere of the natural ethical life of the family.

The form of civil society can only be properly understood against this background: it presupposes the process by which the individual emerges from the organic ethical life of the family, which only liberates the child for the possibility of ethical life to the extent that it pushes the child to move beyond this first shape of ethical existence. The one who has grown up and leaves the family does so precisely by coming back to his nature once again in a new way. The supersession of the organic second nature of the family does not take place by directly progressing toward a thoroughly self-conscious ethical life. It first takes place, surprisingly, in terms of a dissolution or regression: at once, a step beyond the family and a step back from the form of sociality and ethical existence that is already achieved in the family. The one who leaves the family does not determine what he has become as an expression of a universal form of ethical life in which the resulting individual is entirely sublated or taken up. Rather, he interprets what he has become, and also what he has remained in the face of his education and upbringing, as his *individual nature*. He appropriates the product of this education—both what has been transformed and what was revealed as recalcitrant to the process—as something that is given, as something that is once again or still remains natural: "a totality of needs and a *mixture of caprice and natural necessity*" (Hegel 2008,

§182, p. 180–81; my emphasis). In leaving the family, the individual finds itself in a sphere that corresponds to what Hegel describes in the *Phenomenology of Spirit* as the dissolution of organic Greek ethical life: "The universal being thus split up into a mere multiplicity of individuals, this lifeless spirit is an *equality*, in which *all count the same*, i.e. as *persons*" (Hegel 1977, ¶477). In his essay *On the Scientific Ways of Treating Natural Law*, Hegel characterizes the corresponding condition of civil society as "the inorganic nature of ethical life" (1999, 146; my emphasis).

Thus, if this civil society can be called "second nature," this cannot be understood in the organic sense that is characteristic of the family. Rather, this can only signify an inorganic—a *technical, mechanical*, or *machine-like*—arrangement. And herein lies the apparently paradoxical regression involved in civil society. At the same time, this inorganic order is one of arbitrarily acting subjects that do not stand under the immediate compulsion of their respective urges or tendencies. This is precisely the step that civil society, the *spiritual* animal kingdom, takes beyond the merely organic form of ethical life which had replaced the compulsions of given nature with the acquired and developed nature of habituation. In the shape of civil society, ethical life is realized in the mode of its own loss (Hegel 2008, §181Z, p. 180): it is realized through superseding the compulsions of its organic second nature and finds itself confirmed even in the condition of its own dissolution and decomposition. Thus, civil society, far from representing an original state of nature, constitutes a sphere generated within the state through its self-diremption, a sphere in which the ethical enters into an inorganic aggregate condition of atomistic disintegration. Civil society presents itself as a *stage of difference* in which ethical life seems to have dissolved; at the same time the members of civil society here are not simply pre-ethical or unethical beings, but individuals who have already moved beyond a first limited form of ethical life, who here appropriate for themselves what they have become in a new way as a quasi-natural given.

The seemingly unethical relationship of a multitude of particular beings—for whom in each case their own particularity is the primary and fundamentally determining factor—does not only rest upon an already accomplished process of ethical development but also continues to *form* these particular individuals for ethical universality through their relations of cooperation and competition with one another. Civil society is therefore subject to two principles at the same time: on the one hand, the principle of the concrete person "who as a *particular person* is his own end" (Hegel 2008, §182, p. 180) and, on the other hand, the principle of universality that does not manifest itself in a direct manner but shows itself indirectly by the way in which particular persons in each case can only exist by being essentially "*related* to other particular persons" (2008, §182, p. 181). The various persons in question can only assert themselves insofar as they are mediated through one another. Inasmuch as it shapes the particular persons for universality through this process of mediation, civil society performs the work of ethical life; but it does so in a nature-like manner, rather than in one that is itself ethically free.

This nature-like character of civil society thus leaves its mark on both sides of the relationship: on the one hand, on the side of the particular person, we are dealing with beings that present themselves in their particularity as a mixture of caprice and necessity; their actions are governed by their given particular needs and by their arbitrary will, that is, by inner and outer contingency and thus by two symmetrically opposed forms of natural existence. On the other hand, on the side of the principle of universality, civil society presents itself as nature-like in character as well. For the actors, there is no shared or transparent order that they could recognize as their own, but merely an interconnection between particular individuals that each particular person experiences as a kind of limitation or restriction. The universal thus makes itself felt as a factual constraint (*Sachzwang*), as a kind of natural necessity, that remains abstract in the sense that it is seemingly brought about solely through the concatenation of other purely particular factors which the particular person encounters and finds himself dependent upon as he pursues his own particular ends: "this medley of arbitrariness" (*Wimmeln der Willkür*) and "this apparently scattered and thoughtless sphere" give rise to a necessity which "automatically enters it" (Hegel 2008, §189Z, p. 187) without this being known or willed in advance by the individuals in question. Through this necessity, the social-spiritual order is realized as a kind of natural happening. Insofar as this necessity only arises through our activity we can indeed understand it in a distinctive way as "one of our own making alone" (Hegel 2008, §194, p.189); yet it is not intended as such and only arises in a nature-like way like some natural event.

It is worth noting that Hegel describes what transpires through this confrontation of individuals in their ungrounded particularity on the one hand and the universal in its non-transparent necessity on the other hand as a process of *Bildung*. We are not to think of this as a process that the particular person, in contrast to the asymmetrical relationship involved in being educated, finally accomplishes in relation to itself in a conscious and deliberate way—in the sense, for example, that the particular individual might attempt to form itself in accordance with some self-chosen image or ideal. The formation or *Bildung* at issue here is a process that is accomplished through the systemically concatenated pursuit of particular interests by different individuals who all contribute to this process behind their backs. In this sense, the universality and necessity involved in civil society is "of our own making," although not self-conscious. The *Bildung* described by Hegel here encompasses both the unfolding and the formation of the particular: natural needs are not just externally limited or restricted within

the system of needs but are unfolded and developed in a way that simultaneously frees them and allows them to be controlled or modulated through their
will. On this pathway of *Bildung*, it is not, therefore, just a question of discipline
by limiting or restraining—as Kant's description of the culture of training had
perhaps suggested—but rather of discipline by a process of liberation. In other
words, the system of needs is realized, in the first instance, as the unfolding and
development of particular needs "in all directions" (Hegel 2008, §184, p. 181).
This development implies a multiplication, division, and refinement of needs
through ever more specific and complexly substitutable partial needs, along
with the generation of those social needs for recognition by means of which our
natural needs are effectively over-determined. In this sense, human needs are
not held back through prohibition or restriction but are made available through
their development and variegation. This process of multiplying, breaking down,
and refining needs moderates their compulsive character in the particular case,
and this compulsive character is replaced by that of an endlessly expanding system of needs that the individual can hardly escape any longer. The satisfaction
of these multiplied, variegated, refined, and socially expanded needs can only
be met through the process of exchange and the division of labor. To exert any
social effect, individuals must procure recognition for their needs and their abilities and must consequently bring those needs and abilities into a general social
form. Thus the freeing up and the free development of the particular nature of
the individual "in all directions" ultimately leads to a hard struggle of the individual in relation to itself: to the "*hard labour* against the pure subjectivity of
demeanour, against the immediacy of desire, against the empty subjectivity of
feeling and the arbitrariness of inclination" (Hegel 2008, §187A, p. 185). Once
again Hegel describes the result of this labor as a "liberation" (2008, § 187A, p.
185). Yet this is a liberation that is not enacted by but "happens" to those who
are liberated, and it only transpires in a process of division through which the
particular nature of the specific individual and the social nature of their reciprocal dependency work against and with one another. As Hegel puts it:

> Spirit attains its actuality only by creating a division within itself, by imposing
> this limitation and finitude upon itself in the shape of natural needs and the
> network of these external necessities, and by overcoming them and attaining
> objective existence in them precisely by *developing itself in them* (*sich in sie
> hinein bildet*). (2008, §187A, p. 184–85; translation modified, my emphasis)

The way in which spirit acquires objective existence through this process
of formation and development, however effective it may be for unfolding
the *presuppositions* of the ethical order and for *extending* ethical life beyond
its limited forms, is itself problematic as a form of ethical existence. Civil
society takes hold of individuals on the side of their natural particularity and

binds them into a system through which they are both individualized and universalized, becoming capable of further liberation and further realization of freedom. But it accomplishes this not through the free exercise of our powers as "spiritual" beings, but through an ethically ungrounded capacity for arbitrary choice and through apparently "spiritless" forms of external necessity. Thus, civil society too requires us to go beyond the particular way in which it realizes ethical life.

In this connection, however, civil society assumes a form that makes the liberation from it evidently more difficult and demanding than the liberation from the sphere of the family. The one who has grown up, who has become an adult, outgrows the intra-familial power that is exercised upon him precisely to the extent that this education and upbringing proves successful. It is an essential aspect of this process that the person also resists that exercise of power and thereby releases himself from this context of organic ethical life within the family. Civil society, on the other hand, makes us dependent upon processes that imply forms of impersonal structural compulsion and develop a logic of their own that seems to escape any simple kind of control or responsibility; their functioning appears almost automatic rendering any normative objections or expressions of resistance pointless. Civil society disciplines its subjects without manifesting itself as a form of intended and consequently accountable normalization: what operates here seems to be a merely factual constraint (*Sachzwang*), the expression of the externally necessary interconnections of social nature. Civil society thus exercises its formative power in a way that, makes it seem futile to respond to it with "the wish to grow up."[20] On the other hand, civil society, if it is actually supposed to make ethical life in the full sense possible, seems to depend on a comparable impulse to go beyond itself.

In both of these forms, in education within the family and in the formation of civil society, it becomes clear that ethical life involves achieving a liberation from our given nature. This liberation does not come about as the simple negation or supersession of nature, but as a complex process of development and transformation accomplished in relation to nature itself, a process that has nature as and makes nature into its own presupposition. The process of liberation transpires in a different manner in each case as a process of socialization. This socialization does not simply exercise various forms of power in relation to living nature; it thereby also institutionalizes social hierarchies—between the educator and the educated, between the nature of the social world and the individual who confronts it. The unfolding of civil society produces a condition of inequality between different classes, and indeed a further dynamic of inequality which produces "a large mass of people" which "falls below a certain subsistence level—a level regulated automatically as the one necessary for a member of society" (Hegel 2008, §244, p. 221). Civil society thus excludes a part of those who make it up, although it does not thereby release them from itself. It therefore becomes evident that the liberation from nature and the formation of a second nature, accomplished in different ways in the family and in the civil society, are processes that begin as subjection to social power, particularly profound and unsettling in civil society.[21]

On Hegel's account, civil society certainly realizes the right of the particular individual in a deeper way than the sphere of the family does, but at the same time it does so in a limited and distorted form. Even if the particular individual can be taken up into ethical life through civil society, it is thereby also brought into a form that distorts it: individual freedom is posited as the freedom of one's own choice and one's own individual need, rather than as the free capacity of the individual for self-determination. Thus we are free to pursue our needs or our arbitrary choices, that is, free to follow our nature in the double sense of necessity and contingency.[22] The freedom in question is limited in an equally external and nature-like way, since the exercise of this freedom is limited in relation to the given needs or aims of others and to the necessities involved in the interconnected social process, in other words, to things which the individual cannot directly control and which it can only attempt to influence in a strategic way. If the *right of particularity*, the *freedom of the individual*, and the *demand for equality* which civil society produces and claims are in fact to be fulfilled, it is necessary to move beyond civil society itself.

POLITICIZATION: THE APPROPRIATION
OF SECOND NATURE

The move beyond one's incorporation in the family and the discipline associated with the process of upbringing, on the one hand, and beyond the complex process of individualization and normalization promoted by civil society, on the other hand, for Hegel cannot be accomplished through a process of moralization, as it can be for Kant. For it requires a political dimension in which individuals see themselves neither as members of the organic whole of the family, nor as atoms caught up in the mechanism of civil society, but rather understand themselves as citizens of a self-determining political whole. In this sense ethical life requires not just an *organic* and a *technical* form of second nature, but a *political* form of second nature too.[23] And it does so for internal reasons in each case: if education (*Erziehung*) is supposed to be an art that serves to liberate the human being, this clearly requires that the pupil eventually leaves that relationship and understands himself as an *I* that can itself speak for the *We* that the teacher initially claimed to represent exclusively for himself. And if formation (*Bildung*) is supposed to be the "absolute point of transition" for the liberation of spirit (Hegel 2008, §187A, p. 185), this cannot simply consist in the limited release of particularity and an accommodation to objective forms of factual constraint. Rather, it must lead the one so formed precisely to the point where it becomes possible for him to appropriate this process of formation: to recognize it as a process that we have exercised upon ourselves and that we—as those who have been formed in this way—can endorse or must repudiate as such after the event.[24] Given the constitutive lack of transparency that belongs to this process of formation, a necessity that appears to unfold by itself, as something unwittingly produced by the agents themselves, we are here confronted with a difficult task: those who have been formed in this way must attempt to appropriate this process of formation after its event, for it is only through such appropriation that we can constitute our own formation as a form of liberation. But, in doing so, the subject has to face the critical question as to whether precisely in appropriating this process of formation it may already be taken in through its ruses. The intransparency of the process of formation and the inevitably "belated" character of our appropriation means that we can always ask whether we are perhaps only prepared to affirm the processes we have undergone because we have already been malformed by them.[25] And in the context of the apparent naturalness behind which social power has been concealed, the already formed subject must ask itself to what degree it is really the truly universal alone, and not perhaps the interests of individuals that have prevailed in this formative process of civil society. This entails asking how far the formed subject, in unreservedly appropriating the content of its own process of formation, blinds itself to the power relations and exclusions that have arisen in the processes of civil society behind the backs of the subjects involved. Even there where the formed subject is able to and wishes to affirm what it has become, it must still develop a relationship to the fact that the second nature of civil society essentially extends spirit beyond what has already been recognized and intended and acquires a certain surplus character which cannot simply be reduced to consciousness. The appropriation of second nature in this sense would then also imply an express recognition of this surplus character in all its irreducibility.

The appropriation of the liberation which has become second nature within ethical life cannot simply require affirmation, namely the self-conscious endorsement of what we have unconsciously produced. What it requires is that, in relating back critically to our second nature, we continue to make ourselves what we are. It requires those who have been raised to freedom to pose the political question whether they can in fact continue to produce themselves and can wish to live in the way they currently do through the forms of their organic and technical second nature. This political question can only be asked by an *I* that can have recourse to a *We* that is something more than it, and other than the *One* or the *They* of the anonymous and necessary social processes. If the universal is to become accessible in this way as a *We*, this requires more than a multiplicity of individuals working away their immediacy and particularity in interaction with one another, thereby producing something general in which they convene. There is a We only where the I dares to say what We want. There is ethical life only where there is the arrogation of the I and contention with regard to what *we* know, what *we* want, what *we* do.[26] Ethical life only becomes *possible* inasmuch as individuals are socialized through upbringing, education, and culture and are thereby liberated from and in their nature; yet, it only becomes *actual* inasmuch as these individuals grasp the social forms of their liberation from and in nature and liberate themselves from and in those forms.

This can only be achieved by a process of politicization that goes beyond the process of formation and grasps, in a new way, the relationship between the individual and the universal which has determined that process. It may seem plausible to understand the process of formation as one that leads beyond itself and anticipates ethical life specifically insofar as the process is realized as a universalization of the particular individual, in which the content of its particularity is brought into a formally free and general form thus compatible with ethical life. Yet this hardly does full justice to the particularity involved in the formative process of civil society itself, since it was precisely the *infinite* right to this particularity that civil society was supposed to show. From the standpoint of the ethical appropriation of formation in the process of politicization, we must therefore understand formation itself as something that itself already points beyond the merely formally free and universal individuality of the self-interested subject of civil society. This is the condition of possibility of the I that can say We. In other words, the I must recognize civil society as *our* act and product and ask the question whether *we* wish to continue producing this civil society in this way and thus continue to form ourselves through it in the way we do. Only in such an I—which claims to speak for a We and thereby exposes itself to the contention of other individuals regarding this We—it is possible to attain a form of individuality that is inwardly determined by the universal rather than being externally limited by it.

Here we can recognize a *desideratum* that Hegel's *Philosophy of Right* reveals, which is yet only inadequately developed. Hegel's account of civil society and the process of formation required by it implies that civil society must become the "point of absolute transition" to ethical life, but does not fully explore whether or how the current form of civil society actually allows this to happen.[27] Although Hegel's treatment of the issue makes it clear that any movement beyond civil society can only come about through a process of political appropriation beyond the mere administration of civil society (Hegel 2008, §258A, p. 228–29), in his theory of the state Hegel does not actually develop in any detail the politics of second nature that would consequently be required. Instead of specifically showing how the second nature of the family and of civil society can be critically appropriated and questioned in the context of the political process, Hegel limits himself to the state as the presentation of the unity of the spheres of the family and the civil society.

This means that the critical potential of Hegel's own re-conceptualization of second nature is developed in an insufficient way. In the preceding discussion, I have tried to show that ethical life in the form of the family, civil society, and the state realizes itself as second nature in a quite different manner in each case. Neither the organic nor the technical form of second nature can have the last word here, for they point us toward a genuinely political dimension of ethical life in which alone the development of organic and technical second nature can contribute to an ongoing form of liberation. It is not a question of dissolving the family and civil society in the state, but rather of conceiving a process of politicization that can recognize the irreducible character of these forms of second nature, at the same time questioning them through a critical appropriation and supersession of these forms. As soon as we attempt to define such a process of politicization more precisely, the question immediately arises as to how far the forms of organic and technical second nature which are produced in our contemporary societies facilitate or allow this kind of political recognition, appropriation, and surpassing. As far as civil society is concerned, the issue is not just whether in unfolding our predispositions and potentialities it really provides the instrumental achievements it promises, or whether it creates problems in the process that it cannot itself resolve. The further question is whether civil society as currently constituted is of such a kind that we can appropriate it as a mechanism of liberation as we try and move beyond it. It seems clear that the economic, juridical, and ideological form that civil society has assumed in the present makes critical questioning urgently necessary, while the neoliberal conception of politics as a matter of securing and administering civil society obscures the important task of such an appropriation. Civil society can only become a mechanism of liberation if it makes the recourse to the inorganic nature of society into a means for questioning the limitation of the organic forms of ethical life, allowing the "spirit" to renew itself by developing further beyond what it has already consciously understood, recognized, and striven for.[28] The reification of living needs, impulses, and forces in the form of interests, capitalizable skills, and arbitrary powers, along with a political process that sees its task in the mere regulation rather than the critical appropriation of civil society, turns and distorts the mechanism of liberation into its own negation. The task of a critique of civil society is to understand more clearly and precisely how civil society is becoming less a "prelude of unification in society" (Kant 2007c, 8:118) than an obstacle to it.[29]

NOTES

1. For further discussion of the modern conception of second nature as culture, which is connected with an aesthetic, dialectical, and objective turn of the concept, see Khurana (2016).

2. For the further development of this ambiguity in detail, see Khurana (2017, 389–409).

3. In this regard see Kant's exemplary formulation of "the perfect art" which "again becomes nature, which is the ultimate goal of the moral vocation of the human species" (Kant 2007, 8:111).

4. For this particular dialectic, compare Hegel's characterization of habit in the *Encyclopaedia* and in the *Philosophy of Right*: "In habit man's mode of existence is habit, and for that reason he is unfree in it; but he is free in it in so far as the natural determinacy of sensation is by habit reduced to *his* mere being, he is no longer different from it, is indifferent to it, and so no longer interested, engaged, or dependent with respect to it" (Hegel 2007, §410A, p. 131); "Therefore although, on the one hand, by habits man becomes free, yet, on the other hand, habit makes him its *slave*" (Hegel 2007, §410Z, p. 134); "The human being also dies from habit, i.e. when he has once come to feel completely at home in life, when he has become spiritually and physically dull, and when the opposition between subjective consciousness and spiritual activity has disappeared [. . .] When this has been fully achieved, activity and vitality are at an end, and the result—loss of interest in life—is spiritual or physical death" (Hegel 2008, §151Z, p. 159–60).

5. "Where it [i.e. spirit] comes from—that is from nature; where it is going—that is its freedom. What spirit *is*, that is precisely this movement of liberating itself from nature" (Hegel 1968, 249).

6. See also the *Encyclopaedia* (Hegel 2007, §386, p. 22), where Hegel says that gaining freedom *from* a found and given world and gaining freedom *in* the world "are one and the same."

7. See e.g. Kant (2000, 5:431): "As the sole being on earth that has reason, and thus a capacity to set voluntary ends for himself, he is certainly the titular lord of nature, and, if nature is regarded as a teleological system, then it is his vocation to be the ultimate end of nature; but always only conditionally, that is, subject to the conditions that he has the understanding and the will to give to nature and to himself a relation to an end *that can be sufficient for itself independently of nature, which can thus be a final end, which, however, must not be sought in nature at all*" (my emphasis). See also Kant (2000, 5:435): "I have said above that the final end cannot be an end that nature would be sufficient to produce in accordance with its idea, because it is unconditioned. *For there is nothing in nature (as a sensible being) the determining ground of which, itself found in nature, is not always in turn conditioned; and this holds not merely for nature outside of us (material nature), but also for nature inside of us (thinking nature)—as long as it is clearly understood that I am considering only that within me which is nature. A thing,*

however, which is to exist as the final end of an intelligent cause necessarily, on account of its objective constitution, must be such that in the order of ends it is dependent on no further condition other than merely the idea of it" (my emphasis).

8. See Kant's remark that "the history of freedom [. . .] is the work of man [. . .]. Thus the history of *nature* begins from *good*, for that is the *work of God*; the history of *freedom* from evil, for it is the *work of the human being*" (1997c, 115).

9. "Thus amongst all his ends in nature there remains only the formal, subjective condition, namely the aptitude for setting himself ends at all and [. . .] using nature as a means appropriate to the maxims of his free ends in general" (Kant 2000, 5:431).

10. As we shall see below, the analogous transition from civil society to the state in Hegel requires not so much moralization, if we take this to mean the development of personal morality, but rather the transition to a different form of free and ethical sociality. But in Hegel too the character of this different form of sociality is defined by the fact that it is not simply ruled by *discipline* and *habituation* but by the power of *will* and *thought*, where "will" is understood as a kind of thinking: "The merit of Rousseau's contribution to the search for this concept is that, by adducing the *will* as the principle of the state, he is adducing a principle which has *thought* both for its form and its content, a principle which is indeed *thinking* itself, not a principle, like the social instinct for instance, or divine authority, which has thought as its form only" (Hegel 2008, §258A, p. 229–30).

11. In the third *Critique* Kant presents an aesthetic model for the creation of such a "second (supersensible) nature." For further discussion of this idea, see Khurana 2016; Khurana 2023.

12. It is by no accident that Kant's "Doctrine of Right" in contrast to the "Doctrine of Virtue" employs specifically mechanical analogies. In his *System of Transcendental Idealism*, Schelling takes up these Kantian pointers when he claims that the system of right reconstructs the compulsion of nature on a higher level: "A second and higher nature must, as it were, be set up over the first, governed by a natural law quite different, however, from that which prevails in visible nature, namely a natural law on behalf of freedom. As inexorably, and with the same iron necessity whereby effect follows cause in sensible nature, an attack upon the freedom of another must be succeeded, in this second nature, by an instantaneous counter to the self-interested drive. A law of nature such as that just depicted is to be found in the rule of law, and the second nature in which its authority prevails is the legal system, which is thereby deduced as a condition of the continuance of consciousness" (Schelling 1978, 195). In this context, the system of right appears as nothing more than an artificial "mechanism of nature" that is created through freedom.

13. At the beginning of his treatise on pedagogy, Kant introduces an initial rather rough distinction between physical and practical education along the following lines: "Pedagogy or the doctrine of education is either physical or practical. Physical education is the education part which *the human being has in common with animals*, or maintenance. Practical or moral education is the education by which the human being is to be formed so that he can live as a freely acting being. (We call practical everything which has a relation to freedom.) Practical education is education towards personality, the education of a freely acting being who can support itself and be a

member of society, but who can have an inner value for itself" (2007b, 9:455; my emphasis). Further along, Kant, however, provides a more subtle version of this distinction insofar as there is a preparatory part of practical education which he also describes as "physical," namely "culture": "The positive part of physical education is culture. *In this respect the human being differs from the animal.* Culture consists particularly in the exercise of one's mental powers" (2007b, 9:466; my emphasis). This cultivation refers not only to physical or corporeal development in the narrow sense but also includes the culture or development of the human soul: "We come now to the culture of the soul, which in a way can also be called physical. One must, however, distinguish between nature and freedom. Giving laws to freedom is something entirely different from forming nature. The nature of the body and that of the soul agree in this, that in the formation of each of them one seeks to prevent some corruption—and that art furthermore adds something to both of them. *One can therefore call the formation of the soul in a way just as physical as the formation of the body. However, this physical formation of the mind is distinguished from the moral formation of the mind in that the latter aims solely at freedom; the former solely at nature.* A human being can be highly cultivated in physical terms, he can have a well-formed mind, but still be poorly cultivated in moral terms and thus be an evil creature" (2007b, 9:469f; my emphasis).

14. It is plausible to say that this system will privilege in a quite particular fashion the pursuit of those ends which can also function as a general means. If we can regard money as the general means of a market-driven civil society, insofar money permits the acquisition of other concrete means of whatever kind, then it seems that money is what is sought as the ultimate end in civil society. To pursue money in this sense is to determine one's end in such a way that it also always constitutes a means. This expresses the essence of the system of needs.

15. For this "liberation from nature," see also various passages in the *Encyclopedia*'s *Philosophy of Mind* (Hegel 2007, §382Z, p. 17 and §386Z, pp. 22, 24, §410A, p. 131, §441Z, pp. 167–68, §443, p. 170, §485, p. 217, §548–49, p. 246). Consider also: "[B]ut if we ask what spirit is, then the immediate answer is: spirit is this movement, this activity, *this process of starting from nature, liberating itself from nature, this is the being of spirit itself, its substance*" (Hegel 2008a, 151f.; my emphasis).

16. On Hegel's break with the tradition of natural teleology, see Riedel 1974, 109ff.

17. "A philosophical attempt to work out universal history according to a plan of nature that aims at the perfect civil union of the human species, must be regarded as possible and even as furthering this aim of nature. It is, to be sure, a strange and apparently absurd stroke, to want to write a history in accordance with an idea of how the course of the world would have to go if it were to conform to certain rational ends; *it appears that with such an aim only a novel could be brought about*" (Kant 2007a, 8:29; my emphasis).

18. For the claim that the "bad infinity" and contingency of the sensuous desires are appropriated and even turned into a conscious principle through such freedom of choice, see Khurana (2015, 198f). Compare also Hegel's claim that the sphere of civil society contains "natural and *arbitrary* particularity" (2008, §200A, p. 192; my emphasis) and

through this arbitrary freedom succeeds in grasping external contingency as inner contingency (2008, §194, p. 189).

19. From Hegel's marginal notes not included in the English translation.

20. It is an internal aspect of civil society itself that in the course of our formation we acknowledge its necessary features, and it is quite possible that we also recognize these necessary features as "self-made" ones. From the perspective of civil society, however, these regular processes of social nature only interest us insofar as we can exploit them for our particular interests in each case; if we do recognize them as "self-made," this simply yields new contexts and opportunities for securing our own aims by attempting to manipulate the necessities involved. But it does not seem part of the inner logic of civil society itself that we should appropriate these necessities as our own shared act, that we specifically grasp them as a means for the collective self-determination of our form of life and in this sense also go beyond them.

21. On the idea that the liberation from nature begins as social subjection, see also Weil (1970, 19).

22. For the notion that "nature" is the realm of necessity and contingency, see Hegel (1970b, §248, p. 17): "Nature exhibits no freedom in its existence, but only necessity and contingency."

23. A political form of second nature allows us once more to adopt and express a relationship to the organic and technical second nature of the family and civil society insofar as we are able to appropriate these forms of second nature in a critical fashion as expressions of our own activity. Here the political process itself once again needs to embody itself as second nature and take on an independent form of its own; but this process can only lead beyond the family and civil society if it is capable of relating to the institutions that emerge from it and that make it possible in a way that involves more freedom and awareness than is present in the organic or technical second nature. In other words, the political process must not only enable a level of critical reflection and separation with regard to the second nature both of the family and civil society, but must equally exercise a level of critical self-reflection with regard to its own second nature.

24. On the necessity of appropriating our second nature in a properly self-conscious fashion, if we are supposed to be able to understand it as the realization of freedom, see Hegel's remarks in his lectures on the philosophy of religion: "This sublation, this self-subjection to the ethical, and this process of habituation through which what is ethical and spiritual becomes the second nature of the individual is the very work of education and culture. *This reconstruction of the human being must now be brought to consciousness on this standpoint, because it is the standpoint of self-conscious freedom, so that this reversal (Umkehrung) is recognized as what is required*" (Hegel 1970a, 146; my emphasis).

25. As already formed and no longer merely natural beings, we can thus come back to our own nature in a different way and assert it against what the process of formation has made out of it. This is evidently a complex operation that can easily generate a false self-conception as trying to return to a supposedly original nature, or inner core, that was distorted by the process of formation. Yet it is only this process, against which the subject here turns, that has placed the subject in a position to come

back to its own nature in this way and thus, in turning back once again to the process of its own becoming, to put what it has become into question.

26. See Cavell 1979, 20: "The philosophical appeal to what we say, and the search for our criteria on the basis of which we say what we say, are claims to community. And the claim to community is always a search for the basis upon which it can or has been established. I have nothing more to go on than my conviction, my sense that I make sense. It may prove to be the case that I am wrong, that my conviction isolates me, from all others, from myself. That will not be the same as a discovery that I am dogmatic or egomaniacal. The wish and search for community are the wish and search for reason."

27. On this question see the pointed discussion by Sandkaulen 2014, 436–38. On Sandkaulen's diagnosis of the problem, Hegel reduces "the process of formation (*Bildungsprozess*) to a movement towards the universal" and "thereby transforms his concept of formation, even at 'the standpoint of division,' into an entirely affirmative enterprise." Thus the "potential of formation in the sense of a critical participation in public affairs" is not developed at all, which is why it remains entirely unclear how the process of formation can actually become this "absolute point of transition" (2014, 436).

28. This productive surplus character is underlined by Hegel's consistent emphasis on the fact that civil society is a "play": even before characterizing civil society as hard labor, as competition, as a fight of each against all and as an inevitable exclusion of the ones included in it, civil society presents itself as a play—a "play of variegation, decomposition, and refinement" of needs ad infinitum; as a "medley of choice" (Hegel 2008, §189Z); as a "display (*Schauspiel*) of retroactive necessity," as "one playing into the hands of the other" (*Ineinanderspielen*) (Hegel 2007, §189Z). It is this self-active play which first makes intelligible why civil society is not just a helpful mechanism in the capitalization and regulation of individual resources but an intensification of liberation. In the course of Hegel's treatment highlighting the formative and generalizing effect produced by civil society, this element of "play" recedes more and more into the background.

29. This paper was finalized in the context of the research project "The Comedy of Political Philosophy," generously supported by the EU and directed by Dr. Birte Loeschenkohl. I would like to thank Birte Loeschenkohl for instructive comments on the above. In addition, I am indebted to participants of the conference of the Hegel Association in Stuttgart and of a colloquium at Goethe University Frankfurt am Main for comments on an earlier draft. Finally, I would like to thank Daehun Jung, Haeng Nam Lee, and Ralf Beuthan for their insightful remarks on the penultimate version, delivered as one of my Hegel-Lectures at Seoul National University.

REFERENCES

Aristotle. 2009. *The Nichomachean Ethics*. Oxford: Oxford University Press.
Cavell, Stanley. 1979. *The Claim of Reason: Wittgenstein, Skepticism, Morality, and Tragedy*. New York/Oxford: Oxford University Press.

Hegel, G. W. F. 1968. "Fragment zur Philosophie des subjektiven Geistes," in *Gesammelte Werke*, 15. Hamburg: Meiner.

Hegel, G. W. F. 1970a. *Grundlinien der Philosophie des Rechts oder Naturrecht und Staatswissenschaft im Grundrisse* in *Theorie-Werkausgabe*, 7. Frankfurt a. M.: Suhrkamp.

Hegel, G. W. F. 1970b. *Philosophy of Nature*, A. V. Miller (trans.). Oxford: Oxford University Press.

Hegel, G. W. F. 1970c. *Vorlesungen über die Philosophie der Religion* in Theorie-Werkausgabe, 16–17. Frankfurt a. M.: Suhrkamp.

Hegel, G. W. F. 1977. *Phenomenology of Spirit.* A. V. Miller (trans.). Oxford: Oxford University Press.

Hegel, G. W. F. 1999. *On the Scientific Ways of Treating Natural Law, on its Place in Practical Philosophy, and its Relation to the Positive Sciences of Right* in *Political Writings*, L. Dickey, and H. B. Nisbet (eds.). Cambridge: Cambridge University Press.

Hegel, G. W. F. 2007. *Philosophy of Mind.* A. V. Miller (trans.), and M. Inwood (rev.). Oxford: Oxford University Press.

Hegel, G. W. F. 2008. *Philosophy of Right.* M. Knox (trans.), and S. Houlgate (ed.). Oxford: Oxford University Press.

Hegel, G. W. F. 2008a. *Vorlesungen über die subjektive Philosophie des Geistes*, in Gesammelte Werke, 25.1. Hamburg: Meiner.

Kant, Immanuel. 1933. *Critique of Pure Reason*, N. Kemp Smith (trans.). London: McMillian.

Kant, Immanuel. 1996. "Toward Perpetual Peace," in *Practical Philosophy*, M. J. Gregor (trans.). Cambridge: Cambridge University Press.

Kant, Immanuel. 2000. *Critique of the Power of Judgment*, P. Guyer and E. Matthews (trans.). Cambridge: Cambridge University Press.

Kant, Immanuel. 2006. *Anthropology from a Pragmatic Point of View*, trans. and ed. by R.B. Louden. Cambridge: Cambridge University Press.

Kant, Immanuel. 2007a. "Idea for a Universal History with a Cosmopolitan Aim," in *Anthropology, History, and Education*, A. Wood (trans.). Cambridge: Cambridge University Press.

Kant, Immanuel. 2007b. "Lectures on Pedagogy," in *Anthropology, History, and Education*, R. B. Louden (trans.). Cambridge: Cambridge University Press.

Kant, Immanuel. 2007c. "Conjectural Beginning of Human History," in *Anthropology, History, and Education*, A. Wood (trans.). Cambridge: Cambridge University Press.

Khurana, Thomas. 2015. "The Self-Determination of Force: Desire and Practical Self-Consciousness in Kant and Hegel," *International Yearbook of German Idealism*, 13: 179–204.

Khurana, Thomas. 2016. "Die Kunst der zweiten Natur. Zu einem modernen Kulturbegriff nach Kant, Schiller und Hegel," *WestEnd. Neue Zeitschrift für Sozialforschung*, 13 (1): 35–55.

Khurana, Thomas. 2017. *Das Leben der Freiheit. Form und Wirklichkeit der Autonomie*. Berlin: Suhrkamp.

Khurana, Thomas. 2023. "The Art of Second Nature. Modern Culture after Kant," *Graduate Faculty Philosophy Journal*, forthcoming.

Riedel, Manfred. 1974. "Natur und Freiheit in Hegels Rechtsphilosophie," in *Materialien zu Hegels Rechtsphilosophie*, 2, M. Riedel (ed.). Frankfurt a. M: Suhrkamp.

Sandkaulen, Birgit. 2014. "Bildung bei Hegel—Entfremdung oder Versöhnung?" *Hegel-Jahrbuch*, 2014(1): 430–38.

Schelling, Friedrich W. J. 1978. *System of Transcendental Idealism*, P. Heath (trans.). Charlottesville: University Press of Virginia.

Weil, Simone. 1970. *First and Last Notebooks*. Eugene: Wipf & Stock.

Chapter 4

1880: First Philosophical Critique of Adaptationism

Nietzsche, Reader of Herbert Spencer

Barbara Stiegler, translated by
Borhane Blili-Hamelin

> *The madman's privilege of being unable to adapt himself.*
>
> —Nietzsche 1997a, 190

Nietzsche was the first philosopher to diagnose a new disease that brutally emerged during the second half of the nineteenth century and whose virulence has yet to stop growing. I propose to call this illness *adaptationism*, a term that Nietzsche did not coin, and that I borrow from Stephen Jay Gould, Richard Lewontin, and Richard Levins (Gould and Lewontin 1979; Levis and Lewontin 1985). These three influential twentieth-century biologists popularized the term in their own effort to denounce the rampant use of the concept of adaptation: by evolutionary biologists, and by Neo-Darwinists, who— beginning from the mid-twentieth century—attempted to impose the concept of adaptation on all fields of life without exception. Gould and Lewontin do not deny the importance of adaptative processes and do not take issue with adaptation as such (1979). However, they object to the hegemonic and totalizing application of the biological concept of adaptation to life in general, along with the incorrigible tendency to seize the anthropological field of morality and society. Nietzsche's contribution helps amplify this tendency by identifying some of its much earlier manifestations. *Adaptationism* means the unwarranted extension of the biological concept of adaptation—at first overstated in biology and then eventually spread to all domains of our lives. "*Adapt!*" is the new injunction sounded everywhere, all the way up to the political sphere: the guiding principle of the "new liberalism" that emerged decades after

Nietzsche and persists to this day.[1] Such is the importance and seriousness of the phenomenon that Nietzsche first uncovered. He may not have named it; yet, he measured its acuteness and diagnosed it with the highest precision. For he correctly identified the first theorist of adaptationism: not Darwin but Herbert Spencer, the notorious instigator of Social Darwinism, the first to attempt to draw the social and political consequences of the Darwinian revolution. In attacking adaptationism, did Nietzsche also take on Darwin and Darwinism? Or did he find a sufficiently powerful antidote against adaptationism and its budding hegemony within *On the Origin of Species*?

Nietzsche didn't have firsthand knowledge of Herbert Spencer's thought until he read *Data of Ethics* in 1880, which he went on to address straight away, point by point, in *Daybreak*. The posthumous fragments of 1880 are thus vital. These fragments are also the source of one of Nietzsche's most important discoveries in biology. This discovery—praised by Stephen Jay Gould in his latest book *The Structure of Evolutionary Theory* (2002)—is that the origin of an evolutionary phenomenon has strictly nothing to do with its utility, as Nietzsche would fiercely reiterate in a well-known passage from *On the Genealogy of Morality* (2007, §12). The history of life is made of countless emergencies with no basis in utility. Utility, when it happens, is mostly introduced after the fact by life and the living.

For Gould, who delivers a fascinating commentary of around twenty pages on this passage from the *Geneology*, Nietzsche was the first to grasp that the utilitarian approach implicit in adaptationism entirely misses the reality of evolutionary processes (Gould and Lewontin 1979).[2] Instead of a cumulative process accruing the *optimum* of utility and progressively eliminating the harmful as negative, Nietzsche grasped the reality of evolution as a resolutely unpredictable conflict between the old and the new. He discerned, much better than Darwinians themselves, the historical nature of evolution. He also understood—before Gould—that evolution, unlike a machine engineered to run on utility, looks much more like an architectural construction structured by a web of constraints and heritages, which are most often impossible to justify. More like a cathedral than a machine, evolution is weighed down by heavy structural constraints inherited from the past, themselves devoid of any function and utility. These structural constraints are what Gould and Lewontin call "spandrels" (1979)—after the triangular space or "pendentive" left empty when building a vault or dome.

Where there is utility, it is invented and springs forth after the fact, as in the case of the spandrels of the Basilica di San Marco, which ended up being used, much later, as mere decorations. Originally drab and useless, these wasted spaces now have the accidental function of letting the golden light of Byzantine mosaics shine brighter. This brings us to the other essential characteristic of history and evolution that Nietzsche grasped so well.

Like the cellars and attics of our buildings, historical processes are cluttered with remains of the past. At the same time, they are always open to unpredictable reversals of significance: an element may prove useful after the fact, or completely shift in its use. These reversals are what Gould and Elisabeth Vrba—in another influential article—call "exaptation" (Gould and Vrba 1982). Rather than seeing evolution as a cumulative optimization process—rather than forcing it to comply with the utilitarian and functionalist engineering mindset that dominates among Darwinian biologists— Nietzsche is one of the few to have respected the creative historicity of evolution. He thereby anticipated both Michel Foucault's warnings against the Hegelian and Marxist hurry to find "reason in history" everywhere (1994), but also Bergson's worries against Herbert Spencer and his false evolutionism (2008).

No doubt, Gould would have been glad to learn about these passages by Nietzsche's *Daybreak*, which already spelled out very clearly the theses revisited seven years later in the *Genealogy*. Consider, for instance, §37 of *Daybreak*:

> *False conclusions from utility.*—When one has demonstrated that a thing is of the highest utility, one has however thereby taken not one step towards explaining its origin: that is to say, one can never employ utility to make it comprehensible that a thing must necessarily exist. But it is the contrary judgment that has hitherto prevailed—and even into the domain of the most rigorous science. (Nietzsche 1997a, 26)

All "of the most rigorous" contemporary "science," particularly in the domain of life, is indeed based on this utilitarian prejudice. Utility is supposed to provide the reason for the emergence of anything. Utility also gives adaptation its central place: selection retains what is *adapted*, that is to say, *useful* for the survival of the organism and its descendants under their given conditions. The old principle of sufficient reason of early modern metaphysics (Leibniz) is dethroned by its contemporary successor, with *utility* at its helm: utility is likewise taken "to make it comprehensible (*verständlich*) that a thing must necessarily exist," by subjecting it to the logical demands of our understanding (*Verstand*). Here, Nietzsche seems to target both Spencer's evolutionism and Darwinian selection.

However, nothing in life happens quite like this. On this point, Nietzsche favors the example of caring for one's offspring. For Spencer, as for many biologists, this behavior is explained by its utility for the preservation of the species. For Nietzsche, this is but a naïve prejudice. Parents don't care for their offspring for the sake of the species. Instead, they do so for a whole series of obscure and extremely labile motives—a variability that depends on the context and is vastly amplified by the multiplicity of motives within the same living organism: "Love for the brood is not something simple! as is believed! but product, property, entertainment, something harmless, something obsequious, that one dominates, something warm—many reasons for agreeability!" (Nietzsche 1967ff, 7[224]; my translation).

Care for the young can be explained in myriad ways, and by a multiplicity of instincts: appropriation instinct, play instinct, domination instinct, or the simple need for warmth. These contradictory "reasons" for obtaining pleasure—which should instead be called motives or drives, in the sense of simple impulses (*Trieb*)—have nothing to do with the rational utility life would accrue, allegedly accumulating an *optimum*. Far from caring for the young out of altruism, or out of a would-be "instinct for the preservation of the species," some species of fish even mistake their eggs for food to be protected:

[. . .] some species of fish keep guard by their eggs and fend off hostility. I suspect that here, as in other cases in the animal world, the parents consider the eggs and the young as food that must be preserved and protected; in many cases, the animals also live on it. (Nietzsche 1967ff, 3[85]; my translation)

This behavior, initially useful for nutrition, could prove to have a different utility after the fact: such as that of propagating the species. But this diversion of function was neither predicted nor predictable by the initial utility. This is precisely what Gould and Vrba would call "exaptation" (1982):

The species that have taken the most care of this kind of food [. . .] have the best chances of reproducing themselves, and the habit of caring for the eggs and the young transmits itself more and more strongly, until finally becoming a mighty drive for itself, in which the first motive is forgotten. (Nietzsche 1967ff, 3[85]; my translation)

The remarkable polysemy of utility explains these many changes of direction. Completely unpredictable and "quirky," says Gould, these changes make evolution a radically open history (1983). Nietzsche said the same thing when insisting upon the "unexpectedness" at the core of evolution: "The actions with unexpected results, undertaken for another purpose— e.g., an animal guarding its eggs as food, and suddenly sees in front of itself beings in its like" (Nietzsche 1967ff, 1[54]; my translation). If the history of life is made of all of these quirky functional changes, if it never functions as the accruing of the same *optimum*—that is, the "in-itself useful" and the "maximization of well-being"—it is because the same complexity of drives underlies all of these behaviors, from care for the young to procreation, and even nutrition:

Procreation is an occasional but frequent consequence of a kind of satisfaction of the sexual impulse: not its intention, not its necessary effect. The sex drive has no necessary relation to procreation: occasionally, this result [i.e., procreation] is also achieved through it [i.e., the sex drive], like nutrition through the pleasure of eating. (Nietzsche 1967ff, 6[141]; my translation)

Spencer, like all utilitarian evolutionists more generally, glimpses a unitary reason behind all behavior, a reason that natural selection would have been championing, by ensuring the accumulation of the most useful variations and the elimination of the most harmful. This same rationale would have been then encapsulated by utilitarian morality seeking the maximization of happiness in the human species. Nietzsche objects that all behavior stems, on the contrary, from a web of drives within which pleasure and utility are not necessarily coupled—a decoupling which no utilitarian, since Jeremy Bentham, can think. For this is precisely the first fallacious maxim of utilitarianism: what is useful is what maximizes the sum of pleasure and happiness.

Spencer and utilitarian biologists do not understand that their would-be criterion, utility, proves to be extremely labile, heterogeneous, and indeterminate. In seeking to import Darwinian explanatory schemes into morality, evolutionist ethics also introduces all the ambivalence of the criterion of utility. However, "happiness is achieved through opposing ways. Hence it is not possible to determine an ethics (against Spencer)" (Nietzsche 1967ff, 8[12]; my translation). This is what §106 of *Daybreak* repeats very clearly, still against Spencer, while also refusing any "definitions of the goal of morality":

Against the definitions (Definition) of the goal of morality. Everywhere today the goal of morality is defined (*bestimmen*) in approximately the following way: it is the preservation and advancement of mankind; but this definition is an expression of the desire for a formula, and nothing more. Preservation *of what*? is the question one immediately has to ask. Advancement *to what*? (Nietzsche 1997a, 61)[3]

In applying the Darwinian scheme to moral questions, in taking morality to retain what is most useful for preservation and growth, Nietzsche shows, we inevitably sink back into one of the classic problems of Darwinism. Is the unit of selection the organism or the group? And, if it is the group, is it the relatives, the species, or the clade?

How should one act? So that the isolated individual preserves itself as much as possible? Or so that the breed preserves itself as much as possible? Or so that another race preserves as much as possible? (Morality of Animals) Or so that life is preserved in general? Or so that the highest species of life are preserved?

The interests of these different spheres diverge. But what are the highest species? (Nietzsche 1967ff, 1[4])

Utility for preservation is at the bottom merely a formula—one that leaves the question of the criteria for evolution utterly unanswered. Instead of this fictitious univocity, life is made of a multiplicity of conflicting points of view. One of them is the conflict between the old and the new, running through all living organisms, be they individuals or groups—a conflict to which prevailing theories of evolution, with their obsession with the selection for the *optimum*, have become oblivious. For Nietzsche, evolution requires the joint action of two contradictory tendencies which necessarily come into conflict: the tendency to preserve the like and the inverse tendency to experiment with the new. He sees neither tendency as superior to—or more "useful" than—the other. In threatening to supplant the other, each tendency threatens the very continuation of evolution. Speaking of these, §224 of *Human, All Too Human* says that

> [. . .] two things must come together: first, an increase in the stabilizing force [. . .]; and second, the possibility of attaining higher goals as degenerate natures turn up and, in consequence, partial weakenings and woundings of the stabilizing force occur [. . .]. (Nietzsche 1997b, 154)

Deviation from the species—literally *Ent-artung*—always leads to weakening and greater vulnerability. In that sense, we could say that it is harmful. It is nevertheless, at the same time, a challenge necessary for the emergence of the new: "Precisely in this wounded and weakened spot, the collective being is inoculated, as it were, with something new [. . .] Degenerate natures are of the highest significance wherever progress is to ensue" (Nietzsche 1997b, 153–55). Yet, life can only sustain this tendency when conjoined with its countertendency, namely stability. Harmed or wounded by the "infection of what is new," the organism's "strength as a whole must be great enough to absorb this new thing into its blood and to assimilate it" (Nietzsche 1997b, 154). This is precisely what utilitarian biologists are unable to comprehend with their simplistic criterion of the "struggle for existence"—that is, of preservation and reproduction, or of what contemporary Darwinian, with distant echoes of Spencer, calls "fitness":[4]

> Seldom is any degeneration, any mutilation, even a vice or any physical or moral damage whatsoever without an advantage in some other respect. [. . .] someone with one eye will have one stronger eye; a blind person will see more deeply within and will in any case have sharper hearing. To that extent, the renowned struggle for existence does not seem to me to be the only point of

view from which the progress or strengthening of an individual or a race can be explained. (Nietzsche 1997b, 154)

What adaptationists don't want to see—in elevating utility as an absolute criterion—is the driving role of the negative within evolution. Hence Nietzsche's insistence on the vocabulary of vulnerability ("wounded," "weakened," "damaged"), of pathology ("infection," "mutilation"), and of maladaptation. Without the maladapted, who take the risk of experimenting with other ways of living, there would never be evolution:

> It is the more unconstrained, the much more uncertain and morally weaker individuals upon whom spiritual progress depends in such communities: these are the people who attempt new things and, in general, many different things. Because of their weakness, countless individuals of this kind perish without much visible effect [. . .] it is precisely the weaker nature, as the more delicate and free, that makes any progress possible at all. (Nietzsche 1997b, 153–55)

The champions of the "survival of the fittest"—the famous expression that Darwin borrowed from Spencer—cannot see this value of weakness, illness, and maladaptation. Nor can they begin to see the struggle that ceaselessly threatens the two tendencies that are necessary for life. For, if the new always threatens the stability of the old, the stability of the old also always threatens to prevent the new from emerging. For Nietzsche, this constitutive tension— between the force of the old and that of the new—is the Machiavellian question of power as the tension between two sources:

> As for what concerns the state, Machiavelli says that [. . .] "the great goal of the art of politics should be durability, which outweighs everything else, since it is much more valuable than freedom." Only when the maximum durability has been securely grounded and guaranteed is steady development and refining inoculation possible at all. (Nietzsche 1997b, 154–55)

But Machiavelli also has the lucidity to affirm the necessity of the countertendency, that of freedom and novelty. The new always risks suffocation under the domination of the establishment—be it the political state, or whatever state (*stato*) for its duration: "Admittedly, the dangerous associate of all durability, authority, will generally resist that" (Nietzsche 1997, 155). That is, authority, with all its might, shall oppose evolution: "The danger for these strong communities based upon individuals who all share a similar character is a gradual increase in inherited stupidity, which trails all stability like its shadow" (Nietzsche 1997b, 154–55).

While utilitarian evolutionists picture evolution as a cumulative process of optimization, Nietzsche situates it under the aegis of conflict and the negative.

Now, this is precisely what the American biologists that I mentioned at the beginning themselves do. Richard Lewontin, in particular, by associating with Richard Levins, explicitly professed a *dialectical* biology of evolution (1985): finally getting rid of the primacy of adaptationism and its allergy to any form of negativity—by placing conflict and tension at the heart of evolution.

For them, the tension systematically masked by adaptationism is not solely between the old that lasts and the new that breaks forth. It is also between the organism and its environment. In their words, "the metaphor of adaptation [. . .] is pure Cartesianism" (Levins and Lewontin 1985, 3). That is, for Darwinian biology, everything happens as if environment and organism were two separate entities, like subject and object.

While the organism is understood as an alienated object, which must adapt to its given conditions, the environment is the subject of evolution which imposes its conditions on life. Against adaptationism, it is therefore essential to assert the capacity of organisms for proactivity, as active subjects in the construction of their environments:

> The incorporation of the organism as an active subject in its own ontogeny and in the construction of its own environment leads to a complex dialectical relationship of the elements in the triad of gene, environment, and organism. [. . .] The organism is, in part, made by the interaction of the genes and the environment, but the organism makes its environment and so again participates in its own construction. Finally, the organism, as it develops, constructs an environment that is a condition of its survival and reproduction, setting the conditions of natural selection. So the organism influences its own evolution, by being both the object of natural selection and the creator of the conditions of that selection. Darwin's separation of ontogeny and phylogeny was an absolutely necessary step in shaking free of the Lamarckian transformationist model of evolution. [. . .] Darwinism cannot be carried to completion unless the organism is reintegrated with the inner and outer forces, of which it is both the subject and the object. (Levins and Lewontin 1985, 105–106)

In his precocious fight against the prejudices of Darwinism, Nietzsche prefigures this same conception of the biological activity of organisms. But in the famous passage of the *Genealogy of Morals* praised by Stephen Jay Gould, Nietzsche clearly shows that it was less Darwin himself than Herbert Spencer who actually locked evolutionism into adaptationism: by reducing the living to passive and amorphous material, forced to adapt without resistance to "external circumstances," and by systematically "spiriting away" its activity:

> The whole of physiology and biology [. . .] have spirited away their basic concept, that of actual activity. On the other hand, the pressure of this idiosyncrasy forces 'adaptation' into the foreground, which is a second-rate activity,

just a reactivity, indeed life itself has been defined as an increasingly efficient inner adaptation to external circumstances (Herbert Spencer). (Nietzsche 2007, 52)

At its core, adaptation is nothing but the subjection of the new by the old. Hence, by definition and as for the Machiavellian state (*lo stato*), the latter essentially strives to last: "Education, continuation of procreation. The entirety of life is adaptation of the new to the old" (Nietzsche 1967ff, 1[12]; my translation). The fact remains that this tendency, necessary for life, must accept its countertendency: the resistance of the new to any form of adaptation. This is precisely what Spencer is incapable of understanding, going so far as to define in a fixed and final manner the requirements of the environment: "an increasingly efficient inner adaptation to external circumstances" (Nietzsche 2007, 52).

For Nietzsche, struggling against the industrial society advocated by Spencer, it is fundamental to learn to respect "the madman's privilege of being unable to adapt himself"(Nietzsche 1997a, 190).

Education, insofar as it continues the process of procreation and evolution, must not only ensure the "adaptation of the new to the old" (Nietzsche 1967ff, 1[12]; my translation). Education must likewise understand the essential value of wound, damage, disability, and, more broadly, maladaptation, without which the new can be neither attempted nor inoculated: "the educator has to inflict wounds upon [the individual] or to use the wounds that fate inflicts, and when pain and need have resulted from this, something new and refined can be inoculated into the wounded places" (Nietzsche 1997b, 154).

Denying the constitutive and necessary tension between the old and the new—and with it the pains of maladaptation—adaptationism gives itself a fictitious unity: utility in-itself, toward which all the evolutionary processes are supposed to converge. We therefore understand how the utilitarian tendencies of the Darwinians pushed them to a vision of evolution entirely subservient to optimization and, ultimately, to progress. However, as Nietzsche reminds us in §122 of *Daybreak*, Darwin himself is the one who insisted on the role of "chance," and on the need to abandon any reference to the "purposes" of teleology:

Purposes in nature.—The impartial investigator who pursues the history of the eye and the forms it has assumed among the lowest creatures, who demonstrates the whole step-by-step evolution of the eye, must arrive at the great conclusion that vision was not the intention behind the creation of the eye, but that vision appeared, rather, after chance had put the apparatus together. A single instance of this kind—and "purposes" fall away like scales from the eyes! (Nietzsche 1997a, 77)

For Nietzsche, the Darwinian principle of blind and random variation, which gives considerable weight to chance, holds for all historical processes: "Principle: in the entire history of mankind to date, no goal, no secret rational direction, no instinct, but chance, chance, chance—and some favorable. These are to be brought to light" (Nietzsche 1967ff, 1[63]; my translation).

By accommodating the random emergence of variation, entirely decoupled from any goal and any finality, the Darwinian revolution has rightly rid us of any teleological picture of evolution, in which history would have a pregiven meaning and direction. It is in the name of Darwin and of Darwinism itself, as Stephen Jay Gould would later show, that we must fight at once against optimization, utilitarianism, and adaptationism—which surreptitiously reintroduce the illusions of teleology, and with them the principle of sufficient reason. However, this is the whole problem of the nature of Darwinian *selection*, which intervenes after the fact on the stochastic material of variation. To be sure, and since the history of life is nothing like a rhapsodic chaos of variations, it is necessary to think of something like an anti-chance process accounting for the multiple coherent directions of evolution and history. This is precisely the role that natural selection plays for Darwin. But, for Nietzsche, these directions can be explained neither by the falsely unitary criterion of utility nor by that of adaptation—which reduces living things to passive material, subjected to the demands of the environment. At the bottom, they can only be explained by the presence of "active forces" in individual and collective organisms, which introduce after the fact a creative function for what arises at random. This is what Nietzsche maintains at the end of the famous passage of the *Genealogy of Morals* against adaptationism:

> But this is to misunderstand the essence of life, its will to power, we overlook the prime importance that the spontaneous, aggressive, expansive, re-interpreting, re-directing and formative forces have, which "adaptation" follows only when they have had their effect; in the organism itself, the dominant role of these highest functionaries, in whom the lifewill is active and manifests itself, is denied. (Nietzsche 2007, 52)

The whole point of the history of life is precisely that a multiplicity of necessarily conflicting active forces introduce the function, meaning, and direction of evolutionary processes after the fact.

Nietzsche converges with Machiavelli here again—this time, the Machiavelli of the *Discourses on Livy*, who understands history as the necessary conflict between the point of view of the dominant and the resistance of the multitude:

The "development" of a thing [. . .] is a succession of more or less profound, more or less mutually independent processes of subjugation exacted on the thing, added to this the resistances encountered every time, the attempted transformations for the purpose of defense and reaction, and the results, too, of successful countermeasures. (Nietzsche 2007, 51)

The whole history of morality is shot through with the same conflict—between dominant forces seeking to last and new forces seeking to emerge. However, it is precisely this conflict that Spencer's teleological evolutionism denies, by projecting the adaptation of all living things to a final goal, a sort of Hegelian "suspension" or "sublation" (*Aufhebung*) of all contradictions:

An adaptation like the one Spencer has in mind is conceivable, but so that every individual becomes a useful tool and only feels itself as such: thus as a means, as a part—that is, with the abolition of individualism. [. . .] But then individuals become weaker and weaker. (Nietzsche 1967ff, 10[D60]; my translation)

Evolution supposes a multiplicity of conflicting ends and goals, uniquely reinvented each time by individuals, and impossible to abolish in a final "sublation." Adaptationism eschews the reality of evolution by giving itself an ultimate *telos*—like the philosophies of history—a stationary and permanent end state:

Humanity has no goal, just as the dinosaurs did not have one, but it has a development: that is to say, their end is no more significant than any point in their journey! NB. Consequently, one cannot determine the good in such a way that it would be the means to the "goal of humanity." (Nietzsche 1967ff, 6[59]; my translation)

This is the very meaning of the "industrial society" that Spencer theorized as the end state of the history of life and rigorously described in §174 of *Daybreak*. Denying everything that constitutes the reality of evolution, Spencer projects a large global market of cooperation in which all forms of conflict, difference, or deviation will ultimately be abolished and sublated by the adaptation of each to all others:

Moral Fashion of a commercial society. Behind the basic principle of the current moral fashion: "moral actions are actions performed out of sympathy for others," I see the social effect of timidity hiding behind an intellectual mask: it desires, first and foremost, that all the dangers which life once held should be removed from it, and that everyone should assist in this with all his might: hence only those actions which tend towards the common security and society's sense of security are to be accorded the predicate "good." [. . .] Are we not, with this tremendous objective of obliterating all the sharp edges of life, well on the way to turning mankind into sand? (Nietzsche 1997a, 105–106)

Here is the recurring theme of the "sand of mankind," looming throughout the dark visions of *Daybreak*: massification, as the ultimate effect of the adaptationism that dominates "industrial society." All of Nietzsche's rupture with his close friend Paul Rée will play out, from this time, around this question. Rée's work on *The Origin of the Moral Sensations*, by replicating all the errors of utilitarian evolutionism, and by dreaming like Spencer of the final reconciliation of egoism and altruism, in fact merely celebrates the massification of industrial societies and encourages the destruction of individuation.

Nietzsche shows that by projecting final salvation and calling for the cooperation of all individuals in the same unified body, Rée and Spencer's evolutionism remains—just like the philosophies of history of Hegel and Marx—gorged with the last shadows of God. The Darwinian revolution could have led to the definitive disqualification of Christian eschatology. Yet the reign of adaptationism in biology and evolutionary ethics paradoxically reveals "the echo of Christianity" and its pastoral model—where the shepherd is supposed to lead his flock in the ultimate direction of salvation:

> *The echo of Christianity in morality.* [. . .] Today it seems to do everyone good when they hear that society is on the way to adapting the individual to general requirements, and that the happiness and at the same time the sacrifice of the individual lies in feeling himself to be a useful member and instrument of the whole: [. . .] one hopes to manage more cheaply, more safely, more equitably, more uniformly if there exist only large bodies and their members. Everything that in any way corresponds to this body and membership-building drive and its ancillary drives is felt to be good. (Nietzsche 1997a, 82–83)

To this prospect of a final negation of evolution in economic optimization, Nietzsche opposes a path much more faithful to Darwin, that of "the experiment stations (*Versuchs-Station*) of humanity" (Nietzsche 1967ff, 1[38]; my translation) and of "little *experimental states* (*Versuchsstaaten*)" (Nietzsche 1997a, 191), whose function would be to explore the multiplicity of ways of living: "numerous novel experiments (*Versuchen*) shall be made in ways of life and modes of society" (Nietzsche 1997a, 101).

As for Darwin's evolutionism, which Nietzsche here honors, life ceaselessly carries out new experiments: "Experiments are also necessary among humans, as in Darwinism!" (Nietzsche 1967ff, 10[B42]; my translation). But if the ethical experimentation proposed by Nietzsche is indeed Darwinian, it cannot be reducible to the randomness of variation and trial and error. As with evolution guided by natural selection, the account must envisage a controlled process testing a multiplicity of directions each time, rather than relying on chance: "We must not [. . .] rely on chance. It is in most cases a senseless destroyer" (Nietzsche 1967ff, 1[63]; my translation).

By controlling random variations and imposing goals on them, culture continues the selecting activity which, since the beginning of life, sorts through the raw material of chance by giving it a multiplicity of directions. Except that, for Nietzsche, selection cannot proceed, as in Darwin, from the falsely unitarian criterion of utility and adaptation. The only possible selection consists instead in "providing air and light to new drives" (Nietzsche 1967ff, 1[33]; my translation), especially as they are seriously threatened by Spencer's "industrial society" and its dominant adaptationism: "Free spirits experiment [*versuch*] other ways of life, invaluable! moral people would make the world wither. The experiment stations [*Versuchs-Station*] of humanity" (Nietzsche 1967ff, 1[38]; my translation).

However, for Nietzsche, the experimentation of evolution necessarily requires the negative that are pain and delay. Nothing is more contrary to the experimental approach than an imperative of optimization, which would lead to the continuous capitalization of utility and the trending suppression of the negative: "There is a tremendous amount of pain on the experiment stations of new ways of life, of new utility—it is of no help; may it at least help others! may they recognize what failed experiment was attempted here" (Nietzsche 1967ff, 1[39]; my translation).

Because utility is only invented after the fact, and always in the conflict of the multidirectional attempts of life, there is no point in raising the useful and the harmful into absolute criteria. To respect life and its capacity to evolve rather requires, for Nietzsche, that we preserve the possibility of the negative and of conflict, and that we recognize the "privilege" of disability, illness, and madness "of being unable to adapt" (1997a, 190).

A few years after Nietzsche, the pragmatist philosopher John Dewey will articulate the very same objections against Spencer's "industrial society"—brought up to date by the evolutionism of Walter Lippmann and other neoliberals.[5] Fighting both Spencer and Lippmann, Dewey will also draw from the Darwinian revolution's call to experiment with a multitude of ways of living. And he too will challenge any attempt to eliminate the driving force of the negative and conflict from life. Yet, unlike Nietzsche, he will do so through a completely different concept of adaptation, also much more faithful to Darwin than Spencer's adaptationism. For Dewey and the pragmatists, adapting in no way means bending to the requirements of the environment like "putty" (Gould 1983, 157). Instead, as in the dialectical biology of American evolutionists, adapting means actively constructing one's environment while allowing oneself to be transformed by it. The problem thereby becomes to know whether, as Dewey believes, the concept of adaptation can measure up to the conflicting tensions of evolution; or rather, as Nietzsche thinks, it necessarily leads to the excesses of adaptationism. Such is the question we inherit from this fundamental disagreement between Nietzsche and Dewey on the status of adaptation that, a century later, the ongoing conflicts of contemporary Darwinism still have not resolved.

NOTES

1. I mean *neoliberalism*, which also became hegemonic beginning in the second half of the twentieth century. I show its deep connections to biological adaptationism in Stiegler (2022).
2. For a detailed commentary on Gould's reading, see Stiegler (2015).
3. On this theme, see also the following posthumous fragments: Nietzsche (1967ff, 3[171] and 6[59], 6[123], 6[125], 10[B 48]).
4. The terminology of *fitness* was introduced by Herbert Spencer in 1864, in an attempt to describe Darwinian natural selection. Darwin went on to add the term to a later edition of *The Origin of Species*.
5. See my previously cited Stiegler (2022).

REFERENCES

Bergson, Henri. 2008. *L'évolution créatrice*. Paris: Puf.
Foucault, Michel. 1994. "Nietzsche, la généalogie, l'histoire," in *Dits et écrits*, 2: 136–56. Paris: Gallimard.
Gould, Stephen J. 1983. *Hen's teeth and horse's toes*. New York: Norton.
Gould, Stephen J. 2002. *The Structure of Evolutionary Theory*. Cambridge: Cambridge University Press.
Gould, Stephen J., and Lewontin, Richard. 1979. "The Spandrels of San Marco and the Panglossian Paradigm: A Critique of the Adaptationist Programme," *Proceedings of the Royal Society of London*, 205 (1161): 581–98.
Gould, Stephen J., and Vrba, Elisabeth. 1982. "Exaptation—A Missing Term in the Science of Form," *Paleobiology*, 8 (1): 4–15.
Levins, Richard, and Lewontin, Richard. 1985. *The Dialectical Biologist*. Harvard University Press.
Nietzsche, Friedrich. 1967ff. *Werke: Kritische Gesamtausgabe*, G. Colli and M. Montinari (eds.). Berlin: W. de Gruyter.
Nietzsche, Friedrich. 1997a. *Daybreak: Thoughts on the Prejudices of Morality*, R. J. Hollingdale (trans.). Cambridge: Cambridge University Press.
Nietzsche, Friedrich. 1997b. *Human, All Too Human*, 1, G. J. Handwerk (trans.). Stanford: Stanford University Press.
Nietzsche, Friedrich. 2007. *On the Genealogy of Morality*, C. Diethe (trans.). Cambridge/New York: Cambridge University Press.

Stiegler, Barbara. 2015. "L'hommage de Stephen Jay Gould à l'évolutionnisme de Nietzsche," *Dialogue. Revue canadienne de philosophie*, 54: 409–53.
Stiegler, Barbara. 2022. *Adapt! On a New Political Imperative*. New York: Fordham University Press.

Chapter 5

Experimentalism, Naturalism, and the Grounds of Social Critique

Steven Levine

INTRODUCTION

A persistent criticism of Dewey, one made by Mumford, Hartz, Diggins, Horkheimer, and Marcuse, is that he is a philosopher of liberal technocracy. Dewey's experimentalism, they claim, is an account of instrumental rationality, of means to realizing socially sanctioned ends, an account that has no way of critically putting those ends into question. Though Dewey makes a distinction between the desired and the desirable, the valued and the valuable, and gives us a theory of the process by which we go from one to another, his theory has no resources to address the question of whether the ends we find valuable are those we *ought* to find valuable—no resources to derive norms, criteria, or standards in light of which certain ends are genuinely *justified*. Dewey's experimentalism in this reading is an instrumental and not normative doctrine: rather than grounding norms or standards to judge or critique the worth of ends and the modes of social life in which such ends are embedded, it simply helps us to act more intelligently, that is, efficiently, given the ends we already have (see Festenstein 1997).

There is another, and in my view far more accurate, reading of Dewey's experimentalism (Jaeggi 2018). This reading sees Dewey as trying to slip between the Scylla of dogmatism—where valid norms and standards of judgment are taken to be a priori or as stemming from objective normative properties—and the Charybdis of conventionalism or relativism—where valid norms and standards are simply found in a historical community. This reading agrees with the technocratic reading that Dewey's experimentalism does not aim at giving an independent ground for standards of judgment. But, instead of evaluating this negatively, this reading sees Dewey as correctly adhering to the left-Hegelian insight that norms and standards of judgment and critique are immanent to social reality. However, instead of simply enumerating the norms and standards that one's community happens to have, which would lead back to conventionalism, Dewey's experimentalism makes a genetic turn: it traces how norms and standards are the product of a kind of historical learning process. Norms and standards are tools or instruments that are developed experimentally in historical times to solve problems, and they are subject to revision when the practices they recommend fail to facilitate joint action and communicatively mediated social cooperation. In this reading, Dewey's experimentalism gives a proceduralist answer to the question of justification: standards of judgment are justified if they are the product of free and open experimental learning processes and if the practices they recommend sustain and deepen such processes going forward.

While these two views disagree about whether Dewey is able to answer the question of justification, they agree that any answer can only be based on his experimentalism. It is this presupposition that I wish to question in this paper. I argue that Dewey's philosophy contains two theoretical strategies over and above his experimentalism to derive and ground standards of judgment and social critique, a social-ontological strategy and a perfectionist strategy.[1] Those strategies are not based on a historical-experimental account of norm revision but on certain aspects of Dewey's naturalism. I do not deny that Dewey's experimentalism is central to his social and political vision. Yet, I think something critical goes missing if we do not see that his answer to the question of justification is concerned not only with how we ought to go on in our practices but also with what substantive social practices we ought to have given the nature of social life and the kind of creature who participates in this life. Or better, that something goes missing if we do not see that in the development of norms and standards, the question of how we ought to go on in our practices is for Dewey intertwined with the question of what practices are suitable for creatures like us.

THE EXPERIMENTAL METHOD OF CRITIQUE

Contravening the view that he eschewed normative theorizing, Dewey was interested throughout his career in deriving a criterion, measure, or standard by which to judge the worth of social phenomena.[2] Indeed, the articulation of a criterion was a central goal of what Dewey called his social philosophy.[3]

Social philosophy for Dewey is meant to help us evaluate social phenomena (2008, MW 15, 231). In this, it contrasts with both moral philosophy and descriptive social science. Social philosophy is like moral philosophy in that both are evaluative enterprises that are brought about when settled values and practices come into conflict. However, social philosophy is not brought about by a conflict between two goods that an actor cannot achieve at once, but by conflicts between social groups, groups that have different habits, practices, and standards of value. While moral philosophy is a higher-order thinking through of the factors at play in an agent's attempt to solve a moral problem, social philosophy

> carries further the process of reflective valuation which is found as an integral part of social phenomena, apart from general theorizing. It does not differ from any thoughtful judgment upon the value of an institution or proposed policy or law except in greater generality and effort at system. (Dewey 2008, MW 15, 232)

Social philosophy contrasts with descriptive social science because it rejects the idea that we can "discover purely descriptive social laws, free from all element of valuation" (Dewey 2008, MW 15, 234). Descriptions of social phenomena or social facts cannot lead, through a kind of induction, to the development of value-free social laws, because the facts that they describe are not those that "condition human activity," but those that "are conditioned by human activity" (Dewey 2008, LW 2, 240). In other words, the facts or phenomena described by social science are, in Hegel's terms, "spiritual," meaning that their genesis and reproduction are the direct product not of objective conditions (genes, climate, the operation of autonomous social systems, etc.) but of such conditions *as mediated by* historically formed beliefs, desires, and aims of social agents. This mediation "modifies the subsequent course of society" (Dewey 2008, MW 15, 235) and so modifies the object of social philosophy. Furthermore, our theoretical grasp of this object, developed in social philosophy, *itself* alters the subsequent course of social development. "Social inquiry brings the fact of human conduct to consciousness and this very bringing of our own behavior into reflection changes its career [. . .] The knowledge and judgment of social inquiry thus becomes an integral factor in the phenomena itself" (Dewey 2008, MW 15, 235). The judgments of value rendered by social philosophy are therefore not just *about* the social world but are moves *in* the social world itself. They "exist as part of social phenomena, also they modify other social phenomena, both to confirm them and to demand their alteration" (Dewey 2008, MW 14, 231).

But if social philosophy aims to influence the future course of society, then there must *already be* standards or criteria by which we judge whether social phenomena ought to be preserved or modified. But how are we to go about identifying these standards or criteria? Dewey wishes to avoid two methods of identification, the "transcendental" and the "positivistic." The transcendental method is characterized by its attempt "to find a standard [. . .] outside of social phenomena" (Dewey 2008, MW 15, 234). There are two versions of this method: the first tries to ground standards in the "ultimate nature of things—God, the Universe, Man, Reason" (Dewey 2008, LW 2, 233), while the second tries to find universal principles internal to our subjectivity—conscience, the moral law, and so on. Both these methods have something to say for themselves in that they "avoid the circle involved in criticizing social facts by standards derived from the facts" (Dewey 2008a, 234). Dewey recognizes that simply pointing to standards implicit in social practices is not enough to justify those practices. But while the transcendental method avoids circularity, and an infinite regress of standards, it does not avoid dogmatism or foundationalism.[4]

In epistemology, dogmatism is the positing of an unjustified justifier, an item that is able to pass on a warrant to the other propositions that comprise a system of knowledge but whose own warrant is completely independent of that system. In the case we are discussing, dogmatism entails positing a norm or standard which can justify our judgments about the value of features of the social-historical world but whose own warrant is completely independent of this world. There are two problems with this. First, such a standard cannot leave the realm of judgment and enter into the stream of action, for, if the reasons that speak in favor of the standard are not embodied to some degree in actually existent values and practices, then they can get no purchase on acting agents. Second, a standard posited in this external way will not be able to effectively connect means and ends, "since effective means must be found in what already exists" (Dewey 2008, LW 7, 344). In other words, if one posits a standard by which to judge the worth of social phenomena from outside those phenomena, one will have no sense of the powers and forces by which such phenomena can be brought about. Since the goal of social philosophy is to help us "render the social criticism and projection of policies which is always going on more enlightened and effective" (Dewey 2008, MW 15, 233), the standard it renders must be able to bridge the gap between means and ends. If social philosophy is to be possible, we must find an alternative method.

As I said, social philosophy as a more general kind of reflection on the worth of social phenomena is in continuity with the kinds of valuations made in everyday social life. As such, "goods and bads and selective bias, exist as matter of fact prior to theorizing and reflective criticism, they antecede not follow standards" (Dewey 2008, MW 15, 232). It is the "task of social philosophy to derive the norm from [social] phenomena" (Dewey 2008, MW 15, 231), to derive norms and standards of judgment from this pre-reflective sense of good and bad. So, Dewey's account of standards is an immanentist account. But while "the standard of valuation is derived from the positive phenomena," we should not think of it as "a mere record of given valuations" (2008, MW 15, 231). If it were a mere record of given valuations, one's method of identifying the standard would be "positivistic." On this account, the standard by which to judge the worth of the practices of a community would be set by the valuations that are internal to those practices. But how could one then judge that these practices are deficient, not what they ought to be? While the transcendental method leads to a kind of moral utopianism in which the ends always outstrip what is, the positivistic method leads to a kind of relativism or conventionalism that vitiates the possibility of critique, of judging that we ought to go beyond what is the case. So, the question is: how can we slip between the Scylla of transcendental dogmatism *and* the Charybdis of positivism or conventionalism?

Dewey's strategy is to claim that standards of worth are ideals that are nonetheless based on existing features of social reality:

> We cannot set up, out of our heads, something we regard as an ideal society. We must base our conception upon societies which actually exist, in order to have any assurance that our ideal is a practicable one. The ideal cannot simply repeat the traits which are actually found. The problem is to extract the desirable traits of forms of community life which exist, and employ them to criticize undesirable features and suggest improvements. (2008, MW 9, 88–89)

An ideal can be based in, and yet transcend, existing reality, because it is formed by an act of the imagination in which "an actual tendency [is] projected to its *limit*" (Dewey 2008, MW 15, 238). This projection, which is provoked by the need to overcome felt tensions and social conflicts, can go in two ways: it can project a tendency within a context where it is already developing, or it can project the tendency into a new context. Take the concept of equality. This was originally a concept, implicit in developing social arrangements, having to do with the standing of citizens before the law. Once this concept has been explicitly expressed we could, through imagination, expand the category of people to whom equal standing before the law is accorded, thus developing suggestions as to how to go about this expansion. Here we push the concept to its limit, but within the domain in which it was originally developed. Alternatively, we can also project the concept of equality into different contexts, for example, relationships at home or in one's workplace. Through this imaginative projection, we can grasp how actually existing relationships are deficient in certain respects, and we can suggest improvements so as to make them more equitable.

But if we are to intervene into social reality, we cannot remain within imagination. We must instead institute "experiments in living" by changing our practices in light of these suggestions. These changes may lead to desirable outcomes in some respects and perhaps undesirable ones in other respects. Noting these outcomes we learn something, not just about the consequences of this projection for our living, but also about the very meaning of the concept of equality. Equality is a richer and more complex concept than it was before we ascertained the consequences of its application in these contexts. Based upon this richer concept, we may develop a revised criterion or standard of judgment going forward, one that says that modes of social life that are equitable in this richer sense are to be favored and those that are not to be disfavored.

This, Dewey argues, is "the method by which the criterion should be reached and the spirit in which it should be employed, namely, the *experimental*." Dewey goes on:

> That statement concerns the form of the criterion rather than its content or substance. It indicates [. . .] that it should be a generalization from the experiences of the past; a generalization which does not, however, merely repeat or restate in a literal fashion the experience of the past, but is stated in such a way that it will apply to changed conditions of the present and future; that it will serve as an intellectual instrument of survey and criticisms and will point out the direction in which effort at change and betterment should move. It indicates that the generalization should be a hypothesis, not a dogma; something to be tried and tested, confirmed and revised in future practice; having a constant point of growth instead of being closed. (2008, LW 7, 343)

The experimental method is an immanent method, both in the sense that criteria are based on features found in social reality and in the sense that the critic identifying such criteria is an agent coping with this reality from within. But while immanent, it is not positivistic because it does not simply reproduce criteria found in social reality. Rather, the method aims, by a careful survey of the past and the present, at modifying criteria so that actions informed by them may successfully cope with developing social conflicts and changing social conditions. In light of this, the critic, unlike the dogmatist, has *concrete reasons* to sustain or revise a norm that has come into question due to changed social conditions. As such, the "genuine alternatives are not an immanent and transcendent standard but an immanent principle which is dogmatic, uncritical, based ultimately upon the unquestioned authority of a class or group, and an immanent principle reached by reflective comparison and discriminating criticism" (Dewey 2008, MW 15, 232).

But even if we grant that Dewey has correctly identified the form of criteria for social critique, *how* they are to be achieved, we still have no inkling about *what* substantive criteria are justified by reflective comparison and discriminating criticism. Many commentators argue that Dewey purposely avoids answering this, for the question of what criteria or standards ought to be formed through idealization and projection can only be answered contextually, in light of the specific problems faced by a historical community.[5] But I think Dewey has a more general, less contextual, answer to this question. In fact, he has three.

The first, which is internal to his experimentalism, says that the norms and standards that govern the procedures of the experimental process must also govern the norms and standards that are the *outcome* of the process.[6] While the specific norms and standards that are established by a community through the use of this process can only be determined contextually, these norms and standards, whatever they are, must themselves comport with the reproduction of the very process that produced them. Here, the pragmatic *dictum* to not block the way of inquiry does substantive work: to have reason to endorse a norm or standard, whatever its specific content, it must be the product of the right kind of experimental learning process, one that is open and unconstrained rather than blocked, and the practices that the norm judges to be of worth must sustain and deepen such learning processes going forward—sustain and deepen our collective ability to creatively cope with variable situations. Based on this we can derive a substantive measure for the worth of social phenomena: any mode of social life that blocks reflection, criticism, and inquiry does not meet the standard, while any mode that fosters free and open experimental learning processes does.

It is important to point out that while this standard is substantive, its substance is still concerned with how we are to go on in our social practices, with how they are to be reproduced. The content of the standard, therefore, remains proceduralist. But this is not Dewey's last word on the question. Dewey has two additional strategies to derive norms and standards, one grounded in his social ontology and the other in his perfectionism. Let us take these up in order.

THE SOCIO-ONTOLOGICAL STRATEGY

In the *Syllabus: Social Institutions and the Study of Morality*, Dewey gives an argument about the process of idealization that takes a step beyond his experimentalism. He says:

> A social criterion must (1) express the intrinsic defining principle of human associations as they actually exist, but (2) in such a form that the idea or principle must be contrasted with existent concrete forms. Certain conditions have to be fulfilled in order that there may be a social group at all; these traits, abstracted, define society. This definition becomes a criterion when actual phenomena are compared with it to see how fully they realize or express it. (2008, MW 15, 238)

While the doctrine expressed in this passage agrees with the thought that idealization must proceed from social traits that actually exist and must contrast with existent forms, it takes a step beyond Dewey's experimentalism in holding that the traits that exist are those that define the society. On this account, a social criterion is not a tentative hypothesis, a guide for experimental action, but something that *expresses the nature of the social*. Before evaluating this argument, let's get the traits that define the social on the table.

For Dewey, the fundamental concept of social ontology is the social group, which for him occupies "the place which traditional theory has claimed either for mere isolated individuals or for the supreme and single political organization" (2008, MW 12, 196). In other words, instead of seeing society as reducible to atomic individuals, or thinking of society as a supra-individual organization that determines the values and ends of its members, Dewey thinks that both concepts depend on a more basic concept, the social group.

The social group is more fundamental than that of individuals because individuals are what they are only through participation in social groups. "Human beings are generated only by union of individuals [. . .] Apart from the ties which bind him to others he is nothing" (Dewey 2008, LW 7, 323). We only doubt the absoluteness of this claim because "*an* individual can be disassociated from this, that and the other grouping, since he need not be married, or be a church member, or a voter"; in light of this, "there grows up in the mind an image of a residual individual who is not a member of any association at all" (Dewey 2008, LW 2, 355). But there is no asocial core at the heart of the individual; rather, one is the individual one is through a kind of negotiation in which one integrates the habits, values, and aims of the groups with which one associates into a stable and formed character. This point is both genetic and structural: children become individuals through socialization into the habits and customs of the various groups in which they stand, and individuals maintain their identities through time through a simultaneous process of diversification and unification provoked by their association with other individuals and groups. It is not that Dewey is denying the importance of individuality, as it is sometimes claimed. On the contrary, Dewey's ultimate goal, as we shall see, is to identify the conditions by which individuals can flourish and grow. However, we can only discern these conditions if we abandon the social ontology that posits a conflict between a fundamentally asocial individual and the society that stands over against them, which supposedly obscures or represses their individuality. Individuality rather concerns the *way* in which one creatively appropriates the associations that one necessarily has; it does not have to do with getting back to and expressing a core self that stands independent of those associations.[7]

The social group is also more fundamental than "society," the supposedly supreme single group that sets ends and ways of living for its members. It is more fundamental because there is simply no such single group. "Society is one word but infinitely many things. It covers all the ways in which by associating together men share their experiences, and build up common interests and aims" (Dewey 2008, MW 12, 194). Individuals associate in many social groups simultaneously: family, clan, peer group, school, professional association, union, corporation, political party, city, state, and so on. The concept of "society" that is often used in social theory is a reification of the processes by which these groups, and the individuals within these groups, interact and associate. "Society is the *process* of associating [. . .] To this active process, both the individual and the institutionally organized may truly be said to be subordinate" (Dewey 2008, LW 12, 198). There is therefore no interaction, and so no "conflict between *the* individual and *the* social. For both of these terms refer to pure abstractions" (Dewey 2008, LW 7, 324). Rather, there is interaction, both conflictual and cooperative, between groups and between the individuals who stand in those groups. The fact that groups and their members interact with other groups and their members is the first trait that defines social groups.

But what intra-group traits define a social group? The development of a social group is based on the natural fact that "associated or conjoint behavior is a universal characteristic of all existences" (Dewey 2008, LW 3, 41). Indeed, "[h]uman beings combine in behavior as directly and unconsciously as do atoms, stellar masses and cells [. . .] Associated activity needs no explanation; things are made that way" (Dewey 2008, LW 2, 330). But associated activity does not by itself add up to the activity of a social group. For there to be a social group, the individuals in that group must associate in two specific ways: they must share interests and must communicate. Let us take these in order.

A social group is comprised of individuals who, through a process of education and socialization, form similar interests. An interest, for Dewey, is not equivalent to what we standardly mean by this word, for instance when we say that a tax break is in one's interest. Rather, for Dewey, an interest is any "concrete case of the union of the self in action with an object and end" (2008, LW 7, 290).[8] If one is interested in something, for example, music, one will have the tendency to pursue opportunities to perform, listen to, or discuss music. These objects are internal to this interest. If one does not pursue these objects, if this interest is not "manifested in action," then "it is unreal" (Dewey 2008, LW 7, 291). The interest is *objective*, we could say, because it involves an *actualization* of a habitual tendency to act toward certain objects, which reinforces the susceptibility to act toward them in the future. And yet an interest is also *subjective* insofar as these objects would not be objects of one's interest if one did not *care* about them. For one to have an interest in an object, "impulse and desire" must therefore be "enlisted" (Dewey 2008, LW 7, 290). But impulse and desire should not be thought of as discrete inner psychological states. Rather, the impulse or desire to pursue an object is embedded in our affective and bodily way of responding to an object or class of objects, which is to say that their direction depends on our pre-existing habits.

Dewey argues that it is a subject's interests that motivate it to act. So, subjects are motivated to act neither by desire nor by desire endorsed by reflection, but directly by the objects that are inherent to their interests. One has become, through the acquisition of certain habits, the type of individual who directly responds to such objects. If members of a social group have come through a process of education to take on the same interests, it follows that they are motivated to act by the same objects. So, a group is composed of individuals who, in having joint interests, are motivated to engage in modes of action that aim at securing or sustaining the same objects and ends.

However, joint interests, while necessary, are not sufficient for there to be a social group. A number of individuals "do not [. . .] compose a social group because they all work for a common end. The parts of a machine work with a maximum of cooperativeness for a common result, but they do not form a community" (Dewey 2008, MW 9, 8). A group is only a social group if the pursuit of a common object or end is "consciously sustained" (Dewey 2008, LW 2, 330) by the members of the group *in light of* their common understanding of what they are doing. And this, Dewey argues, depends on communication:

> Society not only continues to exist *by* transmission, *by* communication, but it may fairly be said to exist *in* transmission, *in* communication. There is more than a verbal tie between the words common, community, and communication. Men live in a community in virtue of the things which they have in common; and communication is the way in which they come to possess things in common. What they must have in common in order to form a community or society are aims, beliefs, aspirations, knowledge—a common understanding—like-mindedness. (2008, MW 9, 7)

So, members of social groups not only have *shared* interests centered in their habits, they *share* their interests—make them common—by communicating with each other about them. Through sharing, both the communicator and the recipient of communication come to be part of "the same inclusive situation" (Dewey 2008, MW 9, 35). The recipient, on the one side, comes to have "an enlarged and changed experience. One shares in what another has thought and felt and in so far, meagerly or amply, has his own attitude modified" (Dewey 2008, MW 9, 8). The communicator, on the other side, has their experience modified as well, for the "experience has to be formulated in order to be communicated. To formulate requires getting outside of it, seeing it as another would see it, considering what points of contact it has with the life of another so that it may be got into such form that he can appreciate its meaning" (Dewey 2008, MW 9, 8). So, genuine communication comes with a double reciprocity requirement: a requirement that each share in the other's thoughts and feelings, and each get outside of their own experience so as to grasp it as their interlocutor would. In this way, each subject can transcend its egoistic perspective and take part in a *common* and *cooperative* endeavor, one determined by the unfolding communicative process itself.

Our having interests and our communication about those interests are not separate features of social groups. For the ends that are internal to a social group's members' interests, which are embedded in their habits, are achieved through a communicatively mediated and historically based social learning process; now, the common understanding that comes about through these communicatively mediated processes is founded by the standing habits and interests that group members already have. This two-way process is dynamic, and it is the ultimate basis by which individuals associate in social groups.[9] The fact that through this process we come to have interests in common is the second trait that defines social groups.

One last point about social groups before we move on. Above, I said that the natural fact that all things associate is not enough to explain the forma-tion of social groups. This should not lead us to think that social groups are supernatural, something over and above the physical and biological associa-tions of material and living things. For Dewey, the social is itself a natural phenomenon because the associations that comprise social life merely take up and manifest properties already nascent in the less complex associations and interactions of the physical and especially the organic world. When something organic is "taken up into the wider and more subtly complex association which forms human society it takes on new properties by release of potentialities previously confined because of absence of full interaction" (Dewey 2008, LW 3, 48). In other words, when something organic is caught up in the complex patterns of interaction found in social life, "new potentiali-ties are actualized" (Dewey 2008, LW 3, 48)—potentialities that it already has but requires the social to release.[10]

The point is easy to see with associations based on shared habits and inter-ests. Human habits are from an ontological point of view nothing over and above the organic mechanisms found at work in animal habits. But human habits have properties not found in animal instincts, namely variability and flexibility. Human habits have these additive properties not because they are made of a different kind of stuff, or operate in line with biological mecha-nisms not found in the rest of living nature, but because meeting the demands of the more complex interactions found in social life requires the actualiza-tion of potentialities that not realized in animal instincts or habits. Here we have a transformation and augmentation of an organic capacity by the social, but one where there is no discontinuity between the organic and the social.

Dewey tells a similar but much more complex story about our communi-cation-based associations. Very briefly, Dewey argues that certain organic events, that is, animal cries, become meaningful as they are used in new ways, namely when they are used linguistically to coordinate the behavior of two creatures vis-à-vis an object or end. While there is a significant distinction between creatures that can use meanings in this way and creatures that can't, the distinction is not an unbridgeable dualism, because such linguistically conferred meanings are themselves natural. Meaning is not found in nature independently of the development of language as the communicative medium of our cooperative behavior, nor is it projected onto nature by us. Rather, meaning is a natural occurrence bound up with complex social relations and associations, which brings out powers and potentialities in nature that would not be actualized without them. Meaning is "a genuine character of natural events when these attain the stage of widest and most complex interactions with one another" (Dewey 2008, LW 1, 7).

The upshot is that the socio-ontological strategy to derive standards from the traits definitive of social groups is a naturalistic strategy insofar as the actualization of these traits is itself an actualization of certain powers and potentialities found in nature. But what normative criteria can be derived from this fact?

INTERACTION, COMMUNICATION, AND ISOLATION

To sum up the results of the last section, the social groups in which individuals stand are defined by two key traits: they interact with other social groups, and their members communicate and in so doing consciously share interests. How does this bear on the identification of a standard for judgment and social critique? Dewey in a long passage says this:

> Now in any social group whatever, even in a gang of thieves, we find some interest held in common, and we find a certain amount of interaction and cooperative intercourse with other groups. From these two traits we derive out standard. How numerous and varied are the interests which are consciously shared? How full and free is the interplay with other forms of association? If we apply these considerations to, say, a criminal band, we find that the ties which consciously hold the members together are few in number, reducible almost to a common interest in plunder; and that they are of such a nature as to isolate the group from other groups with respect to give and take of the values of life. Hence, the education such a society gives is partial and distorted. If we take, on the other hand, the kind of family which illustrates the standard, we find that there are material, intellectual, aesthetic interests in which all participate and that the progress of one member has worth for the experience of other members—it is readily communicable—and that the family is not an isolated whole, but enters intimately into relationships with business groups, with schools, with all the agencies of culture, as well as with similar groups, and that it plays a due part in the political organization and in return receives

support from it. In short, there are many interests consciously communicated and shared; and there are varied and free points of contact with other modes of association. (2008, MW 9, 89)

Based on these two examples, the criminal band and the well-organized family, we could say that groups that foster free communication of interests and open interaction with other groups meet the standard, while groups that narrow the interests of their members by preventing communication and interaction do not meet it.

In *Democracy and Education*, Dewey generalizes the point by claiming that groups that meet this standard are *democratic* and those that do not are *authoritarian*. Authoritarian groups cannot allow the free communication of interests or interaction with other groups. They must isolate individuals and their interests from one another, making sure that areas of shared concern are narrow and interaction between groups paltry. They must do so because free and open communication and interaction would lead to an expansion of a member's interests, which would possibly lead to torn allegiances. To ward this off, the group must foster habits in its members that are *rigid* and lack flexibility (Dewey 2008, MW 9, 91–92). The group as a whole, therefore, cannot "interact flexibly with other groups; it can act only through isolating itself. It must prevent the operation of all interests save those which circumscribe it in its separateness" (Dewey 2008, LW 2, 328). But this comes at a great cost for group members, "the cost of repression of those of his potentialities which can be realized only through membership in other groups" (Dewey 2008, LW 2, 328).

Let us now turn to democratic groups. Dewey's account of the democratic group is not an account of democracy as a form of government. Rather, the concept applies to "all modes of human association, the family, the school, industry, religion" (Dewey 2008, LW 2, 325). Democracy in this sense is a general mode of human association that "repudiates the principle of external authority" (Dewey 2008, MW 9, 93). More specifically, it is a mode that repudiates external authority by promoting the free communication of interests within a group and open interaction with other social groups. A democratic group, we could say, is one that is open to a process in which its interests, and the interests of its members, are *simultaneously varied through interaction yet integrated through communication.* Through open and free communication, a widening number of individuals can "participate in an interest so that each has to refer his own action to that of others, and to consider the action of others to give point and direction to his own." Through this identification of mutual interests, there is a "breaking down of those barriers of class, race, and national territory which kept men from perceiving the full import of their activity" (Dewey 2008,

MW 9, 93). Democratic groups, therefore, engage in a kind of collective learning process in which the interests of all, and not just some, are communicated, made common, and become the basis of joint action. But in widening the areas of common concern, democratic groups simultaneously vary their interests, for this widening requires interaction with persons and groups with whom one is not already familiar. Open interaction with other groups and modes of life brings about "a greater diversity of stimuli to which an individual has to respond." And the need to flexibly adjust one's habits and interests brings about, on the part of the individual, "a liberation of the powers which remain suppressed as long as the incitations to action are partial, as they must be in a group which in its exclusiveness shuts out many interests" (Dewey 2008, MW 9, 93).

We derive a criterion or standard for judgment and social critique from the defining traits of the social by projecting traits that already exist to some degree to their limit. In this way, democratic forms of association, which instantiate these traits, not only meet the standard, they *set* the standard in the first place:

> Regarded as an idea, democracy is not an alternative to other principles of associated life. It is the idea of community life itself. It is an ideal in the only intelligible sense of an ideal: namely, the tendency and movement of something which exists carried to its final limit [. . .] [Never] has there ever been anything which is a community in its full measure, a community unalloyed by alien elements. The idea or ideal of a community presents, however, actual phases of associated life that are freed from restrictive or disturbing elements, and are contemplated as having attained their limit of development. (Dewey 2008, LW 2, 328)

While the existence of these defining traits is contingent (in the sense that the associations that comprise the social did not necessarily exist), given that they did come to exist, the social realizes certain powers and potentialities that already are there in nature. All groups communicate, and by doing so they hold interests in common, and all groups interact with other groups, *to some degree.* These traits are just augmentations of the associational activity that pertains to nature generally. But in forming a standard by which to judge existing social reality, we go beyond this reality by imaginatively carrying these traits to their final limit. We imagine what it would be like for communication and interaction to be fully realized. By comparing actually existing social phenomena with this imagined realization, we are able to get a purchase on the elements that restrict or disturb their full actualization. Dewey calls these elements "alien" because, while they are *within* the social, they are not *themselves* social insofar as they do not realize the traits that define the social.

There are two main alien elements: the first disturbs the open interaction between groups and the second is the free communication within groups. The first kind can be seen, for instance, in cases when a hegemonic class dominates another class by falsely universalizing its interests, or when an institutional power complex, a corporation for example, imposes its interests on a community without that being the communicatively established intention of the community. In these cases, the interactions between those in the dominant group and those in the subservient group are narrow, rigid, and stereotyped, channeled into patterns that reproduce unequal social relations. Here, the kind of open interaction with other groups that is characteristic of democratic groups is completely missing. The second alien element can be found in groups that "call for some to rule and others to be ruled" (Dewey 1973, 92), groups where there are masters and slaves.[11] In this situation, we have "relations which are not as yet social." For when social relations are based on "physical superiority, or superiority of position, skill, technical ability, and command of tools, mechanical or fiscal," there is "no true social group, no matter how closely their respective activities touch one another. Giving and taking of orders modifies action and results, but does not of itself effect a sharing of purposes, a communication of interests" (Dewey 2008, MW 9, 8). When members of a group cannot reciprocally share interests and experiences in a free and open manner, the communicative space is distorted, with some experiences and interests dominating and crowding out others due to factors external to the communicative relationship itself, factors that while determining the social are not themselves social.

DIRECT AND INDIRECT INTERESTS

The socio-ontological strategy has two main difficulties. The first is that it seems to fall prey to the naturalistic fallacy insofar as it grounds norms and standards, which concern the social arrangements that we ought to have, in factual traits that define the social. Here, we seemingly derive an ought from an is. I take up this difficulty in the last section below. The second difficulty is that this strategy builds into the definition of the social the very traits— open interaction and free communication—that the standard recommends. The strategy, therefore, could be seen as a result of a kind of theoretical gerrymandering, where the theorist finds in the object of investigation what they wish to find there. To avoid the charge of gerrymandering we need—without recourse to a prior definition of the social—an answer to the question of "why we prefer democratic and humane arrangements to those which are autocratic and harsh. And by 'why,' I mean the *reason* for preferring them, not just the *causes* which lead us to the preference" (Dewey 2008, LW 13, 17). If we could give such a reason, we would have firmer ground for our standard.

In *Experience and Education*, Dewey gives this reason:

> Can we find any reason that does not ultimately come down to the belief that democratic social arrangements promote a better quality of human experience, one which is more widely accessible and enjoyed, than do non-democratic and anti-democratic forms of social life . . . Is not the reasons for our preference that we believe that mutual consultation and conviction reached through persuasion, make possible a better quality of experience than can otherwise be provided on any wide scale? (2008, LW 13, 18)

But if this is to be more than a bare assertion, we need a reason, a reason for the belief that democratic social arrangements promote a better quality of experience than non-democratic arrangements. I think Dewey's reason is this: we have learned through experience that non-democratic arrangements, by including the alien elements discussed above, distort and degrade the experience of individuals by making their interest in their activity or experience indirect, while democratic arrangements tend to foster a better quality of experience by bringing about conditions in which individuals can develop a direct interest in their activity or experience. Let me explain.

In an overlooked yet important text, *Interest and Effort in Education*, Dewey argues that there are two ways in which an individual can be interested in their activity or experience: directly or indirectly. When one is directly interested in a course of activity, it

> puts itself forth with no thought of anything beyond. It satisfies in and of itself. The end *is* the present activity, and so there is no gap in the mind between means and ends [. . .] The existing experience holds us for its own sake, and we do not demand that it take us into something beyond itself. (2008, MW 7, 162–63)

In this case, the interest that attaches to the end attaches equally to the steps necessary to reach the end, and the interest in the means is not "externally tied on to interest in an end; it suffuses, saturates, and thus transforms it" (Dewey 2008, MW 7, 164). When one is indirectly interested in a course of experience, in contrast, one is interested in some parts of that experience just because one is interested in a specific part of it. Or, put better, one is *not really interested* in some parts of the experience at all but only pursues them in order to bring about the other part of true interest. Dewey illustrates the contrast between these two cases in this way:

> One student studies to pass an examination, to get promotion. To another, the means, the activity of learning, is completely one with what results from it. The

consequence, instruction, illumination, is one with the process [. . .] means and end coalesce. (2008, LW 10, 201–202)

In the former case, the means are what Dewey calls "*mere* means," means that are "external to that which is accomplished" (2008, LW 10, 201). The end is not an internal fulfillment of the activity but is "set up from without" (2008, MW 9, 107). The end is merely the welcome cessation of the unwelcome activity. The student would be glad to reach the end (passing the exam) without having to endure the means (studying). In such case, the means are *constituents* of the end, which is absorption in the ongoing activity itself. We can still make a distinction between means and end within the ongoing activity, but the distinction is not between the process and its distinct result, but between the activity's earlier stages and its final stage. While the earlier stages, which we could call the means, are of intrinsic interest, in being part of a temporally unfolding course of activity or experience, they nonetheless anticipate what is to come at the later stages of the experience. This final stage, which we could call the end, is not merely the cessation of this ongoing activity but the fulfillment or consummation of these anticipations. As a fulfillment, this phase is "not a mere last thing in time; it completes what has gone before; it settles, so to speak, the character of the theme as a whole" (Dewey 2008, MW 7, 166).

When interest is direct, the anticipations of the earlier stages are fulfilled, not merely broken away from, and this fulfillment brings out the *meaning* of the earlier stages and so of the activity as a whole. So, there is here a kind of two-way mediation: of the end by the means that lead to it and of the means by the end which brings out their full import. Here we have a course of experience in which the earlier stages are valued both for their own sake and for their role in the development of the meaning of the overall experience, and in which there "runs a sense of growing meaning conserved and accumulating toward an end that is felt as an accomplishment of a process" (Dewey 2008, LW 10, 45). A course of experience that displays these characteristics Dewey calls a proper "experience," that is, an experience that lives up to what an experience can be at its best.[12]

The alien and restricting elements enumerated above inhibit the ability of an individual to have "an experience." They do so by bringing about an indirect interest in one's activity, which is "either a symptom or a cause of arrested development in an activity" (Dewey 2008, MW 7, 172).[13] A course of experience involves an indirect interest if interest in one part of it blocks or inhibits the power of that experience to cumulatively realize its meaning. Dewey focuses on three cases: when one's activity is aimless, mechanically efficient, or determined by someone else (2008, MW 7, 183). In aimless actions—perhaps done out of excitement or amusement—there is no development of meaning toward a fulfilling end; in mechanically efficient actions one does not find intrinsic satisfaction in the means to the end; and in actions whose nature and end are determined by someone else, one finds intrinsic satisfaction in neither the means nor the end.

If we focus on the latter two cases, which are more important for us here, it is easy to see how they are related to the presence of the alien or disturbing elements. These elements are present whenever

> social relations are not equitably balanced. In this case, some portions of the whole social group will find their aims determined by external dictation; their aims will not arise from the free growth of their own experience, and their nominal aims will be means to more ulterior ends of others rather than truly their own. (Dewey 2008, MW 9, 107)

In other words, when there is a hierarchy between groups and within groups, the dominant party substitutes its ends for those of the subservient party and demands that their ends are brought about through the most efficient means possible. Dewey argues that modern capitalism, with its scientifically managed division of labor, involves such a hierarchy:

> Plato defines a slave as one who accepts from another the purposes which control his conduct. The condition obtains even where there is no slavery in the legal sense. It is found wherever men are engaged in activity which is socially serviceable, but whose service they do not understand and have no personal interest in [. . .] Efficiency in production often demands division of labor. But it is reduced to a mechanical routine unless workers see the technical, intellectual, and social relationships involved in what they do, and engage in their work because of the motivation furnished by such perceptions [. . .] Intelligence is narrowed to the factors concerned with technical production and marketing of goods. No doubt a very acute and intense intelligence in these narrow lines can be developed, but the failure to take into account the significant social factors means none the less an absence of mind and a corresponding distortion of emotional life (2008, MW 9, 90–91).

Dewey's critical theory, if we wish to call it that, is concerned with the distortions in individual experience that flow from disturbances of the social. We grasp the disturbances of the social by comparing actually existing social conditions with the traits that are definitive of the social when projected to their limit, and we identify the distortions in experience by comparing distorted experiences to the kind of experience when it is not distorted, when one's experience is able to grow freely of one's own accord. In the latter case, we derive standards for judgment of worth not from traits that define the social but from "the inherent value of different experiences" (Dewey 2008, LW 13, 18). This gives us our third and last strategy to ground standards of judgment and social critique based on Dewey's perfectionism.

THE PERFECTIONIST STRATEGY

The claim that Dewey has a perfectionist strategy to derive norms and standards of judgment is contentious because it entails that Dewey is a perfectionist. Many scholars reject this not only because Dewey gave up his early ethics of self-realization, which clearly was perfectionist, but also because perfectionism seems to clash with Dewey's ethical pluralism. While perfectionism posits that human beings have a single highest good, their realization or perfection, Dewey's pluralism claims not only that there is a multitude of human goods but also that the good is only one moral principle among others.[14] However, on my account, Dewey is a kind of perfectionist not because he gives us an account of what the perfect human life looks like or of the single end appropriate for this life, but because he holds that the meaning of the activities and experiences undertaken in light of the multitude of human goods can be fully realized or expressed. This realization, as we are about to see, is a matter of the *way* activities or experiences unfold, not of their end.

Dewey's perfectionist strategy utilizes what he calls "the principle of continuity of experience" as its "criterion of discrimination" (2008, LW 13, 18). The principle of the continuity of experience concerns how one experience is continuous with another through time. Experiences are continuous because "every experience both takes up something from those which have gone before and modifies in some way the quality of those which come after" (Dewey 2008, LW 13, 19). They do so not because there is a self who synthesizes experience through time by attaching the "I think" to it, but rather because we are creatures who take on habits:

> The basic characteristic of habit is that every experience enacted and undergone modifies the one who acts and undergoes, while this modification affects, whether we wish it or not, the quality of subsequent experiences. For it is a somewhat different person who enters into them. The principle of habit so understood obviously goes deeper than the ordinary conception of *a* habit as a more or less fixed way of doing things, although it includes the latter as one of its special cases. It covers the formation of attitudes, attitudes that are emotional and intellectual; it covers our basic sensitivities and ways of meeting and responding to all the conditions that we meet in living. (Dewey 2008, LW 13, 18)

Like his socio-ontological strategy, Dewey's perfectionist strategy is naturalistic. It is naturalistic because the capacity that Dewey references here to develop a standard by which to discriminate between the inherent worth of different experiences is, as we saw earlier in the chapter, continuous with, and merely an augmentation of, capacities found in the rest of the animal kingdom.[15] In line with animal instincts and habits, human habits are based on physiological mechanisms. "Habit is impossible without setting up a mechanism of action, physiologically ingrained, which operates 'spontaneously,' automatically, whenever its cue is given." But, Dewey says, "mechanization is not of necessity *all* there is to habit" (2008, MW 14, 50). It is not, because human habits, in being mediated by reflective thought and feeling, grow more flexible, "more varied, more adaptable" (Dewey 2008, MW 14, 51–52). In this way, human habits can come to be "intelligent" and not just "routine" (Dewey 2008, MW 14, 51).

But how specifically does the fact that experiences have continuity through time by involving habits bear on the development of a criterion or standard for judgment and social critique, especially given that there is some kind of continuity in all sapient experience? "It is when we note," Dewey says, "the different forms in which continuity of experience operates that we get the basis of discriminating among experiences" (2008, LW 13, 19). There are certain forms of continuity of experience that are inherently valued by agents, and certain forms that are not. The basis of the argument has already been outlined in the previous section: a course of experience whose meaning is arrested in its development is not valued by an experiencing subject for its own sake, but only for the sake of one of its parts (or for something outside of the experience altogether), while absorption in a course of experience whose meaning freely grows or develops toward a fulfilling end is valued for its own sake. To put it simply, experiences that are growing freely are inherently valuable, while experiences that are not are not valuable per se.[16]

Within Dewey's perfectionism, the standard for judging the worth of social phenomena is derived from their role in fostering growing experiences. As Dewey puts it, "it may be said, without exaggeration, that the measure of the worth of any social institution, economic, domestic, political, legal, religious, is its effect in enlarging and improving experience" (2008, MW 9, 9). Democratic social arrangements meet this standard because, by promoting free interaction and free communication between and within groups, they provide individuals with the various and variable stimuli necessary for them to develop and sustain intelligent habits, and with the opportunity to cooperatively share and develop joint interests and experiences. These arrangements thereby bring about a growing self:

> The *kind* of self which is formed through action which is faithful to relations with others will be a fuller and broader self than one which is cultivated in isolation from or in opposition to the purposes and needs of others. In contrast, the kind of self which results from generous breadth of interest may be said alone to constitute a development and fulfillment of self, while the other way of life

stunts and starves selfhood by cutting it off from the connections necessary to its growth. (Dewey 2008, LW 7, 302)

As we saw above, every experience modifies the self by altering their habits. An arrested course of experience modifies the self by reinforcing their routine habits, habits formed in light of the need to act in a mechanically efficient manner, or the need to submit to the command of another. The social arrangements that tend to bring about arrested courses of experience produce and reproduce selves who are adjusted to those very arrangements. A course of experience that grows freely of itself, on the other hand, modifies the self by reinforcing their intelligent habits, habits that in being mediated by thought and feeling are varied, flexible, and able to support a self's engagement with varied and changing situations. The social arrangements that tend to bring about experiences that freely grow of their own accord tend to produce and reproduce selves who perpetuate those very arrangements.

That fact that a growing self develops habits that allow them to continue to grow enables Dewey to meet an obvious objection to his account, namely that the concept of growth seems applicable to individuals in authoritarian groups. If this were the case, then growth as a standard would not be able to distinguish between the worth of democratic social arrangements and authoritarian ones. It would therefore be a quite useless standard. Dewey poses the problem in this way:

The objection made is that growth might take many different directions: a man, for example, who starts out on a career of burglary may grow in that direction, and by practice may grow in to a highly expert burglar. Hence, it is argued that "growth" is not enough; we must also specify the direction in which growth takes place, the end towards which it tends. (2008, LW 13, 19)

But if growth requires more than becoming efficient at something, if it requires engaging in courses of experience reinforcing the habits that allow for the growth of the self in the future, then this objection does not hold. For does becoming a better burglar "create conditions for further growth, or does it set up conditions that shut off the person who has grown in this particular direction from the occasion, stimuli, and opportunities for continuing growth in new directions?" (Dewey 2008, LW 13, 19). It is clear that this path sets up conditions that routinize the burglar's habits and narrow their interests, and so does not meet the standard. If growth can only be counted *as* growth if it opens up conditions for the self to freely grow in the future, then we have a criterion that is able to do substantive work in guiding our judgments concerning the worth of social conditions.

INTERRELATIONS AND CRITICISMS

How are the three strategies that I have discussed interrelated? We can approach this question from two sides: from the side of the standards they derive or from the side of the grounds they give for this derivation. Let us take these in order.

I said in the Introduction that Dewey's account of standards concerns both *how* we ought to go on in our social practices and *what* social practices we ought to have given the nature of social life and of the selves who participate in this life. We can now see how this maps onto the three strategies I have laid out. The standard derived by Dewey's experimentalism informs judgments about how we ought to go on in our social practices, namely through open and free experimental learning processes, while the standards derived by his socio-ontological and perfectionist strategies inform judgments about what practices we ought to have, namely those that realize the traits definitive of the social and those which foster the free and full development of experience. But this way of breaking things up, distinguishing between formal and substantial standards of worth, is in fact overdrawn, for Dewey thinks that form and substance intertwine. They do because the experimentalist standard does substantive normative work, and the socio-ontological and perfectionist standards concern the form that our practices ought to take. Dewey's experimentalist standard is substantive and not just formal because its application promotes a certain form of life, one that values democratic social arrangements and individual traits like autonomy, curiosity, and flexibility; the social-ontological and perfectionist standards, on the other hand, are formal and not just substantive because they, respectively, concern *how* social groups and their members ought to interact, not the content of these interactions, and *how* experience ought to unfold, not the content of an unfolding experience.

Based on this, we can see how the standards of all three strategies work together. On the one hand, it is by engaging in successful learning processes that selves grow and social groups intelligently steer their behavior—and this reinforces the habits and customs that allow for continued growth and realization of democratic modes of association. On the other hand, groups that foster the growth of their members do so by promoting open interaction and free communication, and members of such groups interact and communicate through experiment, inquiry, and criticism—through open and free learning processes.

When we turn to the other side, to the grounds for the derivation of these standards, things are more complicated. This is because there seems to be a divide between the experimentalist strategy on the one side and the socio-ontological and perfectionist strategies on the other. As we have seen, in Dewey's experimentalism standards are hypotheses formed to address specific historical problems and which are tested by experiments in living. This is a kind of trial and error process. It must be, because, given the uncertain and unpredictable nature of the problems we collectively face, given their contingency, we must be able to flexibly and creatively adjust our evaluative schema to cope with new contexts and circumstances. Based on the historical success of this process in addressing social problems, we develop a more general standard: we ought to foster social arrangements that sustain and deepen experimental learning processes. The normative force of this *ought* is grounded by the success of the social processes governed by the standard. Here we have a kind of pragmatic justification, one based on what *works*. But if standards are derived from traits that must exist for there to be social groups at all, and ultimately from the inherent worth of growing experiences, then standards are not grounded in what works, but rather in the need for social groups and experiencing selves to *actualize what they are.* We ought to foster democratic social arrangements to fully actualize the social, and we ought to do this to fully actualize the experiencing self. The normative force of these oughts is grounded in the fact that in doing these things we realize certain potentialities for meaning that are implicit in nature, potentialities that we find to be inherently valuable.

I think that there is a genuine tension here. But it can be mitigated if we see that Dewey's experimentalism is itself formed in light of his naturalism, and that his socio-ontological and perfectionist strategies involve historical learning processes.

On the one hand, Dewey's historical experimentalism is developed in light of the fact that the physical and social environment that we act on and within is both stable and precarious.[17] By seizing on the stable elements, we are able not only to cope with but to make over, to some degree, the environment in light of our values and ends. But because the stable elements are necessarily intertwined with those that are precarious, any such formed equilibrium eventually breaks down, requiring us to revise our practices, values, and standards. While this breakdown is a threat to our settled practices, values, and norms, it is also the means by which the *meaning of our social and individual experience can grow*—an experience in which we do not just reproduce what already is, but take steps beyond it.[18] The conditions that necessitate Dewey's historical experimentalism are therefore also the conditions in which the social and the experiential are actualized.

On the other hand, we have to learn about the tendencies that can be actualized by society and experience, because for Dewey these tendencies are only given *within* experience. They do not lie behind experience and are not the realization of hidden forms, essences, or natures. We have to learn, through a historical process, about democratic social arrangements, arrangements that foster the free growth of our experience, because they are restricted or blocked by the social deformations to which they are bound. There is no necessity that these deformations will be removed, or that the kinds of social conditions that foster growth will be *discovered through inquiry and reproduced through the development of the right kinds of customs and habits.* There is no inevitable *telos* leading to democratic social arrangements. But what is not contingent is the fact that *if* such restrictions are removed in various domains of social life and democratic arrangements are instituted, then individuals will come to experience these arrangements as inherently valuable to their lives, as promoting their growth.

Two potential criticisms emerge at this point. First, has not Dewey committed the naturalistic fallacy? For, while standards of judgment of worth are normative, that is, concern the social arrangements that we ought to sustain and foster, the traits that define the social and our growth are natural given facts about us and our form of life. Second, has not Dewey reinstated the transcendental method by grounding his perfectionist standard in something external to the socio-historical world? Let me take these in order.

As we would expect, Dewey does not accept the philosophical picture that leads to the idea that there is a fallacy in deriving an ought from an is, for this picture accepts a dichotomy between facts and values. Ought is not the product of an autonomous reason projecting obligation onto nature, nor is it a pre-existent essence that can only be intuited; rather, it is the product of the fact that we have experience of certain tendencies in social life and in experience that can, or cannot, be realized through our doings. The social traits that *in fact* define the social nevertheless *ought* to be actualized, because, given the social deformations with which they are bound, they are never fully actualized; and we *ought* to grow, rather than simply growing as a matter of fact, because, though the potential for growth is natural to the kind of creature we are, this potentiality is only actualized in selected circumstances, that is, when social conditions and one's habits have the right form. So, ought-ness stems from a deficiency in the way things are, from the fact that the actualization of these tendencies is blocked. But while these tendencies are natural, they are not value-neutral. We stand within them, and find them, when they are realized to some degree, to be inherently valuable. This is the origin of the normative force of the standards that say that we ought to realize the traits definitive of the social and bring about the free and full growth of the experiencing self.[19]

However, if the perfectionist standard is grounded in the inherent worth of growth, has not Dewey reinstated the transcendental method by grounding it in something outside of the socio-historical world? The answer is no, because Dewey's two naturalistic strategies depend upon each other. Dewey would reinstate the transcendental method only if it were possible to ascertain the inherent value of growing experiences independently of the social conditions of their actualization. But there is no such position from which one could ascertain this, a position in which our experience is not already enmeshed in the associations that comprise social life. This is so because these associations are not merely conditions for growth, they enter into growth. In other words, the myriad social relations that a self has—familial, professional, civic, political—and the myriad interests that are their result are not just the basis for their growth, they are constituents of it. There is a speculative identity here: to actualize the traits definitive of social groups is to actualize the growth of the individuals in those groups, and to actualize the growth of those individuals is to realize these social traits. While we can analytically distinguish between the socio-ontological and the perfectionist strategies, the realization of each of their objects depends on the realization of the other. In light of this, we see clearly how Dewey's perfectionism avoids reinstating the transcendental method: the value of growth can only be discerned immanently to the social because the social is *internal* to growth.

NOTES

1. In arguing that Dewey aims at providing a ground for the derivation of norms and standards, I am not only opposed to those who deny that Dewey has a normative theory but also to many Deweyians who argue that Dewey's anti-foundationalism entails that he was not interested in any kind of grounding project. However, to ground a norm or standard of judgment is not necessarily to provide it with a foundation, it is merely to justify it in light of more general considerations. I argue that Dewey gives three distinct kinds of consideration.

2. See for example *Ethics* (1908), *Democracy and Education* (1916), *Lectures in China* (1919), *Reconstruction in Philosophy* (1920), *Syllabus: Social Institutions and the Study of Morals* (1923), *Ethics* (1932), and *Experience and Education* (1938). In *Democracy and Education*, Dewey talks about deriving a "measure" for judging modes of social life, in the *Syllabus* he talks about a "norm or standard" of judgment, in *Reconstruction in Philosophy* he talks about a "test" for measuring the worth of social goods, and in the *Lectures in China, Experience and Education*, and the 1908 and 1932 *Ethics* he talks about a "criterion" for judging social and political conditions. I use these terms interchangeably.

3. For Dewey's social philosophy, see Mitgarden (2012); Frega (2015, 2017); and Renault (2017).

4. Dogmatism is one of the legs of Agrippa's trilemma, the others being circularity and infinite regress.

5. See Pappas (2008) for this kind of contextualist reading.

6. I follow Jaeggi (2018) in thinking that Dewey's experimentalism gives him the resources to articulate a less contextual (she says "non-contextual") answer to the criteria question. Our focus, however, is slightly different. She is interested in the criteria by which we can judge the rationality of learning processes, whereas I am

interested in the criteria by which to judge the worth of social phenomena developed in light of these processes. See her chapter 10 in particular.

7. For an excellent account of this point that draws on Dewey, see Jaeggi (2014).

8. For more on Dewey's concept of interest, see Levine (Forthcoming) and Santarelli (Forthcoming).

9. For more on the relation of habit and communication, see chapter 6 of Levine (2019).

10. For more on the social as a natural phenomenon, see Honneth (2017) and Särkelä (2017).

11. Recently there has been a debate about the role of this language in Dewey's social philosophy. The debate has been focused on Dewey's *Lectures in China*, where Dewey discusses the domination of some by others more overtly than in many other of his texts (1973). On the one side of the debate are those who wish to claim that domination is *not* a key concept in Dewey's social philosophy. They attribute its prominent role in the *Lectures* to the unusual way this text was produced: through a translation back into English of the Chinese translation of Dewey's original lectures. These commentators argue that this procedure altered the very substance of the views expressed in this text, which are not in line with Dewey's genuine position (Frega 2015). On the other side are those who argue that while this procedure did affect the language of this text, sprinkling it with Marxist inflected terms not typically used by Dewey, it did not affect the substance of his account of domination (Särkelä 2013; Testa 2017). I, on the whole, agree with the second view, as I do not see the account of domination and social conflict given in the available text of the *Lectures* as substantially different from the ones found in *Democracy and Education* and the 1932 *Ethics*. The language of mastery and slavery threads all of *Democracy and Education*, and the account of social conflict in the 1932 *Ethics* is very close to the one found in the *Lectures*. While perhaps the *Lectures* offer a more "functionalist" social theory than these other texts, one more concerned with questions of social stability (which is understandable given the political situation in China at the time), all three containing the thought that democratic forms of associated life are characterized by free interaction and communication, and that their articulation is blocked by group hegemony and hierarchical social relationships.

12. The concept of "an experience," par excellence, comes from *Art as Experience*. The concept, however, applies beyond aesthetic activity to intellectual and practical activity. What accounts for these differences in kind is the *quality* that saturates the experience. Though this qualitative dimension of an experience is very important for Dewey, I leave it to the side here. See Dewey 2008, LW 10, 3 for more.

13. Indirect interests are not always pernicious. For example, one might eat an energy bar because one is working on something strenuous in the yard and needs more energy. Here, one is not interested in the means for their own sake, or in the end as a fulfillment of the meaning of prior experience.

14. For more on this, see Dewey 2008, LW 7, as well as Honneth 1998 and Levine Forthcoming.

15. Confusingly, there are two major principles of continuity in Dewey, one concerning the continuity of different experiences through time and the other involving

the idea that those phenomena that are seemingly recalcitrant to naturalistic treat-ment—intentionality, meaning, value, and so on—are continuous with the rest of nature. The latter principle of continuity "excludes complete rupture on the one side and mere repetition of identities on the other; it precludes reduction of 'higher' to the 'lower' just as it precludes complete breaks and gaps" (Dewey 2008, LW 12, 30).

16. Diggins, a representative of the instrumental reading of Dewey that I outlined in the Introduction, says this about Dewey: "With pragmatism in particular, the use of experience only prepares for future experience, without experience being imme-diately self-illuminating or self-rewarding" (Diggins 1994, 20). While Dewey would reject the notion of self-illumination and the idea that there are non-mediated experi-ences, we can now see that his philosophy is concerned precisely with the question of how human beings can live lives comprising experiences that in being consummated are—to use Diggins' term—"self-rewarding." The instrumental reading, hypnotized by the colloquial meaning of the terms "pragmatic," "instrumental," and so on, misses Dewey's point entirely.

17. See Dewey 2008, LW 1, chapter 2 in particular.

18. For more on this, see Särkelä 2017.

19. This account has its origin in a naturalization of Hegel's account of *ought*. Ought-ness, for Hegel, is not the product of the fact that there is an unbridgeable gap between our finite embodied selves and an infinite and universal reason, as it is for Kant. Rather, ought-ness is an ontological feature of *any* finite something (see Book 1, chapter 2 of the *Science of Logic*). All things strive to actualize what they are, to realize their "vocation," though as limited they are not able to do so. This is what pro-duces the ought-to-be-ness at the heart of being. But while Hegel thinks that the finite ought is a permanent feature of being (and so does not think that "bad infinity" is *just* a mistake), he also posits that some things can fully actualize what they in fact are and can be infinite in the sense of self-dependent. Here, the "true infinite" is present in the finite. It is not that we assume a position side-ways on to an activity or experience and identify the conditions necessary for its full realization; it is rather that we have access to this realization *within* the finite activity. For Hegel, the best examples of this are properly structured families and the state, while, for Dewey, they are the instances of participation in democratic arrangements and the having of growing experiences.

REFERENCES

Dewey, John. 1973. *Lectures in China, 1919–1920*, W. Clopton, and Tsuin-Chen Ou (eds.). Honolulu: University of Hawaii Press.

Dewey, John. 2008. *The Collected Works of John Dewey 1882–1953 (Early Works, Middle Works, and Late Works)*, J. A. Boydston (ed.). Carbondale: Southern Illi-nois University Press.

Diggins, John P. 1994. *The Promise of Pragmatism: Modernism and the Crisis of Knowledge and Authority*. Chicago: University of Chicago Press.

Festenstein, Matthew. 1997. *Pragmatism and Political Theory*. Chicago: University of Chicago Press.

Frega, Roberto. 2015. "John Dewey's Social Philosophy: A Restatement," *European Journal of Pragmatism and American Philosophy*, 7: 98–127.

Frega, Roberto. 2017. "A Tale of Two Social Philosophies," *Journal of Speculative Philosophy*, 31: 260–72.

Honneth, Alex. 1998. "Between Proceduralism and Teleology: An Unresolved Conflict in Dewey's Moral Theory," *Transactions of the Charles S. Peirce Society*, 34: 689–711.

Honneth, Alex. 2017. *The Idea of Socialism*. Cambridge: Polity Press.

Jaeggi, Rahel. 2014. *Alienation*. New York: Columbia University Press.

Jaeggi, Rahel. 2018. *Critique of Forms of Life*, C. Cronin (trans.). Cambridge: Harvard University Press.

Levine, Steven. 2019. *Pragmatism, Objectivity, and Experience*. Cambridge: Cambridge University Press.

Levine, Steven. (Forthcoming.) "Dewey and the Identity of Self and Act," in *John Dewey's Ethical Theory: The 1932 Ethics*, R. Frega and S. Levine (eds.). London: Routledge Press.

Midtgarden, Torjus. 2012. "Critical Pragmatism: Dewey's Social Philosophy Revisited," *European Journal of Social Theory*, 15: 505–21.

Pappas, Gregory F. 2008. *John Dewey's Ethics: Democracy as Experience*. Bloomington: Indiana University Press.

Renault, Emmanuel. 2017. "From ["Political Ethics"] to ["Social Philosophy"]: The Need for Social Theory," *Transactions of the Charles S. Peirce Society*, 53: 90–106.

Santarelli, Matteo. (Forthcoming.) "Psychology, Moral Theory and Politics. Dewey's Mature Theory of Interest in *Ethics* (1932)," in *John Dewey's Ethical Theory: The 1932 Ethics*, R. Frega and S. Levine (eds.). London: Routledge Press.

Särkelä, Arvi. 2013. "Ein Drama in drei Akten: Der Kampf um öffentliche Anerkennung nach Dewey und Hegel," *Deutsche Zeitschrift für Philosophie*, 61: 681–696.

Särkelä, Arvi. 2017. "Degeneration of Associated Life: Dewey's Naturalism about Social Criticism," *Transactions of the Charles S. Peirce Society*, 53: 107–26.

Testa, Italo. 2017. "Dominant Patterns in Associated Living: Hegemony, Domination, and Ideological Recognition in Dewey's Lectures in China," *Transactions of the Charles S. Peirce Society*, 53: 29–52.

Chapter 6

From Naturalism to Social Vitalism

Revisiting the Durkheim-Bergson Debate on Moral Obligations

Louis Carré

Quand des consciences, au lieu de rester isolées les unes des autres, se groupent et se combinent, il y a quelque chose de changé dans le monde.

—Durkheim, *Le Suicide*

THE NATURALIST DILEMMA IN SOCIAL PHILOSOPHY

Admitting that one of its main concerns is to define the "nature of society" (and leaving for the moment aside the ambiguity of those terms), social philosophy must deal with the following dilemma: either it views society—like many other phenomena—as grounded *in* nature, or it locates society somewhere *outside of* nature building "an empire in an empire." In other words, either society is an overall natural phenomenon, or it is non- or extra-natural. As with any dilemma, the two branches of the problem are equally unsatisfying. With the first branch, social philosophy loses the specificity of the social by pretending that "everything (society included) is natural." Through the second, it appears also problematic to boldly affirm that "society is everything but natural." Those two positions nevertheless find representatives in contemporary currents of social philosophy. Sociobiologists (Barkow 1992) and tenants of the "cognitive turn" in the social sciences (Clement and Kaufmann 2007) can be labeled "strong naturalists" as they claim that the social consists in the conglomerate of our selfish genes in a given population or in the interconnection of our brain cells. Contractualists (Gauthier 1987) and textualists (Brown 1985) alike can be called by contrast "social constructivists" as they maintain that society results from our voluntary act to agree on conventions or from the rhetoric performativity of our all too human language. However opposite they might look, the two options of "strong naturalism" and "social constructivism" are only the reverse of one another, just as in metaphysics monism is the reversed coin of dualism (and vice versa). There is but one nature (to which society participates), say the strong naturalists, to which the constructivists respond in a rather dualistic fashion that society, by being non- or extra-natural, is diverse in shape and changing through time. Again, the former will face difficulties in specifying the "nature of the social" within nature, whereas the latter will find it difficult to attach "society" to any nature whatsoever.

My contention is that one way to escape the dilemma between "strong naturalism" and "social constructivism" is to abandon from the start the project of *founding* the "nature of society" (be it in brain cells or in speech acts) and to look instead for the *genesis* of "society in nature." Such an approach might be called "genealogical." Unlike naturalism and constructivism, a genealogical social philosophy neither pretends that society is grounded *in* nature nor that it is built on its own ground *apart from* nature, but that it somehow stems *from* nature. When we assume that society has its origins (and not its foundation) in nature, it becomes possible to maintain both terms of the dilemma: society's specificity *and* its naturalness. To do this, a genealogical social philosophy must add that society's natural provenience does not refer to a pre-social, mythical, and almost forgotten past, but that society *persists* in being natural. All in all, a genealogical social philosophy comes with another concept of "nature"—and also of "society"—than that at the center of the never-ending disputes between the strong naturalists and the social constructivists. "Life" seems a good candidate for this other nature, "social life" being the name for a new way to tackle the issue of the "nature of society." The main advantage of the category of "life" compared to that of "nature" monolithically understood is that it leaves plenty of room for the idea of social transformation, without considering society as a splendid exception in the reign of nature. From the perspective of a genealogical and "vitalist" social philosophy, transformation appears in the end as natural as it is social, and "social life" as nature being transformed into a new form that nevertheless remains tied to its natural origins.

In the following, I would like to defend the thesis that, in order to avoid the dilemma sketched above, as social philosophers we must (1) be anti-dualist and anti-monist alike on the ontological level when it comes to defining the relationships between "nature" and "society," (2) adopt a genealogical as opposed to foundationalist attitude toward the problem of "society in nature," and (3) be transformative or "vitalist" in our attempt to discern the "nature of society." I will try to give some flesh to these rather programmatic thoughts by reassessing an old debate between two of the most prominent French thinkers of the beginning of the twentieth century: Émile Durkheim and Henri Bergson. Bergson once presented his last *oeuvre, The Two Sources of Morality and Religion*, as his "sociological book." Much of the *Two Sources* is indeed dedicated to a close, albeit implicit, confrontation with some of the main social theories of his time (Comte, Spencer, Durkheim, Levy-Bruhl, etc.), especially the first chapter which offers an analysis of "moral obligation" that significantly differs from the one proposed by Durkheim throughout his own sociological work. Bergson and Durkheim shared at least one thing in common in their *post-mortem* discussion.[1] Both raise doubts about purely "theoretical" approaches to morality, such as those of deontology (Kant) or consequentialism (utilitarianism), which merely look after its intellectual grounds, be those in an autonomous or a calculating reason. To them, morality is first and foremost a matter of practices upon which the moral theorist can only retrospectively reflect. Reason does not produce by itself the content of the everyday life obligations we have toward ourselves and others, precisely because moral practices are already at work before our intellect tries to rationalize them.[2] If morality is not grounded in practical reason, then its very sources must be found elsewhere, and to excavate those sources means to proceed genealogically. It can be said that Durkheim and Bergson provide each in their own way a "natural history of morals" in the Nietzschean sense.[3] Yet, behind their genealogical approaches to morality lies the crux of the Durkheim-Bergson controversy on which I will focus here. Whereas Durkheim's "sociological naturalism" traces the origins of morality in society as a "*sui generis* reality," Bergson's "very comprehensive" sociobiology views it as a "manifestation of life." As I will show, their *fin de siècle* debate goes far beyond the sole question of the sources of morality. It involves questioning the "nature of society" in terms of "society in nature" and offers a good chance to escape the dilemma of strong naturalism and social constructivism while moving toward a "social vitalism."

DURKHEIM'S "SOCIOLOGICAL NATURALISM"

Durkheim retained from Auguste Comte, whom he considered the "father of sociology," the idea that society consists in a higher "synthesis" of the elements it is composed of. There is "society" as soon as individual consciousnesses associate themselves so that their union gives birth to a "*sui generis* reality" that shows to be irreducible to them taken separately. Association of elements giving birth to new organized forms of existence is a principle that Durkheim borrowed from the biological sciences of his time before applying it by analogy to "social life":

Though a cell contains nothing but mineral elements, these reveal, by being combined in a certain way, properties which they do not have when they are not thus combined and which are characteristic of life (properties of sustenance and of reproduction); they thus form, through their synthesis, a reality of an entirely new sort, which is living reality and which constitutes the subject matter of biology. In the same way, individual consciousnesses, by associating themselves in a stable way, reveal, through their interrelationships, a new life very different from that which would have developed had they remained uncombined; this is social life. (Durkheim 1985, 2)[4]

The analogy of "organic" and "social life" means that "association" (or "organization") corresponds to an overall principle that prevails in different orders of reality: "cells by aggregating together form living beings, just as living beings by aggregating together form societies" (Durkheim 1970, 99; my translation). For Durkheim, it is as if any realm of reality is an association of elements that relatively supersedes them while emerging from them. Stemming from the combination of physical and chemical inert matter, biological processes provide the substratum for individual psychological representations from which social phenomena in the end arise. Not only does the emergence principle tied to association explain the genesis of society, it is also larger in its extent both ontologically and epistemologically. The different orders emerge from each other in a more and more complex way and constitute at the same time the diverse realms that each scientific discipline (physics, chemistry, biology, psychology, and sociology) is in charge to investigate. From physical and chemical matter to social reality by passing through living organisms and psychic life, the continuum of reality spreads out of gradually heterogeneous orders with each one possessing its own irreducible features.

Since reality is a continuum made out of emergent orders, each science is able to develop its proper modes of explanation.[5] The sociologist Durkheim can thereby affirm the specific nature as well as the naturalness of "social life":

We say that social life is natural, [. . .] because it derives directly from the collective being which is, of itself, a nature *sui generis*; it is because it arises from that special process of elaboration which individual consciousnesses undergo through their association with each other and whence evolves a new form of existence. (Durkheim 2013, 98)

Natural in the same sense biological and psychological processes are, "social life" remains nevertheless specific as far as it refers to a "*sui generis* reality" that cannot *de facto*—and must not *de jure*—be reduced to biological or psychological facts. As Durkheim summarizes it, "[i]f the laws of life are to be found in society, then it is under new forms and with specific features"

(Durkheim 2010, 1). As "a new form of existence" as such distinctive from organic beings or mental operations, society requires its own models of explanation that only a fully developed sociology—whose methodological tools still need to be refined, as Durkheim repeatedly admits—can provide. In principle, social phenomena have to be explained by social factors, and by social factors *alone*, Durkheim claims. The self-explanation of social facts in which the *explanandum* tends to coincide with the *explanans* opens the perspective of a "sociological naturalism" that Durkheim conceives as an alternative to the numerous attempts of explaining the social by something other than itself, be it through psychological or brute material factors, attempts that make society appear as a mere "epiphenomenon":

> Beyond the ideology of the psycho-sociologist and the materialistic naturalism of the socio-anthropologist there is room for a sociological naturalism which would see in social phenomena specific facts, and which would undertake to explain them while preserving a religious respect for their specificity. (Durkheim 2010, 15)

Durkheim's "sociological naturalism" presents a naturalism of a very peculiar kind since he sometimes assimilates it to a superior form of "spirituality." Assuming that individual representational life can be characterized as "spirituality," the social that emerges from it can be defined by its "hyperspirituality" meaning that "all the constituent attributes of mental life are found in it, but elevated to a very much higher power and in such a manner as to constitute something entirely new." Strangely enough, society's "hyperspirituality" makes up an integral part of Durkheim's "sociological naturalism," for "[d]espite its metaphysical appearance, this word designates nothing more than a body of natural facts which are explained by natural causes" (Durkheim 2010, 15). In what does the "hyperspiritual" specificity of social life consist, which the sociologist should so "religiously" preserve from the interference of the other realms and the other sciences? Durkheim gives a firm and all too famous answer to this when he identifies "social facts" by their capacity of exercising an "external constraint" on individuals. The two apparently redundant criteria—"constraint" and "exteriority"—are here of equal importance in order to understand what the "nature of society" means for Durkheim. To begin with, "constraints" characterize natural phenomena in general and are therefore not proper to society: "any physical environment exercises constraint upon the beings that are subjected to it, for, to a certain degree, they are forced to adapt themselves to it" (Durkheim 2013, 14; translation modified). On the background of the overall naturalness of constraints, Durkheim extricates what is specific to *social* constraints:

The pressure exerted by one or several bodies on other bodies or even on other wills should not be confused with that which the group consciousness exercises on the consciousness of its members. What is exclusively peculiar to social constraint is that it stems not from the unyieldingness of certain patterns of molecules, but from the prestige with which certain representations are endowed. (Durkheim 2013, 14; translation modified)

The "prestige" associated with collective representations is due to the relative transcendence by society of its members, obliging them to act and think in certain ways. In the sort of sociological version of Rousseau's "general will" Durkheim advocates for, collective representations act on individuals on the basis of the "moral authority" those individuals recognize in society insofar as it derives from their mutual association.[6] Inasmuch as moral rules are established and guaranteed by society, "the obligatory character with which they are marked is nothing but the authority of society, communicating itself to everything that comes from it" (Durkheim 1973a, 162). In other words, where physical constraints *force* individuals to behave in a determinate way, social constraints morally *oblige* them to act in such and such a manner. However, while tracing a thick line between the "physical environment" and the "moral environment" in their respective ways of constraining individuals, Durkheim remains thoroughly loyal to his "sociological naturalism." Moral obligations are best to be explained not, as for Rousseau, through "the skillful artifice of the social contract" (Durkheim 2013, 97; translation modified) but rather by the "natural forces" embodied in society. Social constraint, Durkheim writes, "is not derived from some conventional arrangement which the human will has contrived, adding it on to what is real; it springs from the entrails of reality itself; it is the necessary product of given causes" (Durkheim 2013, 97–98; translation modified).

Next to their morally (and still naturally) constraining feature, Durkheim gives a second criterion to identify what social facts are: "externality." Externality looks prima facie redundant if not tautological with "constraint," since any constraint seems to impose itself from the outside to that which it constrains. Durkheim makes clear however that there are forms of constraint, as for instance instincts or habits that exercise their forces on us *from within*, whereas social practices and beliefs shape us *from the outside*:

It is true that habits, whether unique to individuals or hereditary, in certain respects possess this same property [of constraining us]. They dominate us and impose beliefs and practices upon us. But they dominate us from within, for they are wholly within each one of us. By contrast, social beliefs and practices act upon us from the outside; thus the ascendancy exerted by the former as compared with the latter is basically very different. (Durkheim 2013, 14)

Far from being redundant with constraint, externality is in fact just as crucial for specifying the "nature of society." In Durkheim's mind, it allows no more and no less than to settle "the great difference between animal societies and human societies":

> in the former, the individual creature is governed exclusively from *within itself*, by the instincts (except for a slight degree of individual education, which itself depends upon instinct). On the other hand human societies present a new phenomenon of a special nature, which consists in the fact that certain ways of acting are imposed, or at least suggested *from outside* the individual and are added on to his own nature. (Durkheim 2013, 190)

Durkheim thereby subverts the traditional opposition between human and animal societies in which interiority (in terms of subjective consciousness and free will) used to be a privilege of human beings—whereas non-human beings were supposed to respond blindly to laws that are external to them. For Durkheim, animals are constituted in such a way as to follow their internal instincts and eventually to readjust their behavior depending on what they have learned individually during their existence. Human beings, by contrast, are utterly transformed through their socialization process, and their education is collective and not strictly individual, so that the social institutions in which they are raised (the family, professional corporations, the state, etc.) "take on substance as individuals succeed each other without this succession destroying their continuity" (Durkheim 2013, 190). Being born as an organic "individual," the little human animal is socialized into becoming a moral "person," an attribute that is thus everything but innate, merely resulting from its participation in social life.

This all converges toward Durkheim's anthropological thesis on the duality of human nature (*Homo duplex*). Two classes of "states of consciousness" coexist in the human being that correspond to its "double existence," "the one purely individual and rooted in our organisms, the other social and nothing but an extension of society" (Durkheim 1973a, 162).

> One class merely expresses our organisms and the objects to which they are most directly related. Strictly individual, the states of consciousness of this class connect us only with ourselves, and we can no more detach them from us than we can detach ourselves from our bodies. The states of consciousness of the other class, on the contrary, come to us from society; they transfer society into us and connect us with something that surpasses us. (Durkheim 1973a, 161–62)

Yet the duality of human nature does not contradict Durkheim's "sociological naturalism." In Durkheim, there is no dualism of nature and society, only a duality *within* human nature between the "organic" and the "social" aspects of its existence. Being in itself a natural phenomenon, society is externally added to our basic human nature with the effect of transforming it into a new nature of a "moral" or "hyperspiritual" kind, distinctive as such from our "organic" and "strictly individual" one. Rightly understood, the duality of our nature appears in the end as real as the society in which it originates, so that "[i]nasmuch as he participates in society, the individual *naturally* transcends himself, both when he thinks and when he acts" (Durkheim 1995, 16; my emphasis).

Morality represents, for Durkheim, the social fact par excellence since it fittingly combines the two criteria of "constraint" and "externality." Moral duties are not only the best sign that society imposes its rules upon us, but it does so externally so as to transform our nature toward a higher, more "spiritual," and "civilized" level. Still, Durkheim acknowledges that, when defining social facts by their "external constraints" on individuals, he is not exhausting the realm of "social life." His preliminary definition of the "nature of society" largely proceeds from his methodological requirement of studying social phenomena "from the outside, as external things, because it is in this guise that they present themselves to us" (Durkheim 2013, 37), as it is paradigmatically the case for moral duties. But social life possesses other distinctive features than that of "external constraint," as he admits in the following passage: "while institutions bear down upon us, we nevertheless cling to them; they impose obligations upon us, and yet we love them; they place constraints upon us, and yet we find satisfaction in the way they function, and in that very constraint" (Durkheim 2013, 16). Society is not only constraining us the way moral duties do, we also feel attracted to society as we enjoy our participation in it. "Good" and "duty" are the two faces of our moral life insofar that they share a common origin in society to which we feel internally attracted while it externally constrains us. However, Durkheim remarks, "[t]he good possesses something more internal and intimate than duty, and is in consequence less tangible" (Durkheim 2013, 16). It is because of its higher "tangibility" that the moral phenomenon of duty is preferred to that of good when it comes to defining the "nature of society." Moreover, insisting on the "externality" of social facts is also a way for Durkheim to underline the possibility of reflecting upon them by looking after their "natural causes" with the aid of the social sciences. Self-reflection is another distinctive feature of human societies in comparison to animal societies and their strictly internal regulation. By gaining intelligence of social life, sociologically informed individuals acquire the opportunity of "mastering the moral world" (Durkheim 1973b, 115) that is imposed upon them. Sociological knowledge makes it possible that "the external merge with the internal" (Durkheim 2013, 37), which designates for Durkheim nothing more than the final process of moral autonomy. Individual self-reflection alone does not give access to such autonomy, only social science does, that is, science as a collective—and thus social—enterprise. Hence the three basic components of morality for Durkheim, each one having its origin in society: our moral life as social beings (and we are moral only inasmuch as we are social beings) is composed of (1) discipline (we feel constrained by society), (2) attachment to social groups (we are fond to social participation), and (3) "practical autonomy" (we are able to understand society and thus to reshape it through our knowledge).

BERGSON'S "VERY COMPREHENSIVE" SOCIOBIOLOGY

In the *Two Sources*, Bergson agrees with Durkheim "that society exists, and that hence it inevitably exerts a constraint on its members, and that this constraint is obligation." He refuses however to draw from the constraining existence of social facts that society is self-sufficient, arguing that "for society to exist at all the individual must bring into it a whole group of innate dispositions." Instead, Bergson concludes, "we must search below the social acquisitions, get down to life, of which human societies, as indeed the human species, are but manifestations" (Bergson 1977, 100; translation modified). Against the self-sufficiency of social facts, Bergson develops the counter-thesis according to which "the social underlies the vital" (*le social est au fond du vital*) (Bergson 1977, 193). Yet his sociobiology is clearly not a reductionist one, as he intends to give "to the word biology the very wide meaning it should have" (Bergson 1977, 101). How then must we understand in Bergson that human societies are "manifestations of life" in the broadest sense?[7]

The *Two Sources* begins with an analysis of the "whole of obligation" as the trace both of society in the individual and of the individual in society. In contrast to Durkheim, Bergson's method is indeed introspective instead of extrospective but ends up with the same conclusion: the fact that we feel morally obliged to ourselves and others has its origin in that we are living in an organized society. Our multiple obligations as members of a family, as partners in the division of social labor, or as citizens of a state get their meaning from the whole of society in which we were born and raised. Bergson pushes further than Durkheim the analogy between human and non-human societies, while stressing at the same time their intrinsic differences. From the side of this analogy, he claims, "[w]hether human or animal, a society is an organization; it implies a co-ordination and generally also a subordination of elements; it therefore exhibits, whether merely lived through or, in addition, represented, a collection of rules and laws" (Bergson 1977, 27). From the side of their divergence, animal societies leave no room for their members to act otherwise than out of mere instincts, whereas human societies are based on a system of habits that tend to *imitate* instincts. Social habits on which the "whole of obligation" relies simulate the internal forces and the regularity of natural instincts. Paramount to human societies is "the habit of contracting habits" (Bergson 1977, 26), social habits being "virtual instincts" (Bergson 1977, 28) that operate *as if* they were the instincts that they are *not*.[8] Essentially, Bergson's analysis of the "whole of obligation" rests upon an evolutionary explanation of the point of divergence between human and animal societies *in* nature. During evolution, nature has split itself into distinctive pathways with respect to their societal tendencies, corresponding to the classes of *arthropods* (especially among the *hymenoptera* like bees and ants) and of *vertebras* (especially among humans). The former points in the direction of instincts, the latter in that of intelligence.[9] Although they present two distinctive solutions that nature has found to the problem of coordinating actions, "instinctive societies" and "intelligent societies" remain in fact entangled because of their common origin in nature. One effect of their entanglement is that the latter functions *by mimicry* of the former. Indeed, Bergson notices that

> an activity which, starting as intelligent, progresses towards an imitation of instinct is exactly what we call, in man, a habit. And the most powerful habit, the habit whose strength is made up of the accumulated force of all the elementary social habits, is necessarily the one which best imitates instinct. (Bergson 1977, 26)

Being organized forms of life, human societies are built on a system of habitual obligations, the contents of which are historically contingent while their overall obligatory form remains strictly necessary as it is tied to nature's original intentions.[10] Moral obligations exhibit thereby the paradoxical form of a "necessity with which one can argue" (Bergson 1977, 92). They are necessary for any society to function at all, and still, they are open for discussion insofar as they hold for "a society composed of free wills" (Bergson 1977, 9). The core of Bergson's sociobiological argument against Durkheim now becomes clearer. Unlike Durkheim's "sociological naturalism" and its "hyperspiritualism," Bergson points out the existence of "a substratum of instinctive activity, originally implanted there by nature, where the individual and the social are well-nigh indistinguishable" (Bergson 1977, 37). Below the surface of socially acquired skills and dispositions lays the bottom of instinctual life that obligations mimicry in order for the social organization to exist and to reproduce itself. For Durkheim, biological processes seem to vanish as soon as we enter the realm of social life; for Bergson, on the contrary, natural life persists to trace its way beneath the sedimentations of social habits. He therefore admits that "[t]here is such a thing as fundamental nature," even though "there are acquisitions which, as they are superadded to nature, imitate it without becoming merged into it" (Bergson 1977, 271). To Bergson, the "nature of society" derives from "society in nature."

However, this is not the last word of Bergson's "very comprehensive" sociobiology. Just as for Durkheim "external constraint" does not exhaust social life, the "whole of obligation" constitutes to Bergson but one aspect of life's manifestation. Like Durkheim, Bergson reports a duality within our morality between a "closed" (or "static") and an "open" (or "dynamic") one. The former is characterized by the impersonal "pressure" members of a given society exercise on each other in order to coordinate and organize themselves, the second by the personal "aspiration" toward a higher form of humanity that transcends any given society (and even the natural boundaries of the human species). Between those two morals, Bergson adds, there is no gradual continuity from the most particular (my family, my neighborhood, my country, etc.) to the most general (human kind), but "a single bond" (Bergson 1977, 33) from the "closed" to the "open." Bergson's famous opposition between "closed" and "open" morality and their corresponding forms of society contains again an implicit but all too clear critique of Durkheim's most basic sociological postulates (Lefebvre and White 2010). Because he was trapped in his own methodological presuppositions, Durkheim could only take into account "closed societies" without paying due attention to the way societies "open" themselves to moral change. Durkheim not only wrongly admitted society's self-sufficiency by eluding its natural origins, he was also wrong to confer it "supreme authority" over its members. But if we accept that society "is only one of the aspects of life," then, Bergson concludes,

> we can easily conceive that life, which has to set down the human species at a certain point of its evolution, imparts a new impetus to exceptional individuals (*individus privilégiés*) who have immersed themselves anew in it, so that they can help society further along its way. (Bergson 1977, 100)

Through history, moral heroes (Bergson evokes the figures of Socrates and Jesus) have appeared now and then and their examples gave rise to a "moral transformation" of the societies in which they were living. Their examples continue to emotionally "appeal" to mankind long after their death so that "a mystic society" (Bergson 1977, 84) has gathered around them over the centuries. By contesting society's self-sufficiency in the name of its "vitality," Bergson thus also contests the "supreme authority" of "closed society" in the name of "openness." Bergson's genealogical operation of "getting down to life" appears thereby to pursue a twofold aim. On an "infra-rational" level, it excavates the biological bottom behind the "whole of obligation" with which "closed society" and its inevitable tendency to self-conservation "pressure" its members. On a "supra-rational" level, it sheds light on the way life impulses create changes into human society through the "aspiration" that moral geniuses generate among their centuries-old audience.

Still the closed/open duality does not involve any kind of dualism. It is true that Bergson sometimes refers to "closed societies" as the way human society emerges "out of the hands of nature" (Bergson 1977, 27; translation modified) suggesting that "open societies" contrariwise succeed in escaping for a while the rigidity of nature and its necessary laws. But drawing from this, a dualism of "natural" and "trans-natural" societies would be misleading. Bergson indeed claims that

> the duality itself merges into a unity, for "social pressure" and "impetus of love" are but two complementary manifestations of life, normally intent on preserving generally the social form which was characteristic of the human species from the beginning, but, exceptionally, capable of transfiguring it, thanks to individuals who each represent, as the appearance of a new species would have represented, an effort of creative evolution. (Bergson 1977, 97)

The two sources of morality and their corresponding types of society have their common origin in life, so that "the substratum of pressure [. . .] which is the basis of society" is at least "*capable* of being extended into aspiration" (Bergson 1977, 91; my emphasis). There is unity of the closed/open duality *in* life as being one and the same force "which manifests itself directly, rotating on its own axis, in the human species once constituted, also acts later and indirectly, through the medium of privileged persons, in order to drive humanity forward" (Bergson 1977, 51). Although different by nature, the "closed" and the "open" appear as mixed in the process of society opening itself, just as between rest and motion there is the process of getting in motion. To be sure, during the process of opening "we break with one particular nature, but not with all nature" (Bergson 1977, 58). Bergson makes here the use of Spinoza to claim that "it is to get back to *natura naturans* that we break away from *natura naturata*" (Bergson 1977, 58). Far from setting a dualism, the tension between "closure" and "openness" expresses life itself in its divergent but still complementary tendencies toward self-conservation (life as organization, *natura naturata*) and self-transformation (life as creative effort, *natura naturans*). Life is the force that reconciles the "contradictory requirements" to which each society is confronted: a society "can only subsist by subordinating the individual" and "can only progress by leaving the individual free" (Bergson 1975, 33). Life achieves this in "working both by individualization and integration to obtain the greatest quantity, the richest variety, the highest qualities, of invention and effort" (Bergson 1975, 34).

A subtle but decisive difference between "nature" and "life" intervenes in Bergson as he contrasts "nature's demands for a life in common" with the "impetus (*élan*) [. . .] related to life in general, creative of nature which created the social demand" (Bergson 1977, 269). As *natura naturata* is encompassed by *natura naturans*, the nature out of which (closed) society emerges depends upon the creative process that drives (open) society. Life's creativity that once gave birth to "intelligent societies" in nature can be restarted again at any time and eventually results in new forms of society. In other words, creativity is certainly "exceptional" but not an "exception" in nature seen as a larger life process. "Closure" and "openness" being divergent manifestations of one and the same force, the society that emerges from nature gives way to life pushing society further in its back. Like Durkheim's anthropological thesis on the *"Homo duplex,"* the duality of "nature" and "life" is best to be seen with respect to human beings insofar as it epitomizes a permanent tension between its natural determinacy as a sociable and intelligent species and its ever open-ended humanity.

If it is true that the "nature of society" has its ultimate source in the "life of society," then Bergson's social philosophy is a "vitalist" rather than a "naturalist" one. "Vitalism" here means a philosophical commitment that puts "confidence in the spontaneity of life" and that opposes a "permanent distrust in front of its mechanization" by setting mechanism in its due place within life in general.[11] As a vitalist social philosopher, Bergson strongly believes in the capacity of society to regenerate itself against any attempt to fossilize and to "naturalize" it.[12] Having started with the genesis of society "out of the hands of nature" to finally appeal to the creative efforts of humanity, his "very comprehensive" sociobiology is large enough to depict society's dual tendency toward reproduction and transformation, *and yet* precise enough as to analytically stress the differences between "closure" and "openness" and to resolutely subordinate "nature" to "life."

SOCIAL VITALISM IN BERGSON—AND DURKHEIM?

Durkheim and Bergson have both traced paths to the kind of naturalist social philosophy that I have programmatically announced in beginning. First, it appears that, through their attempts to define the "nature of society," Durkheim and Bergson refuse any sort of dualism between nature and society: Durkheim because he sees in society a natural phenomenon that is part of the overall gradual continuum of reality; Bergson because he conceives society as a "manifestation of life" in its dual tendency toward "closure" and "openness." As Durkheim writes, "even if society is a specific reality, it is not an empire within an empire: It is part of nature and nature's highest expression. The social realm is a natural realm that differs from others only in its greater complexity" (Durkheim 1995, 17). Still, their anti-dualist social philosophies are neither monist nor attached to a reductive naturalism. Both insist on the specificity of human societies without separating them from the rest of nature. Through their anthropological thesis on human duality, Durkheim and Bergson affirm the great "plasticity" of human nature. Because they are relatively indeterminate biologically speaking, human beings are capable of transforming themselves in time and space, be it through the changing features of society itself (Durkheim) or through the "appeal" of moral heroes (Bergson). The higher transformability of human nature in comparison with other animals does not involve that human beings are detached from their natural bounds whatsoever. The *duality* (which is not however dualist) of their nature expresses a permanent and living tension between their primary attachment to nature and their openness to social and moral changes. This kind of anthropology trenches with more classical conceptions that confer to humans the a priori supernatural qualities of consciousness and free will, whereas Durkheim and Bergson see these qualities as a posteriori results of "social life."

Second, their intention is certainly not to ground society in nature but rather to show how society actually stems from it. This seems more decisively the case for Bergson than it is for Durkheim. Bergson's analysis of the "whole of obligation" indeed comes to the conclusion that "the social underlies the vital" without being merged into it. His genealogical uncovering of the biological background (but not foundation) behind social life targets Durkheim's claim about the self-sufficiency of society. However, the "*sui generis* reality" formed by society does not mean for Durkheim that it is somehow self-grounded apart from nature. Rather, the biological as well as psychological substrata from which society emerges continue to be largely effective *within* the social. Durkheim's requirement of explaining social phenomena through social factors must therefore be understood from the perspective of his sociological method, and not—as Bergson suggests—as an ontological statement. In other words, the self-explanatory account of social facts does not imply that everything is thoroughly social in society.[13]

Finally, Durkheim's and Bergson's approaches to the problem of the "nature of society" depart from any mechanistic or narrowly causalist conception of nature in favor of an organic or vitalist model which they share with many others of their contemporaries at the turn of the twentieth century. Affirming the specificity of the "vital" over the "mechanical" is at the very core of their anti-dualism (and anti-reductive monism) as well as of their genealogical (anti-foundationalist) approaches to "society in nature." In Durkheim, the analogy with living beings is paramount to understand his conception of society as a new order emerging from the association of its members. The new and higher "synthesis" represented by society is synonymous with its uncontested "creativity" in comparison with other natural phenomena:

Society does indeed have at its disposal a creative power that no observable being can match. [. . .] A society is the most powerful collection of physical and moral forces that we can observe in nature. Such riches of various materials, so highly concentrated, are to be found nowhere else. It is not surprising, then, that a higher life develops out of them, a life that acts on the elements from which it is made, thereby raising them to a higher form of life and transforming them. (Durkheim 1995, 447).

More influenced by evolutionist theories than by cellular biology as Durkheim is, Bergson's reference to "life" designates the creative process that drives society against its own mechanization. In any case, the paradigm shift from a mechanical and analytically understood nature to an organic and synthetical life enables both authors to "dynamize," as it were, the "nature of society." It helps them to conceive society as a transformative process rather than a pre-given and inert reality. From their "vitalist" perspective, transformation appears as equally natural to society than to the life process from which it continues to emerge.

"Social vitalism" is however a label that seems better suited to Bergson's social philosophy than to that of Durkheim. With his "sociological naturalism," Durkheim intends to give an *explanation* of social transformation assuming that social changes are natural in that they respond to "natural (social) causes." Social transformation especially occurs through sociological self-reflection, that is, when the members of society develop the necessary tools to modify the social processes imposed upon them by understanding their profound causes. Avoiding the kind of rationalist bias he would ascribe to Durkheim's formulation of "practical autonomy" in terms of the "intelligence of morals," Bergson is very far from offering any naturalistic explanation of the "moral transformation" undergone by societies, for this would be at odds with his own idea of "life's creativity." Hence his appeal to exceptional figures of "moral geniuses" who, while rising above society, kickstart new impulses and directions for mankind.[14] To resume, for Bergson, "exceptional individuals" have the mission to *exogenously* transform society; for Durkheim, it is the task of society (including the social sciences as social phenomena) to *endogenously* transform individuals.

The Durkheim-Bergson debate leaves us in the end with two irreconcilable options, which is perhaps a good sign of their social philosophies' *vitality* today. Is the very dynamic of "social life" explainable (in terms of "natural causes" we can understand and therefore master) or is it quasi-miraculous (as a "supra-rational" but nevertheless tangible force that pushes society further in its back)? How are we as naturalist social philosophers to find the right balance between a *too*-mechanical Durkheim and a *too*-vitalist Bergson? If we succeeded to escape one dilemma to land directly into another, my guess is that this one is more fruitful than the clash between strong naturalism and social constructivism.

SELF-DISCIPLINE AND SOCIAL CHANGE

My last remarks are not intended to trench once and for all the debate between Durkheim and Bergson but on the contrary to complicate it even further. I would like to briefly challenge the two main charges Bergson raises against Durkheim—his alleged lack of attention to the biological bottom below (closed) society and to the possibility of transformation toward (open) society—by returning to some passages of the lessons Durkheim dedicated to "moral education" (Durkheim 1973b). In the first lesson, Durkheim discusses "the spirit of discipline" which is composed of regularity through habitual conduct and moral authority: "at the root of moral life there is, besides the preference of regularity, the notion of moral authority" (Durkheim 1973b, 31). Like Bergson in his treatment of "closed morality," Durkheim claims that morality, being a "constant thing," "implies a certain ability of contracting habits, a certain need for regularity" (Durkheim 1973b, 27; translation modified).[15] Habits are "forces internal to the individual," consisting in a certain amount of "accumulated activities" that tend to expand, while moral rules are something outside of us imposing their commandments on the basis of their socially admitted authority. Only the combination of the two forms the "spirit of discipline," morality as a whole being a "system of habitual conducts" *and* "of commandments." Habits and moral duties are thus intertwined in that the former expand from our inside to the outside, whereas the latter consist in the exactly reversed movement of constraining our individual forces from the outside. As the combination of both, moral discipline is "an internal expression of external resistance" which has the double effect of "regularizing" from the inside and "containing" from the outside our conducts.

Interestingly enough, when he attempts to justify "the spirit of discipline" by tracing its social genesis, Durkheim comes up with a biological analogy following which regularity represents "the moral analogue of periodicity in the organism" (Durkheim 1973b, 34). As for any organism, a certain level of regulation is required in moral conducts for society to exist at all: "social life is only one of the forms of organized life; all living organization presupposes determinate rules, and to neglect them is to invite serious disturbance" (Durkheim 1973b, 37). This seems to support Bergson's criticism of Durkheim for remaining trapped in a narrow depiction of a "closed society" that perpetuates itself through the impersonal "training" of its members. However, thereafter Durkheim mitigates his own organicist explanation of discipline as he remarks:

True, social institutions are directed toward society's interests and not those of individuals as such. But, on the other hand, if such institutions threaten or disorganize the individual life at its source, they also disorganize the foundation of their own existence. (Durkheim 1973b, 38)

However "vital" to social reproduction, regulations must not exceed a "normal" level, for it would otherwise transform moral discipline into violence and coercion against that "individual life" at the source of social life. In other words, it is as if the act of morally "containing" from the outside and the propensity of our "individual forces" to expand are *normally* counterbalanced by each other. A society with no regulation at all ceases to be a society, but the same goes for a society that overregulates "individual life" in such an extreme way as to make the moral operation of "containing" impossible. A "normal" society is a society that achieves to maintain equilibrium between the two "pathological" tendencies of *de*regulation and *over*regulation.

The question then is where to put the boundary between "normal" and "pathological" forms of moral discipline. Durkheim's paradoxical but all too consequent answer consists in saying that, while being "natural" to the moral realization of human beings, the social tolerability toward discipline is itself evolving through time: "If discipline is a means through which man realizes his nature, it must change as that nature changes through time" (Durkheim 1973b, 43). The paradox of moral discipline being "natural" to human beings *and* subject to social changes makes sense if we consider Durkheim's deeper anthropological account of its *raison d'être*. Because of its constitutive indeterminacy, each "normally" constituted human being goes in search of determination by means of *self*-discipline (and not merely *social* discipline). For it is otherwise condemned to suffer from "infinity sickness." Far from ascribing to the "ascetic conception of discipline" that sees it as a necessary evil inflicted upon the sinful nature of men, Durkheim conceives discipline as representing for human individuals a "natural" means to self-determination:

If we deem it essential that natural inclinations be held within certain bounds, it is not because that nature seems to us bad, or because we would deny the right to gratification; on the contrary, it is because otherwise such natural inclinations could have no hope of the satisfaction they merit. (Durkheim 1973b, 44)[16]

Self-discipline is not the restriction of freedom; it is its anthropological condition of possibility: "The rule, because it teaches us to restrain and master ourselves, is a means of emancipation and of freedom" (Durkheim 1973b, 49). To freely express oneself, one must first have learned how to limit oneself. The free "expansion" of individual forces presupposes its minimal "containment" at least through the primary inner/outer distinction. The boundaries between "normal" and "pathological" forms of moral discipline might therefore change historically as societies become more and more permissive and sensitive to unnecessary violence and repression, still the anthropologically rooted need for self-limitation remains, as it were, intangible. Durkheim's idea that "[t]he normal boundary line is in a state of continual becoming" (Durkheim 1973b, 44) has thus two sides: first, there *is* a "normal boundary line" which is profoundly rooted in the anthropological need for self-limitation; second, this line remains by definition open to discussion and to permanent change precisely because human nature becomes determinate through its socialization. Self-discipline and social change are not antithetical as the closed/open duality in Bergson suggests; on the contrary, the former is the anthropological condition of the latter. If this is true, then Durkheim *pace* Bergson takes into account some of the pre- or non-social (here "anthropological") conditions of social life, and he does indeed, under his anthropological premise, confront the issue of social changes by asking *how* they concretely occur. For, as Durkheim notes,

> to move toward clear-cut objectives, one after another, is to move ahead in uninterrupted fashion and not to be immobilized. It is not a matter of knowing whether one must move or not, but at what speed and in what fashion. (Durkheim 1973b, 50)

NOTES

1. Durkheim died in 1917, fifteen years before Bergson published the *Two Sources*. They belonged to the same generation and even studied together at the École Normale in Paris, but they never had the chance to publicly confront their positions unless indirectly through their disciples. On the historical background behind their controversy, see Azouvi 2007.

2. See how Canguilhem describes the "rationalist bias" from a vitalist perspective: "Rationalism is an afterthought philosophy. Taken to the letter and in all rigor, rationalism, the philosophy of the scientific man, would end up making man lose sight of the fact that he is a living being" (Canguilhem 2015, 313; my translation).

3. In §186 of *Beyond Good and Evil*, Nietzsche opposes his genealogical project of a "science of morals" which requires "collecting material, formulating concepts, and putting into order the tremendous realm of tender value feelings and value distinctions that live, grow, reproduce, and are destroyed" to that of philosophers who "wanted morality to be *grounded*" (Nietzsche 2002, 75).

4. On the biology inspired social sciences of Durkheim's close predecessors (Saint Simon, Comte) and his contemporaries (Espinas, Worms), see Guillo 2002 and Barberis 2003. Note that the reverse is also true (Vatin 2005), as at that time biology was also influenced by sociology. In his *Introduction à l'étude de la médecine*

fondamentale of 1865, the French physiologist Claude Bernard evokes for instance the "social solidarity" of the cells in an organism.

5. The idea that the differentiated continuum of reality also traces the different domains proper to each science is borrowed by Durkheim again from Comte but also from his former philosophy teacher Émile Boutroux, author of *De la contingence des lois de la nature* in 1874.

6. In the first book of the *Social Contract*, Rousseau described the effects of "association" on its members as follows: "At once, in place of the individual personality of each contracting party, this act of association creates a moral and collective body, composed of as many members as the assembly contains votes, and receiving from this act its unity, its common identity, its life and its will" (1920, 7). Note that Durkheim devoted his Latin dissertation thesis to *Rousseau as a precursor of sociology* in 1892.

7. For an interesting discussion of Bergson's sociobiology, see Caeymaex 2012.

8. In one of his earlier texts, Gilles Deleuze defends a position close to that of Bergson when he claims that "humans have no instincts" and compensate their lack of instincts by "building institutions": "The Human is an animal decimating its species. Therefore, instinct would translate the urgent needs of the animal, and the institution the demands of humanity: the urgency of hunger becomes in humanity the demand for bread" (Deleuze 2003, 21).

9. In chapter II of *Creative Evolution* (Bergson 1944), Bergson defined instincts as organic instruments and intelligence as the capacity to create nonorganic tools. Intelligence shares with instincts its "instrumentality," but, being instinctively poor, it necessitates the capability to create artificial tools, as extensions of the natural organism.

10. As to "nature's intentions," Bergson does not mean by this that nature pursues ends as in the classical (Aristotelian) model of natural teleology. He rather expresses himself "like a biologist, who speaks of nature's intentions every time he assigns a function to an organ" (Bergson 1977, 60). In this case, the obligatory form appears as the best-suited organ to fulfill the function of organizing human societies.

11. I borrow this overall characterization of vitalism from Canguilhem 2008, 64 and 73. For a recent appropriation of Canguilhem in terms of "critical vitalism" as opposed to "substantial" or "ideological vitalism," see Worms (2015).

12. For a contemporary example of "vitalism" in social philosophy with reference to Hegel and Dewey, see Särkelä 2018.

13. As Durkheim puts it in his lessons on pragmatism (1913–1914), "the organic world does not abolish the physical world, and it is not *against* the organic world, but *with* it that the social world is formed" (Durkheim 2002, 146; my translation).

14. The publication of the *Two Sources* has immediately raised criticism among the Durkheimians about the "individualist" account of social changes behind Bergson's conception of "open society" (Pinto 2004).

15. Remember that for Bergson "social life appears to us as a system of more or less deeply rooted habits, corresponding to the needs of the community" (Bergson 1977, 10). For a fruitful discussion of Bergson and Durkheim on the topic of habits, see White (2013).

16. This echoes Hegel's speculative notion of "concrete freedom": "In this determinacy, the human being should not feel determined; on the contrary, he attains his self-awareness only by regarding the other as other. [. . .] Freedom is to will something determinate, yet to be with oneself in this determinacy and to return once more to the universal" (Hegel 1991, 42, addendum to §7). On the "pathologies of freedom" related to indeterminacy, see also Honneth (2000).

REFERENCES

Azouvi, François. 2007. *La gloire de Bergson. Essai sur le magistère en philosophie.* Paris: Gallimard.

Barberis, Daniela S. 2003. "In search of an object: organicist sociology and the reality of society in fin de siècle France," *History of the Human Sciences*, 16 (3): 51–72.

Barkow, Jerome H., Cosmides, Leda, and Tooby, John (eds.). 1992. *The Adapted Mind. Evolutionary Psychology and the Generation of Culture.* Oxford: Oxford University Press.

Bergson, Henri. 1944. *Creative Evolution.* New York: Random House.

Bergson, Henri. 1975. *Mind-Energy. Lectures and Essays.* London: Greenwood Press.

Bergson, Henri. 1977. *The Two Sources of Morality and Religion.* South Bend: University of Notre Dame Press.

Brown, Richard H. 1987. *Society as Text.* Chicago: University of Chicago Press.

Caeymaex, Florence. 2012. "La société sortie des mains de la nature. Nature et biologie dans *Les deux sources,*" in *Annales bergsoniennes*, 5: 311–34. Paris: Presses Universitaires de France.

Canguilhem, Georges. 2008. *Knowledge of Life.* New York: Fordham University Press.

Canguillhem, Georges. 2015. "Note sur la situation faite à la philosophie biologique en France," in *Oeuvres completes*, 4: 307–20. Paris: Vrin.

Clement, Fabrice, and Kaufmann, Laurence. 2007. "Paths Towards a Naturalistic Approach of Culture," *Intellectica*, 46 (2): 7–24.

Deleuze, Gilles. 2003. "Instincts and institutions," in *Desert Island and Other Texts*: 19–21. Los Angeles: Semiotext(e).

Durkheim, Émile. 1970. "Cours de science sociale," in *La science sociale et l'action*: 85–117. Paris: Presses Universitaires de France.

Durkheim, Émile. 1973a. "The Dualism of Human Nature and its Social Conditions," in *Emil Durkheim on Morality and Society. Selected Writings*: 149–65. Chicago: University of Chicago Press.

Durkheim, Émile. 1973b. *Moral Education.* New York: Free Press.

Durkheim, Émile. 1985. "Sociology and the Social Sciences," in *Readings from Emile Durkheim*: 2–7. London: Routledge.

Durkheim, Émile. 1995. *The Elementary Forms of Religious Life.* New York: Free Press.

Durkheim, Émile. 2002. *Pragmatisme et sociologie*. Paris: Vrin.

Durkheim, Émile. 2010. "Individual and Collective Representation," in *Sociology and Philosophy*: 1–15. London: Routledge.

Durkheim, Émile. 2013. *The Rules of Sociological Method and Selected Texts on Sociology and its Method*. London: Palgrave Macmillan.

Gauthier, David. 1985. *Moral by Agreements*. Oxford: Oxford University Press.

Guillo, Dominique. 2002. "Biology inspired sociology of the nineteenth century: a Science of Social 'Organization,'" *Revue française de sociologie*, 43: 123–55.

Hegel, Georg W. F. 1991. *Elements of the Philosophy of Right*. Cambridge: Cambridge University Press.

Honneth, Alex. 2000. *Suffering from Indeterminacy. An Attempt at a Reactualization of Hegel's Philosophy of Right*. Amsterdam: Van Gorcum.

Lefebvre, Alexandre, and White, Melanie. 2010. "Bergson on Durkheim: Society *sui generis*," *Journal of Classical Sociology*, 10 (4): 457–77.

Nietzsche, Friedrich. 2002. *Beyond Good and Evil*. Cambridge: Cambridge University Press.

Pinto, Louis. 2004. "Le débat sur les sources de la morale et de la religion," *Actes de la recherche en sciences sociales*, 4 (153): 41–47.

Rousseau, Jean-Jacques. 1920. *The Social Contract & Discourses*, J. M. Dent (ed.). London/Toronto: E. P. Dutton & Co.

Särkelä, Arvi. 2018. *Immanente Kritik und soziales Leben. Selbstransformative Praxis nach Hegel und Dewey*. Frankfurt a. M.: Klostermann.

Vatin, François. 2005. *Trois essais sur la genèse de la pensée sociologique*. Paris: La Decouverte.

White, Melanie. 2013. "Habit as a Force of Life in Durkheim and Bergson," *Body & Society*, 19: 240–63.

Worms, Frédéric. 2015. "Pour un vitalisme critique," *Esprit*, 1: 15–29.

Part II

EMBODIMENT AND SOCIAL LIFE

ACTION, GENDER, AND WORK

Chapter 7

The Dual Character of Social Interaction

Habit, Embodied Cognition, and Social Action

Italo Testa

INTRODUCTION

In this chapter, I present an understanding of social action based on the notion of habit which to my mind could offer a basis for developing a naturalistic social philosophy and a cross-disciplinary conceptual framework from which both social sciences and cognitive sciences could benefit. The approach that I will present is based on a socio-ontological reconstruction of some basic pragmatist ideas. I will argue that the pragmatist notion of habit is particularly useful as a cross-disciplinary framework for social philosophy insofar as, by overcoming the dualism between routine and skilled action, it can help us to read anew the constitutive role that automation plays for action. This may let us appreciate the importance of a still-understated phenomenon that emerges both in cognitive sciences and social sciences, which I will label as the "two-sided" character of interaction; it's being both active and passive, spontaneous and receptive.

Here is how I will proceed in the argumentation of my thesis. In the first section, "Pragmatist Habit Ontology," I will first reconstruct three key elements of a pragmatist approach inspired by Dewey, that is, (i) methodological and ontological interactionism, (ii) a naturalist understanding of interaction as a process, and (iii) habits understood as fundamental patterns that individuate and stabilize units of interaction. I will present such a habit-based approach providing a socio-ontological framework, insofar as habit formation can account for the interplay between individual behavior, social customs, and collective institutions.

In the second section ("The Reappraisal of Habit in Contemporary Social Theory, Cognitive Sciences, and Neurosciences"), I will reinforce with a short historical survey my argument for the theoretical relevance of the notion of habit for both social and cognitive sciences. First, I will show that the notion of habit, due to a negative understanding which has led to its identification with that of routine, has been put aside in the foundation of social theory in the twentieth century. An analogous dualism between routine and goal-directed behavior has deeply influenced cognitive sciences, whose rise in the twentieth century has led classical cognitive science, as Barandiaran and Di Paolo have argued, to put aside the notion of habit as a theoretical concept and substitute it with the internalist notion of representation (2014). The same has happened in the neurosciences as for approaches to motor action, which have for a long time assumed a dualism between rigid motor routines and higher cognitive, flexible processes. I will show that only recently habit is beginning to be discovered and to regain a role in our understanding of the notions of social practices, cognitive phenomena, and neural processes. This to my mind leads us to reconsider the pragmatist heritage and, in particular, the fruitfulness of the Deweyan habit ontology as a framework which can offer foundational tools apt to highlight some shortcomings of the contemporary debate and to revise some of its presuppositions.

In the third section ("The Role of Automatism"), I will argue that the pragmatist framework overcomes the dualism between customary/traditional behavior and creative action, automatism and active intelligence, a dualism which to my mind still looms at the back of enactivist approaches such as Barandiaran and Di Paolo's. Dewey realizes the constitutive role that automation, understood as the setting up of a mechanism of action, plays for human behavior for both its cognitive enhancement and its economization. This framework accounts for a plurality of forms of automatism of action, which ranges from unintelligent, rigid behavior to flexible and intelligent mechanisms of adaptation. Consequently, habit ontology allows for a plurality of forms of habit and does not oppose routine to skilled action, but rather conceives both as manifestations of habit formation which can be analytically discriminated as different degrees in a continuum of experience. Moreover, this framework lets us appreciate the internal dynamics, the two-sided aspect of automatism in habit formation, which can implement the efficiency and plastic adaptability of behavior but can also turn into a resilient, inertial tendency that blocks action and eventually breaks down.

In "The Two-Sided Character of Social Interaction," finally, I will argue that the habit ontology framework developed so far can allow us to frame a crucial phenomenon that cross-cuts cognitive and social sciences, that is, the phenomenon of the "two-sidedness" of interaction. The notion of habit, by overcoming the opposition between automatism and flexible action, allows

us to realize that interaction is both active and passive, receptive and spontaneous. In this sense the Deweyan conception of interaction as a "two-way"
process, when reconstructed in terms of habit ontology, provides us with a
framework that can make explicit and conceptually systematize the results of
different empirical and theoretical researches—which at the physiological,
cognitive-functional, and phenomenological level have observed that mirror neurons, patterns of primary intersubjectivity, and subjective individual
experience operate in a two-way manner, respectively. At last, I will argue
that such a two-way model of interaction can be captured in social philosophy
by the idea that habits operate as social attractors—as attracted attractors—
which is particularly relevant for how we are to conceive of social practices
and institutions within both social theory and the cognitive sciences.

PRAGMATIST HABIT ONTOLOGY

In this section, I try to reconstruct the basic assumptions of a pragmatist
socio-ontological understanding of action, that is, (i) *methodological and
ontological interactionism,* (ii) a *naturalist understanding of interaction as a
process,* and (iii) *habits understood as fundamental patterns* that individuate
and stabilize units of interaction.[1]

The first assumption (i) of the kind of pragmatist framework I am reconstructing is what could be called a combination of *methodological and
ontological interactionism.* Accordingly, interaction is assumed to be a basic
notion for both the causal explanation and the ontological understanding of
the very being of social phenomena. As such, interaction is not merely a
contextual condition of social phenomena (something that merely influences
X), nor solely an enabling condition (something necessary for X to occur),
but first and foremost interaction is a constitutive condition for them: a part
of X that is a defining element of what social phenomena are. This is an idea
deeply rooted in pragmatism and that can for instance be traced back to three
classic pragmatist texts, namely *Human Nature and Conduct, Experience
and Nature,* and *The Public and its Problems,* where Dewey develops the
idea that social facts are dependent on human activity, and in particular on
"human interaction," and still exhibit an "objective reality" (Dewey 1984,
240; 1981, 153).

As for assumption (ii), the Deweyan pragmatist relational ontology of
interaction is moreover a *naturalist* one. Action is introduced first as a manifestation of a life process, a defining feature of our living nature. Naturalism here is not only a methodological issue—concerning a philosophical
approach that relies on empirical research drawn from a plurality of natural
and social sciences—but also an ontological one, since it concerns the idea

that action is itself a manifestation of a natural process. And the life process of which action is a manifestation is taken to be an interactive phenomenon, a process of organism-environment interaction—where both terms are understood as correlatives, definable only in relation to their continuous interaction (see Johnson 2010, 127).

As for assumption (iii), the pragmatist social ontology which I am reconstructing here is moreover based on the notion of *habits as patterns of action*. The idea is that action always happens in the context of prior action. This expresses not only the process character of action, understood as a phase in an ongoing, self-developing process rather than as a singular event. While happening, actions are cast into a "regulated pattern of behavior derived from prior experience" (Dewey 1973, 85), that is, they lead to the formation of some regular and recurring structures. It is this structure of action's embedment that Dewey understands as a process of habit formation where actions are cast into habitual patterns.

The process whereby actions are cast into patterns is the same as the process of habit formation, in which standing, habitual patterns of action are formed. Following this model, Dewey's ontology of the social world introduces three basic notions—"habit," "custom," and "institution" (Dewey 1983, 43)—understood as different degrees of systematization of the process of habit formation, that is, stabilization of patterns of interactions. Those individuate in turn individuals, groups, and social totality. Units of social interaction are not presupposed by the process of habit formation but rather are individuated as its emerging properties.

We can now begin to see in which sense this kind of habit ontology can inform a naturalistic social philosophy and be helpful, as we shall see in the later sections, to develop it as an interdisciplinary scheme that cuts across social theory and cognitive sciences. Pattern formation is a process of action's embodiment, embeddedness, and extension. Human interaction is at the same time a horizontal transaction between living organisms and a vertical transaction between these organisms and the natural and social environment they inhabit. The formation of habits is thus built into the organic nature of living beings and is sensitive to the affordances of the natural and social environment. The formation of habitual patterns of action, as Dewey argues in *Human Nature and Conduct*, involves a form of embodiment which is both an adaptation of our behavior *to* the natural and social environment and *of* the environment to our behavior (Dewey 1983, 38). In this sense, patterns are incorporated in the living bodies and incorporate within themselves their natural and social environment: which means that such patterns are not only embodied in the individual organisms but are embedded in the environment these organisms interact with. Furthermore, the model according to which patterned social interaction is ontologically constitutive of social facts allows for the idea that habituation is an extended phenomenon. Hence, in this scheme social institutions can be understood as objectivations of social customs rooted in habitual patterns, that is, as a form of symbolic embodiment of interaction in technological, social, and political bodies rather than in organic ones.

THE REAPPRAISAL OF HABIT IN CONTEMPORARY SOCIAL THEORY, COGNITIVE SCIENCES, AND NEUROSCIENCES

Due to a negative understanding of habit identified with dead routine, this notion has for a long time been put aside in the foundation of both social theory, cognitive sciences, and in the neuroscientific analysis of motor action. Only recently the notion of habit is beginning to be re-evaluated as an important theoretical and empirical issue: a reappraisal to which, to my mind, the pragmatist framework can significantly contribute with its conceptual tools, and in particular with a model of patterned interaction that overcomes the dualism between routine and intelligent action that has prevailed in the tradition.

Even though the notion of habit is directly or indirectly to be found in the writings of classical sociological thinkers such as Durkheim, Weber, and Veblen (Camic 1986) in a way that presents some similarities with the pragmatist understanding of this notion (Kilpinen 2012), it is a fact that for a long time this notion has not played a central foundational role in social theory. Analogously to what has happened in the philosophical tradition, in social theory habit has been understood mainly in a negative sense, as they were conceived of as mere mechanical routines and opposed to rational action. Even sociological trends deeply influenced by pragmatism such as symbolic interactionism, with its focus on the interpretative aspect of symbolic interaction between social actors (Blumer 1969), were somehow influenced by the prevailing negative reading of habit, and under this aspect did not fully inherit the pragmatist legacy. Let us consider for instance the so-called "pragmatic sociology of critique," with its focus on the creative aspect of actors in the situation (Boltanski 2011), which has been inspired by pragmatism too. The choice to use the notion of "actor" instead of the notion of "agent" was aimed against Bourdieu's critical sociology and his notion of social agents as having dispositional properties embodied in the forms of habits, allegedly explaining the reproduction of social structures. Here an understanding of habit as something merely passive and deterministic, as opposed to the active, performative, and reflexive character of social action, is at the basis of Bourdieu's criticism and maybe also of some aspects of Bourdieu's understanding of *habitus*.

Still, there is today an increasing tendency to re-evaluate the contribution that the notion of habit could make to the foundations of social theory. As Stephen Turner has noted, the widespread use of the notion of social practices, even if it mostly does not explicitly mention the notion of habits, tacitly assumes that habits sustain practices in time and history (Turner 1994). And the idea that habits are an ineradicable element and a necessary foundation of our understanding of social practices is gaining influence, even if mostly indirectly by use of correlate notions, also in political theory (see Hartmann 2003), and in those currents of contemporary social theory and social philosophy which are sensitive to the interplay between agential and structural aspects of social practices: for example, the morphogenic approach and critical realism (see Archer 2003; Elder-Vass 2012), critical social metaphysics (Haslanger 2012), cultural pragmatics (Alexander 2016), and neo-Durkhemian approaches to the sociology of the ritual and of social performance (Seligman et al. 2008).

The reappraisal of the foundational role of the notion of habit requires us to overcome the dualism between habitual action and creative action upon which the negative understanding of habit as a dead routine was based. And here the classical pragmatist habit ontology suits this purpose very well, since its main idea is that habit is constitutive of every form of action. Hence, even creative, reflexive, and rational action has to be conceived of as being constituted by standing patterns, as some sort of second-order habit consisting in the "habit of changing habits," as Peirce would put it (1976, 142). This is also extremely relevant for contemporary cognitive sciences and neuroscientific approaches to motor action, since a dualism between routine and goal-directed action has for a long time permeated these fields of study and has led to the theoretical abandonment of the notion of habit. As Barandiaran and Di Paolo have noted in a recent genealogical survey, in the approach to mindedness "before the advent of cognitivism, one of the most prominent theoretical ideas was that of habit" (2014, 22). The authors distinguish two trends in the traditional approaches to habit. The tradition they label as "associationism" understands habits atomistically as units that result from the association of ideas or between stimulus and response. Habits are kept here within the realm of reactive sub-personal mechanism and opposed to rational, intentional, and personal levels of cognitive processing. The tradition they label as "organicism" understands habits holistically as dynamic, ecological, and self-organizing teleological structures. Habits are here conceptualized as traversing a continuum from pre-reflexive to reflexive embodied cognitive processes. According to Barandiaran and Di Paolo, the associationist understanding prevailed in the philosophy of mind with behaviorism, which substituted the notion of habit with that of "rate of conditioned response." Finally, the computational and informational theory, emerged as a reaction to behaviorism to inform classical cognitive science, substituted the notion of "mental representation" for that of "habit" (and the notion of "computation" for that of "association") as the theoretically fundamental concept in the approach to mindedness. According to this diagnosis, which I will later evaluate in more detail, the overcoming of the internalist, mentalist, and representational approach of classical cognitive science through the 4E cognition approach (embodied, embedded, enactive, and extended cognition) could give way to a reappraisal of the theoretical role of habit, provided that we are able to overcome the dualism between routine and reflexive, goal-directed action leading to the negative understanding of habit and eventually to its dismissal.

An analogous situation can be detected in the approach of the neurosciences to habits, which has been dominated for a long time by a sort of dualism between habits and actions (see for instance Dickinson 1985). Here, habits were reduced to rigid motor routines—understood as inflexible, automatic, and ateleological stimulus-response pairings with no cognitive control (Sieger and Spiering 2011; Bernacer and Murillo 2014)—and motor behavior was somehow separated from the emotional and cognitive dimension. More recent studies of the neurobiology of habits and social rituals (Graybiel 2008; Smith and Graybiel 2014) are now increasingly overcoming this dualism toward an understanding of motor behavior as being much more flexible, plastic, and integrated with emotional and cognitive processes. And the neurobiology of mirror neurons also offers us here some relevant tools for our understanding of the goal-oriented structure of patterns of motor action already at the sub-personal and automatic level of neural activation (Rizzolatti, Fogassi, and Gallese 2001).

Still, a lot of work remains to be done, for which a reconstruction of the pragmatist approach could offer some important insights. The first thing to note is that, strangely enough, the dualism between motor routine and intelligent behavior, and the associationist and ateleological understanding of habits that has molded the neurophysiological research into habit, has often been traced back to pragmatism, namely to the influence of William James' *Principles of Psychology* (see Sieger and Spiering 2011; Smith and Graybiel 2014). This underestimates the fact that even James, while speaking of habit as the "enormous flywheel of society, its most precious conservative agent," was not merely attributing a passive and inertial character to it. He was at the same time underlining the plastic and teleological structure of habits (1890), or in other terms, as we will see later, was conscious of the two-sided character of habitual interaction. Moreover, it is exactly in the pragmatist tradition, and namely in the work of both Peirce and Dewey, that we can find a sharp criticism of the identification of habits with dead routines which leads Dewey for instance to distinguish between "routine habits" and "intelligent habits," both understood as stabilized patterns of behavior (1983, 32 and 48), and

Peirce to affirm that "habits are not for the most part formed by mere slothful repetition of what has been done" (1976, 143).

THE ROLE OF AUTOMATISM

The truncated reception of the pragmatist heritage is not merely a historical-philosophical question that is worth revisiting. I think that here a deeper understanding of the pragmatist model of habit ontology could also be relevant in order to diagnose some shortcomings of the contemporary reappraisal of the role of habit within cognitive sciences and neurosciences. There is a certain tendency in readings such as those offered by Barandiaran and Di Paolo (2014), based on too sharp a historical and theoretical opposition between the associationist and organicist understanding of habits, to simply convert the negative evaluation of habit as routine into its opposite. Accordingly, in this vitalist picture it is now the active, creative, plastic, reflexive, personal, and intentional side of habit to be exclusively under focus. Habits as a whole tend to be modeled on this picture whereas the automatic, unconscious, pre-intentional side is reduced to a subtype of the first and understood as the result of the decay of higher cognitive functions (see for instance the Aristotelian approach of Bernacer and Murillo 2014, 17). This is not only in contrast with Dewey's naturalist principle of continuity (Dewey 1986, 26), which requires that higher functions be shown to emerge from lower ones (see Johnson 2010, 125). In this pragmatist approach, the continuity between the two sides of habits has to be understood not only as a top-down process but also, more fundamentally, as a bottom-up process. Here the notions of "automatism" and "mechanism," as we shall see, play a crucial role in the understanding of the continuity between routine and intelligent habits and cannot be unilaterally put only on the side of routines, as Barandiaran and Di Paolo (2014) and others tend to do.

Habits, according to the Deweyan framework, emerge out of (and are underpinned by) physiological mechanisms that operate at a sub-personal, pre-reflective, and unconscious level. Automatism is in this sense required for habits to function. The indispensability of the mechanism of automation for habit formation is here related to the idea that habits, in order to emerge, function, and maintain themselves, first need to have physiological correlates. Second, they must be implemented in functional mechanisms that operate at a pre-intentional and sub-personal level. And, thirdly, their being expressed in a phenomenological pre-reflexive, spontaneous dimension is a condition for both the economization and the cognitive enrichment of our experience. As contemporary neurobiological studies on dual tasking also show, automation of motor tasks which at first required many brain areas to be active is a condition for freeing our energies and channeling them toward the development of newer, higher forms of cognitive control (Poldrack et al. 2005). Dewey directly connects the role that automation plays in the economization of action—reducing the expense of physical energy and the use of mental resources, minimizing our efforts and our cognitive load—with his notion of habits. As he writes, "yet all habit involves mechanization. Habit is impossible without setting up a mechanism of action, physiologically engrained, which operates 'spontaneously,' automatically, whenever the cue is given. But mechanization is not of necessity *all* there is to habit" (Dewey 1983, 51). In this sense, automation, understood as some form of "setting up" of a mechanism of action, is for Dewey constitutive of the notion of habit. Of course, not all automatic behavior are habits—consider for instance some automatic bodily reflexes in infants such as sucking and the grasp reflex, which are not acquired by habituation. Nor automation is all that is required to analyze the notion of habit. Still, habitual actions are according to Dewey one type of automatic behavior.

When it comes to understanding the relation between habit and automatism, it is interesting to note that Dewey refuses to reduce mechanisms to "unintelligent automatism" (1981) and tends to think that automatism applies both to unintelligent and intelligent behavior. That's why Dewey sharply criticizes those positions, such as Bergson's vitalism, that assumed a dualism between life and mechanism. On the contrary, for Dewey "all life operates through a mechanism" (1983, 51). The point here is not to oppose again mechanism and intelligent life, but rather to make room for a gradual and evolutionary distinction between different forms of automatism, that is, between simpler and repetitive ones and more complex and adaptable mechanisms, between un-flexible and flexible automatism. As Dewey writes, "the higher the form of life, the more complex sure and flexible the mechanism" (1983, 51). Higher levels of life are not to be understood as merely departing from the mechanical organization, but rather as evolving into more complex and flexible automatisms, where "mechanism is fused with thought and feeling" (Dewey 1983, 51). According to this model, life is constituted by a plurality of forms of automatisms. Automatism of behavior does not rely on one single mechanism, but rather on a variety of mechanisms, which allow different forms of control of behavior, ranging from rigid to more flexible and adaptable ones, up to full-blooded and conscious monitoring. In this sense, automatism of action for Dewey is not identical with what is called in contemporary psychology "mindless automaticity" (Ashforth and Fried 1988; Gersick and Hackman 1990; Louis and Sutton 1991), involving total lack of control and consciousness. Automaticity can be rather instantiated at different degrees of the evolution of life, which instantiate distinct combinations of what Bargh labels as the "four horsemen of automaticity" (1994), that is, efficiency, awareness, controllability, and intentionality. Those are understood as the four aspects into which automaticity can be decomposed, and whose full, minimal occurrence or complete lack can mark an action as being automatic, ranging from mindless automaticity up to intelligent, mindful, flexible action.

Even habits, given the constitutive role that automation plays for them, are to be understood as a plurality of forms. Dewey's ontology of social action is in this sense based on a broad notion of habit, which encompasses both routine behavior and skilled action. Dewey argues against those who assume "from the start the identity of habit with routine" (1983, 32) and thinks that we should also account for the fact that "habit is an ability, an art formed by past experience" (1983, 48). In this sense Dewey, contrary to Ryle (1949), does not oppose "habit," understood now as repetitive routine, to "skill," understood as intelligent behavior. Dewey rather distinguishes between "routine habits" and "intelligent," "creative habits," both understood as manifestations of the genus of habit. Routine habits are qualified as "rigid" responses, pigeon-hole-like rather than intertwining, overspecialized, based on previous patterns that self-perpetuate without transforming themselves. When they are incapable of adapting themselves to varying situations and renewing themselves, they tend to decay into "dead," lifeless schemes, and thus to "sink below the level of any meaning" (Dewey 1983, 146). On the other hand, creative, intelligent habits are characterized as something sensible to practice and exercise, both self-preserving and self-transforming, freely intertwining with other habits, flexible and adjustable to different situations: they are habits capable of answers that fit the unusual and the novel by producing new meanings that are "unique" and "never twice alike" (Dewey 1983, 146). Routine habits are distinguished from creative ones as a matter of degree, that is, they are understood as a poor instantiation of the structure of habit, where expressiveness tends to the zero degree of meaning production. Since mechanism, as we have seen, is constitutive of all forms of life, the point of such a distinction is not to oppose automatism and intelligent life, but rather to make room for a gradual, evolutionary, and contextual distinction between different forms habitual automatism can be taken to manifest, that is, between simple and repetitive mechanisms of habitual behavior and more complex, flexible, and adaptable ones.

Routines and intelligent habits in Dewey's pragmatist framework are not two qualitative distinct and opposite forms but rather can be analytically distinguished as different degrees in a continuum of experience, since they are both manifestations of the same dynamic structure of habit and in this process one can easily turn into the other. In this sense, the automatism that is constitutive of habit can be both an efficiency booster of action, leading to flexible and intelligent adaptation, but can also turn into an inertial tendency that blocks the action and leads to practical errors of adaptation. As Dewey argues, "repetition is in no sense the essence of habit. Tendency to repeat acts is an incident of many habits but not of all" (1983, 32). On the one hand, inertial bare repetition is not the essence of habits, which are pretty compatible with creative adaptation to a changing situation. On the other hand, the dynamics of habitual action at all levels, according to Dewey's diagnosis, can involve some sort of inertial tendency, which can lead skilled behavior to decay into dead and lifeless schemes and to become "unilateral," "rigid," and "fossilized" (2015, 19). In this sense, Dewey's habit ontology is quite aware of the internal dialectics of habit formation understood as a two-sided process, which can manifest both an active, efficient, creative side and a passive, resilient, inertial side. This can be connected to what in organizational theory emerges as the "dark side" of automation (see Makowski 2017, 160–64), and which is being analyzed by the psychological literature on the fragility of habitual skills (Christensen, Sutton, and McIlwain 2015) and their openness to various dynamics of internal collapse and breakdown.

If we now go back to Barandiaran and Di Paolo, the point here is not only that the pragmatist understanding of the role of automatism in habit cross-cuts the bifurcation between mechanist associationism and vitalist organicism, as it has been portrayed by the authors (2014). Most importantly, I think that this lets us appreciate an aspect of the pragmatist legacy which has often been missed in its reception both in social theory and in cognitive sciences. In both cases, the tendency to unilaterally conceive of pragmatism as an activist philosophy neglects the fact that the pragmatist framework is deeply informed by what I would call an understanding of the two-sided character of social action and cognition, that is, by the idea that agency is both active and passive, spontaneous and receptive.[2] And this two-sided aspect of agency is deeply rooted, as we have seen, in the dynamics of habit formation and in the two-sided character of automation.

THE TWO-SIDED CHARACTER OF SOCIAL INTERACTION

In this concluding paragraph I will argue that pragmatist habit ontology, by overcoming the opposition between routine and creative action, provides us with a model that allows us to frame a crucial phenomenon that cross-cuts the social sciences, the cognitive sciences, and the neuroscientific investigation on the action, that is, the "two-sidedness" of interaction. The pragmatist understanding of the two-sided character of social action is deeply related to its habit-based model of patterned action. And the truncated heritage of pragmatism is largely connected with the fact that the two sides of habit have not been taken together, as happened with the reception of James' take on habit, which has been mostly taken to get the passive side of habitual interaction as something separate from its active dynamics. Still, if one really wants to assess the pragmatist legacy in all its depth, one should realize that at the roots of its concept of agency lies the idea of the two-sided character of social interaction, understood not as two separate aspects, but rather as moments of an actual, qualitative whole, which may be analytically distinguished in the occurrence of a problematic situation. As Dewey writes,

> A trans-action does not just go across in a one-way direction, but is a two-way process. There is reaction as well as action. While it is convenient to view some human beings as agents and others as patients (recipients), the distinction is purely relative; there is no receptivity that is not also a re-action or response, and there is no agency that does not also involve an element of receptivity. (1988, 119)

The "two-way process" of interaction has everything to do with the fact that interaction has a two-sided character: action and response, agency and patency, activity and receptivity. The distinction between these two sides is not a fixed one but is relative to different contexts, which can manifest in different ways the two-sided character of interaction. Here emerges the pragmatist model of social subjects as agents which embody a disposition to act and react, rather than as mere social and cognitive actors. And as we will see, it is exactly this dispositional side of action, its being conceived of in terms of stabilized patterns, which allows its two-sided character to be captured.

The two-sided character of interaction is at the core of the naturalist pragmatist theory of social agency but also of its conception of phenomenological experience. This is what Dewey expresses by saying that "the living creature undergoes, suffers, the consequences of its own behavior. This close connection between doing and suffering or undergoing forms what we call experience." (1982, 129). Experience, understood naturalistically as a self-regulatory process of habit formation, has then for Dewey a two-sided character of manifestation. While conceiving of experience in terms that are in accordance with the contemporary dynamic system and enactive approaches (Barandiaran and Di Paolo 2014; Barrett 2014), Dewey at the same time reminds us that, once we understand habits as self-organized stabilities, dynamically configured stable patterns, we should not lose sight of the fact that the active side of self-organization is always intertwined with a receptive, passive side. And this two-sided character of habit formation is manifested not only in the phenomenological experience of subjects and in the structure of their agency but also characterizes the functional organization of habitual patterns as well as their physiological underpinnings, as Dewey's passage on the physiological embodiment of the functional mechanisms of patterned action affirmed.

If we now leave aside for a moment classical pragmatism and look at contemporary research, I think we can appreciate from a different viewpoint how the two-sided character of interaction is a phenomenon that manifests itself at the physiological, functional, and phenomenological levels. For instance, as for the neurophysiological level, Vittorio Gallese has noted that mirror neurons have some sort of dual mode of operation, being both receptive and expressive, passive and active (2001, 45). In fact, mirror neurons respond both as a particular action is performed by the subject and as the same action is performed by another individual. The mirror system seems to constitutively map an agential relation having a relational structure, where the other and I are related as agents and recipients of some action (Gallese 2001; Gallese and Metzinger 2003). If we consider the interactive aspect of this, we can see that mirror neurons are receptive to something—the action performed by other agents—and, as a consequence of this, they activate a response. If we understand the functional explanation of these neural mechanisms in terms of embodied simulation theory, this response consists of an internal (inhibited) motor simulation of the same action (which is to be distinguished from the full-blown activation of the motor system by the acting subject). Here there may be other functional explanations alternative to embodied simulation theory and more in line with a social externalist view, such as enactive models inspired by dynamic system theory, research on primary intersubjectivity, phenomenology, and pragmatism (Hutto and Gallagher 2008; De Jaegher, Di Paolo and Gallagher 2010). But I think that a prerequisite for these explanations to succeed is for them to be able to take into account how the two-sided character of interaction manifests itself in the functional mechanisms and phenomenological experiences (see Testa 2017f).

And, indeed, a two-sided configuration of the intertwinement between receptive and expressive mode is to be found also in much empirical research into the development of primary intersubjectivity, emotional coordination, bodily mimesis (Trevharten 1979; Hobson 2004; Zlatev 2008), as well as in the phenomenological analysis of embodied intersubjectivity ("intercorporeality" in Merleau-Ponty 1962). For instance, in many aspects, human infants start attracting and being attracted by recognition long before they have developed higher competencies to actively recognize others (such as higher-order perspective taking, attribution of intentional states, language, etc.). This emerges not only from developmental analysis of primary intersubjectivity as an embodied enactive process but also from phenomenological accounts of the experience of recognition (Ricoeur 2005). In fact, recognizing is always somehow being moved by something which triggers, elicits, or summons (according to different contexts, experience, and more powerful or less powerful ways of being moved) our acts of recognition as a response to it.

We have seen so far that different empirical and theoretical researches have observed that interaction operates in a two-way manner at the physiological, cognitive-functional, and phenomenological levels. Let us now come back to habit ontology and try to see how this framework, by accounting for the two-sided mode of interaction, can offer a unitary understanding that can frame different findings in social and cognitive sciences. Habit formation, as we have seen (according to the pragmatist hypothesis), is a notion that can apply both to the configuration of neural patterns, of the dynamic functional mechanism of the living body, and of subjective phenomenological experiences. Now, habit itself has a two-sided character. Habits have to be understood as structured and structuring structures, conditioned and conditioning patterns of behavior, which have both a receiving and an expressive side, a passive and an active side. Such a notion of habit goes back not only to Bourdieu's social theory (1990, 53) but is to be found in Dewey and in his image of habits as "structures" (1988, 64–65; see on this also Sullivan 2000, 26), that is, as permanent and stable self-organizing structures such as river banks which both channel the river flow and are also molded by it (1988, 119).[3] In habitual behavior, there is always something that evokes a response—a trigger or elicitor, a set of responses conditioned by previous patterns—which can range from automatic bodily responses to emotional ones, up to reflexive and deliberate ones, and finally an act that is the resulting behavior. We can better understand this if we consider that habits are both sustained *by* the body and inscribed *in* the body. On the one hand, they need to be inscribed in bodily causal chains and become automatic; and yet, on the other hand, they also expressively reshape our bodily behavior. In the philosophical tradition, this has often been expressed by saying that habits are both mechanical and spontaneous, as Dewey himself stated in his understanding of the relation between life and mechanism (1983, 51). Here we can see that habit formation is a process through which we acquire not only new capacities and opportunities to act but also new ways to be acted upon. Habit, as a socio-ontological operator, is a constituent part not only of active agential powers but also of passive agential powers.

Let me add some considerations as to why the two-sided mode of habitual interaction is an important phenomenon to take into account when we come to the interpersonal and the institutional levels of habit formation, that is to those levels of stabilization of action patterns which Dewey labeled as "customs" and "institutions," which are particularly relevant for social theory and social cognition. If we now consider social interaction as a system of customs, as a matter of historically rooted social practices bodily inscribed and stabilized by habit, we can begin to see that the two-sided mode of habituation affects the way we are to conceive of social agents, and of the sort of social cognition whose bearers are stabilized patterns of action. Habituation, as a socio-ontological operator, constitutes not only active agential powers but also passive agential powers. If we now come to see interactive attitudes as embodied habitual attitudes—as standing attitudes—we can better understand why attribution, in social action, is, first and foremost, something which can take place also at the level of embodied background processes, and, second, is always also a response to something. That is also why in social theory and social philosophy habit should be considered as a more fundamental notion than that of attribution of status (Testa 2017a; see on the contrary Searle 2010). The notion of habit accounts for how the attribution of social statuses can be bodily inscribed and for how statuses can become a constitutive aspect of some social objects (which can be embedded in the natural and social environment and extended also beyond the inscription into the individual organic body) and social subjects we respond to. In other words, the notion of habit accounts for how statuses become objective aspects, affordances of the social reality we perceive, and are experienced as having some sort of resilience, as something which is somehow given even if socially produced, resisting our active efforts to change it (see Haslanger 2012). In this sense, the notion of habit accounts for the interplay between the agential and the structural side of social action, or, to put it another way, for how agency can give rise to objective structures which in their turn (and according to some, on different timescales—see Archer 2003) constrain it.

One can also see why the two-sided character of habitual interaction is also very important for how we are to conceive of institutions within both social theory and cognitive sciences, and in general to develop a critical approach to social reality in social philosophy. On the one hand, institutions, such as for instance the system of right, when understood as regulated patterns of social interaction, are to be conceived of as an objective extension of our cognition that symbolically embodies statuses actively attributed to our attitudes. But, on the other hand, we do not only actively constitute social institutions, we are somehow also passively constituted by them. And this has to do directly with the assumption of the primacy of custom in the interactive process of habit formation. This means that bodily individual habits are shaped, maintained, and transformed under social, cultural, and historical conditions which precede the individual. Once we assume that institutions are systematized, regulated, and formalized customs, then we can see that they play a constitutive role in configuring bodily individual attitudes, agential powers, and subjectivity.

If we assume the scheme of embodied, embedded, and extended cognition, and view it through the lenses of the socio-ontological role of habituation, the primacy of custom, and its two-sided character, then we can realize that institutions on the one hand empower our individual cognition, agency, and subjectivity. But, on the other hand, just because they constitute some aspects of our subjectivity, they can also exert on us a constraining effect (Crisafi and Gallagher 2010; Gallagher and Miyahara 2012). We are not only shaping social institutions, but under many aspects we are also exposed to them, and this is essentially connected with the fact that habit on the one hand is a propulsive, active force, but on the other hand has a resilient, inertial, and passive side (see Testa 2017c; 2017d; 2017e). In this sense, the idea that institutions are instances of extended cognition through the habitual embodiment of statuses seems to be a necessary condition for understanding how they can in their turn be constitutive of cognitive and practical aspects of human subjectivity. And the two-sided character of habit accounts for how we can be both active subjects and subjected to this process of social constitution. A socio-ontological account is not only descriptive but also offers conceptual tools for a social philosophy committed to a dynamic and critical redescription of social processes.

A further important aspect of the ontology of the two-sided character of habit and social interaction, and of the kind of constraint we experience here, can be captured by the idea that habits function as social attractors. Felix Ravaisson once wrote that "habit is not an external necessity of constraint but a necessity of attraction and desire" (2008, 57). What Ravaisson meant by using the notion of "attraction" is not completely clear. But I think that a good starting point here is to realize that habitual action has to be conceived of not only in terms of active agential power of doing something but also as involving some passive agential power of undergoing something, and, namely, the power of attracting and being attracted by other action patterns. This leads us back to the pragmatist idea that recurring patterns such as individual habits, social customs, and collective institutions can be understood as different forms of stabilization of centers of attraction—what in dynamical system theory has been called attractor basin or attractor landscape (Rockwell 2016; Barrett 2014). This leads to an understanding of habits as attractor landscapes of social interaction, that is, as patterns produced by interaction, which can be embodied at different levels (sub-personal, personal, interpersonal, and collective) and which attract and are attracted by other interacting forces: they operate as attracted attractors, exerting in this sense some sort of passive and active causal power which plays a central role in social explanation. The notion of attracted attractors, which I cannot develop here in more detail (see more on this in Testa 2017b), could in this sense be apt to capture the two-sidedness of interaction and make available an interesting conceptual tool for a habit ontology. This could be helpful in bridging the gap between the analysis of dynamic systems and extended cognition approaches in cognitive sciences on the one hand, and socio-theoretical analysis of social practices and institutions on the other, and in promoting in both a critical approach to the power dynamics of social cognition and action.

CONCLUSION

In this chapter, I have argued that a pragmatist understanding of interaction inspired by Dewey can offer us a common ontological framework for both social and cognitive sciences. The pragmatist framework—my thesis—allows us to take distance from the negative understanding of habit which has been prevalent in the twentieth-century accounts of action within the social sciences, cognitive sciences, and neurosciences, and that has led to an opposition between motor routine and intelligent action. By overcoming such an opposition, habit ontology can let us appreciate the importance of the phenomenon of the two-sided mode of operation of interaction for both social theory and cognitive sciences. This makes available for us some conceptual tools such as the notion of habits as attracted attractors, which can help us re-conceive of social practices and institutions as two-sided socially extended cognitive systems and contribute to the development of a critical approach within both social and cognitive sciences.

NOTES

1. For a more detailed reconstruction of different aspects of Dewey's habit ontology, see Testa (2017a; 2017b; 2017c; 2017d; 2017e; 2017f). See also Särkelä (2021) and Gregoratto and Särkelä (2021), who focus on the relation between habituation and impulses, that is social reproduction nicely characterized as that "spiral of second nature and first nature" within which social groups and persons are constituted through habituation. Frega (2019) develops rather the pragmatist socio-ontological framework as a counterpart to a political theory of democracy. Frega affirms that "habits," patterns," and "institutional forms" are primitive notions in this social ontology and writes: "to that extent, I disagree with Italo Testa, who considers that a social ontology inspired by pragmatism can be easily reduced to the notion of habit" (2018, 173n). Of course, if one reduces habits to "individual habits," as Frega does, then a pragmatist social ontology cannot be reduced to them. But this is not the Deweyan use of the notion of "habit," which includes individual dispositions, social habits (customs), and collective organizational forms (institutions). Moreover, the notion of "patterns" cannot be isolated from the notion of habit, which in the most encompassing sense refers by Dewey (1983, 31) to the patterned structure of interaction (the fact that action always happens in the context of prior action). In this sense, the three "primitives" Frega introduces are to be understood rather as different levels of habitual pattern formation. Hence habits and interaction are not to be conceived as having different ontological status, as Frega

assumes, and be reduced one to the other—but rather habits, in their adverbial character (see also Steiner, forthcoming), are the way interaction manifests itself.

2. On the combination of the active and the passive side in the history of the philosophical notion of habit, but not in relation to the question of social action, see also Carlisle (2014, 30–34). On the relevance of passivity in relation to the theory of social action, see Joas (1996, 168–69). On habits as an "intermediate zone" between activity and passivity, see also Levine's (2017) interesting remarks.

3. On the complementarity between Dewey's notion of habit and Bourdieu's analysis of *habitus*, see for instance Colapietro (2004) and Inghilleri (2014), who also underline some important differences, since Bourdieu is mostly concerned with the analysis of the production of social structures and the reproduction of domination through habit formation, and does not seem to share Dewey's more optimistic view, related to his democratic theory, about the role that cooperative interaction and discursive acts can play as a means for restructuring the *habitus*.

REFERENCES

Alexander, Jeffrey C., Giesen, Bernhard, and Mast, Jason L. 2006. *Social Performance Symbolic Action, Cultural Pragmatics, and Ritual*. Cambridge: Cambridge University Press.

Archer, Margaret. 2003. *Structure, Agency and the Internal Conversation*. Cambridge: Cambridge University Press.

Ashforth, Blake E., and Yitzhak, Fried. 1988. "The Mindlessness of Organizational Behaviors," *Human Relations*, 41 (4): 305–29.

Barandiaran, Xavier E., and Di Paolo, Ezequiel A. 2014. "A Genealogical Map of the Concept of Habit," *Frontiers in Human Neuroscience*, 8 (522): 22–28.

Bargh, John A. 1994. "The Four Horsemen of Automaticity: Awareness, Intention, Efficiency, and Control in Social Cognition," in *Handbook of Social Cognition*, R. S. Wyer Jr. and T. K. Srull (eds.), 1–40. Hillsdale: Lawrence Erlbaum Associates Inc.

Barrett, Nathaniel. 2014. "A Dynamic System View of Habits," *Frontiers in Human Neuroscience*, 8 (682): 55–57.

Bernacer, Javier, and Murillo, Jose A. 2014. "The Aristotelian Conception of Habit and its Contribution to Human Neuroscience," *Frontiers in Human Neuroscience*, 8 (883): 12–21.

Blumer, Herbert. 1969. *Symbolic Interactionism: Perspective and Method*. Englewood Cliffs: Prentice Hall.

Boltanski, Luc. 2011. *On Critique—A Sociology of Emancipation*. Cambridge: Polity Press.

Bourdieu, Pierre. 1990. *The Logic of Practice*. Cambridge: Polity Press.

Camic, Charles. 1986. "The Matter of Habit," *American Journal of Sociology*, 9: 1039–87.

Carlisle, Claire. 2014. *On Habit*. London: Routledge.

Christensen, Wayne, Sutton, John, and McIlwain, Doris. 2015. "Putting Pressure on Theories of Choking: Towards an Expanded Perspective on Breakdown in Skilled Performance," *Phenomenology and the Cognitive Sciences*, 14 (2): 253–93.

Colapietro, Vincent. 2004. "Doing—and Undoing—the Done Thing: Dewey and Bourdieu on Habituation, Agency, and Transformation," *Contemporary Pragmatism*, 1 (2): 65–93.

Crisafi, Anthony, and Gallagher, Shaun. 2010. "Hegel and the Extended Mind." *S. AI & Society*, 25: 123–29.

Dewey, John. 1981. *Experience and Nature*, in *The Later Works of John Dewey, 1925–1953*, 1, J. A. Boydston (ed.). Carbondale: Southern Illinois University Press.

Dewey, John. 1982. *Reconstruction in Philosophy*, in *The Middle Works of John Dewey, 1899–1924*, 12, J. A. Boydston (ed.). Carbondale: Southern Illinois University Press.

Dewey, John. 1983. *Human Nature and Conduct*, in *The Middle Works of John Dewey, 1899–1924*, 14, J. A. Boydston (ed.). Carbondale: Southern Illinois University Press.

Dewey, John. 1986. *Logic: The Theory of Inquiry*, in *The Later Works of John Dewey, 1925–1953*, 12, J. A. Boydston (ed.). Carbondale: Southern Illinois University Press.

Dewey, John. 1988. *My Philosophy of Law*, in *The Later Works of John Dewey, 1925–1953*, 14, J. A. Boydston (ed.), 116–23. Carbondale: Southern Illinois University Press.

Dickinson, Anthony. 1985. "Actions and Habits: The Development of Behavioural Autonomy," *Philosophical Transactions of the Royal Society*, 308: 67–78.

Elder-Vass, David. 2012. *The Causal Power of Social Structures*. Cambridge: Cambridge University Press.

Frega, Roberto. 2019. "The Social Ontology of Democracy," *Journal of Social Ontology*, 4 (2): 157–85.

Gallagher, Shaun, and Miyahara, Katsunori. 2012. *Pragmatism and Enactive Intentionality*, in *New Directions in Philosophy and Cognitive Science: Adaptation and Cephalic Expression*, J. Schulkin (ed.). New York: Palgrave Macmillan.

Gallese, Vittorio. 2001. "The 'Shared Manifold' Hypothesis: From Mirror Neurons to Empathy," *Journal of Consciousness Studies*, 8 (5–7): 33–50.

Gallese, Vittorio, 2005. "Embodied Simulation: From Neurons to Phenomenal Experience," *Phenomenology and the Cognitive Sciences* 4 (1): 23–48.

Gallese, Vittorio, and Metziger, Thomas. 2003. "The Emergence of a Shared Action Ontology: Building Blocks for a Theory," *Consciousness and Cognition*, 12: 549–571.

Graybiel, Ann M. 2008. "Habits, Rituals, and the Evaluative Brain," *Annual Review of Neuroscience*, 31: 359–87.

Gregoratto, Federica, and Särkelä, Arvi. 2021. "Social Reproduction Feminism and Deweyan Habit Ontology," in *Habits: Pragmatist Approaches from Cognitive Neuroscience to Social Science,* I. Testa and F. Caruana (eds.), 438–57. Cambridge: Cambridge University Press.

Hartmann, Martin. 2003. *Die Kreativität der Gewohnheit: Grundzüge einer pragma-tistischen Demokratietheorie*. Frankfurt a. M.: Campus.

Haslanger, Sally. 2012. *Resisting Reality: Social Construction and Social Critique*. Oxford: Oxford University Press.

Hobson, Peter. 2004. *The Cradle of Thought*. Oxford: Oxford University Press.

Hodgson, Geoffrey M. 2010. "Choice, Habit, Evolution," *Journal of Evolutionary Economics*, 20: 1–18.

Hutto, Daniel, and Gallagher, Shaun. 2008. "Understanding Others Through Primary Interaction and Narrative Practice," in *The Shared Mind: Perspectives on Inter-subjectivity. Converging Evidence in Language and Communication Research*, J. Zlatev et al. (eds.), 12: 17–38. Amsterdam/Philadelphia: John Benjamins Publish-ing Company.

Inghilleri, Moira. 2014. "Bourdieu's Habitus and Dewey's Habits: Complementary Views of the Social?," *Approaches to Translation Studies*, 40: 185–201.

Joas, Hans. 1996. *The Creativity of Action*. London: Polity Press.

Johnson, Mark. 2010. "Cognitive Science and Dewey's Theory of Mind, Thought, and Language," in *The Cambridge Companion to John Dewey*, M. Cochran (ed.), 123–44. Cambridge: Cambridge University Press.

Kilpinen, E. 2012. "Human Beings as Creatures of Habit," in *The Habits of Consump-tion*, A. Warde, and D. Southerton (eds.), 45–69. Helsinki: Helsinki Collegium for Advances Studies.

Levine, Steven. 2015. "Hegel, Dewey and Habits," *British Journal for the History of Philosophy*, 23 (4): 632–656.

Louis, Meryl R., and Sutton, Richard I. 1991. "Switching Cognitive Gears: From Habits of Mind to Active Thinking," *Human Relations*, 44 (1): 55–76.

Makowski, Piotr T. 2017. *Tadeusz Kotarbiński's Action Theory*. Basingstoke: Pal-grave MacMillan.

Peirce, Charles S. 1976. *New Elements of Mathematics*, C. Eisele (ed.), 4. The Hague/Paris: Mouton; Atlantic Highlands: Humanities Press.

Poldrack Russell A. et al. 2005. "The Neural Correlates of Motor Skill Automaticity," *Journal of Neuroscience*, 25 (22): 5356–64.

Ravaisson, Felix. 2008. *Of Habit*, C. Carlisle and M. Sinclair (trans.). London: Continuum.

Ricoeur, Paul. 2005. *The Course of Recognition*, D. Pellauer (trans.). Cambridge, MA: Harvard University Press.

Rizzolatti, Giacomo, Fogassi, Leonardo, and Gallese, Vittorio. 2001. "Neurophysi-ological Mechanisms Underlying the Understanding and Imitation of Action," *Nature Reviews Neuroscience*, 2: 661–70.

Rockwell, Teed. 2016. "The Embodied 'We': Extended Mind as Cognitive Sociology," in *Pragmatism and Embodied Cognitive Science: From Bodily Intersubjectivity to Symbolic Articulation*, M. Jung and R. Mazdia (eds.), 165–82. Berlin: De Gruyter.

Ryle, Gilbert. 1949. *The concept of Mind*. Chicago: The University of Chicago Press.

Särkelä, A. (2021). "Das andere Leben: Deweys naturalistische Sozialontologie und ihre kritische Aufgabe," in *Pragmatistische Sozialforschung*, H. Brunkhorst, F. Petersen, and M. Seeliger (eds.), 151–69 Stuttgart: Metzler.

Seger, Carol A., and Spiering, Brian J. 2011. "A Critical Review of Habit Learning and the Basal Ganglia," *Frontiers in System Neuroscience*, 5 (66): 1–9.

Seligman, Adam B. et al. 2008. *Ritual and Its Consequences: An Essay on the Limits of Sincerity*. New York: Oxford University Press.

Smith, Kyle S., and Graybiel, Ann M. 2014. "Investigating Habits: Strategies, Technologies and Models," *Frontiers in Behavioral Neuroscience*, 8: 39.

Steiner, Pierre. (Forthcoming). "Habit, Meaning, and Intentionality," in *Habits. Pragmatist Approaches from Cognitive Neurosciences to Social Sciences,* I. Testa and F. Caruana (eds.). Cambridge: Cambridge University Press.

Sullivan, Shannon. 2000. "Reconfiguring Gender with John Dewey: Habit, Bodies, and Cultural Change," *Hypatia*, 15 (1): 23–42.

Testa, Italo. 2017a. "Dewey's Social Ontology: A Pragmatist Alternative to Searle's Approach to Social Reality," *International Journal of Philosophical Studies*, 25 (1): 40–62.

Testa, Italo. 2017b. "Recognition as Passive Power. Attractors of Recognition, Social Power, and Bio-Power," *Constellations*, 24 (2): 192–205.

Testa, Italo. 2017c. "Dewey, Second Nature, Social Criticism, and the Hegelian Heritage," *European Journal of Pragmatism and American Philosophy*, 9 (1): 1–23.

Testa, Italo. 2017d. "The Authority of Life. The Critical Task of Dewey's Social Ontology," *Journal of Speculative Philosophy*, 31 (2): 231–44.

Testa, Italo. 2017e. "Dominant Patterns in Associated Living: Hegemony, Domination, and Ideological Recognition in Dewey's Lectures in China," *Transactions of the Charles S. Peirce Society*, 53 (1): 29–52.

Testa, Italo. 2017f. "The Imaginative Rehearsal Model. Dewey, Embodied Simulation, and the Narrative Hypothesis," *Pragmatism Today*, 8 (1): 105–12.

Trevarthen, Colwyn. 1979. "Communication and Cooperation in Early Infancy: A Description of Primary Intersubjectivity," in *Before Speech,* M. Bullowa (ed.), 227–70. Cambridge: Cambridge University Press.

Turner, Stephen P. 1994. *The Social Theory of Practices: Tradition, Tacit Knowledge and Presuppositions*. Cambridge: Polity Press.

Zlatev, Jordan. "The Co-evolution of Intersubjectivity and Bodily Mimesis," in *The Shared Mind: Perspectives on Intersubjectivity. Converging Evidence in Language and Communication Research,* J. Zlatev et al. (eds.), 12: 15–44. Amsterdam/Philadelphia: John Benjamins Publishing Company.

Chapter 8

Sex, Gender, and Ambiguity

Beauvoir on the Dilaceration of Lived Experience

Mariana Teixeira

INTRODUCTION: BEAUVOIR AND
THE SEX/GENDER DIVIDE

The emancipatory implications of the distinction between gender as socially constructed and sex as biologically given are well known: if women are not inclined by nature to certain social roles (wife, mother, caretaker), spaces (the private sphere of the home), and activities (domestic chores such as cleaning and cooking), that is, if these constraints are historically imposed, they can be historically transformed as well. Simone de Beauvoir's conception of femininity as socially constructed in *The Second Sex* is a milestone in this regard. The book's famous quote—*"On ne naît pas femme: on le devient"*[1]— foreruns the sex/gender divide that would become a widely held assumption of feminist theory and activism in the following decades.[2] In this vein, many feminist authors place the material limitations to women's freedom in their bodily specificities, the capacity of bearing children being one of the central factors; for them, women's submission could only be overcome when these biological determinants are eliminated or, at least, mitigated.[3]

As liberating as its effects might have been, this idea was later challenged for its purported detraction of nature as *immanence* in favor of culture as *transcendence*. From the 1980s to 1990s, for example, other feminist strands have pointed out the detrimental consequences of a masculinist emancipation ideal based on the *domination of* rather than *accord with* the body and the surrounding natural world; today, this perspective gains traction once again with critical studies on the Anthropocene, climate change, and animal rights from a perspective of gender. Beauvoir herself has been accused of urging women to "be more like men"; in other words, to abandon the realm of immanence and transcend the merely given via the domination of internal and external nature.

In both cases, however, a rather unmediated sex/gender divide tends to be preserved in its seemingly unsurmountable dichotomy. With a unilateral embracing of one of the poles—either nature or culture, immanence or transcendence—the split is not mediated but negated only on an abstract level. I suggest, in this chapter, that a more compelling treatment of the relation between sex and gender (nature and culture, body and mind, etc.) can be drawn from Beauvoir's own writings. In addition to the paradigmatic formulation of the issue in her 1949 masterpiece, the philosophical essay on *The Ethics of Ambiguity* is also very instructive in this regard. While in *The Second Sex* there is a much stronger emphasis on transcendence, as Beauvoir stresses the many ways women are historically confined to the realm of immanence, in her short book, published two years earlier, she argues more explicitly that the ambiguity or tension between these poles should not simply be done away with, but rather creatively assumed and further explored. To understand the different ways subjects might experience this tension, I propose moreover a distinction between existential *ambiguity* and contingent *dilaceration*: from a Beauvoirian perspective, emancipation would be conceived of not as the elimination of ambiguity between immanence and transcendence. Rather, it would involve the overcoming of an unmediated dilaceration through the reciprocal movement of embodied subjectivities toward one another.

To make this argument, in the first part of the text I present the main features of woman's paradoxical situation as formulated by Beauvoir in *The Second Sex*:[4] at the same time that woman is an existent seeking to transcend the merely given, she is a slave to the biological needs of the reproduction of the human species, which confines her to the realm of pure immanence. The second part explores two opposing ways this idea was received and developed within feminism: it was radicalized by cyber- and specially xenofeminists on the one hand, and vehemently opposed by ecofeminists on the other. While the former see emancipation as transcendence, as the mastery of nature, the latter equate it rather with immanence, a harmonious connection with nature. Based on Beauvoir's works I argue, then, that replacing the opposition between immanence and transcendence with a distinction between ambiguity and dilaceration can provide us with a more complex understanding of the existent's situation as both subject and object, self and other, or nature and spirit. Finally, in the third part, I draw a contrast between Beauvoir's and Alexandre Kojève's readings of Hegel's so-called "master-slave dialectic" in order to show that both her intersubjective conception of selfhood and her refusal of an ontological duality between nature and *Geist* set the basis for a non-masculinist ideal of freedom transcending mere immanence.

BECOMING WOMAN: TRAPPED WITHIN
THE BOUNDS OF IMMANENCE

Simone de Beauvoir describes the situation of woman in *The Second Sex* from different points of view: from the perspective of man,[5] of woman's own lived experience,[6] and of Beauvoir herself.[7] It is important therefore to pay close attention to who is speaking, as it were, when one reads the book or an excerpt of it—otherwise, as has often happened to Beauvoir, one runs the risk of ascribing to the philosopher a viewpoint she is actually merely staging, and oftentimes with a critical intention.

There is a common trace, however, to the book's many voices talking about woman: they all diagnose—with different causes and implications, as well as different normative judgments—woman's subordination to man. In this first part of the chapter, I will present the main features of this *situation*; show how, for Beauvoir, this does not imply a *necessity*; and finally explore her own account of how and why woman *has become* subordinate. This analysis should make explicit the existential premise of Beauvoir's work as the human tendency toward transcendence of the merely given.

Situation

The Second Sex features numerous and lively depictions of woman's subordination to man throughout history, as well as at the time of its writing, in postwar France. This subordination takes up several different forms and expressions but is consistently characterized by Beauvoir as the confinement of woman to passivity. Woman is not a subject in a proper sense: she does not act, she is acted upon. While man creates, transforms the given, pursues his projects, and thus changes the course of history, woman is overwhelmingly kept in a state of dependence, her activities are not creative, but rather mainly reproductive, toward the repetitive maintenance of sameness. Man seeks always to surpass his given situation; woman can, at best, find ways to better adapt herself to it. Man seeks transcendence while woman remains trapped within the bounds of immanence. Man is subject, while woman is object—*the Other*.

For Beauvoir, woman's bondage to immanence manifests itself primarily in how broadly and heavily the reproduction of the human species impacts her body. The physiological processes involved in gestation and childbirth do not bring any direct advantages to woman individually. Pregnancy is pictured by Beauvoir not only as long and often troubled (2011, 66), tiring work that requires serious sacrifices (2011, 64), but also as a form of acute *alienation*: "a hostile element is locked inside them: the species is eating away at them" (2011, 65). Giving birth is a painful and dangerous endeavor, a moment where the "conflict between the species and the individual can have dramatic consequences" (Beauvoir 2011, 64). Even breastfeeding is characterized as an exhausting servitude (Beauvoir 2011, 64) that limits woman's projects and possibilities.

Woman is enslaved to the species, and this reaches beyond pregnancy and the puerperium. The physiological processes connected to the *possibility* of conception also subject woman's body to a number of limiting, threatening events: puberty is experienced as a crisis, for the "body does not accept the species' installation in her without a fight; and this fight weakens and endangers her" (Beauvoir 2011, 61);[8] menopause, with physiological changes opposed to those of puberty, is one last crisis woman has to go through, when the decrease in ovarian activity causes in her "a vital impoverishment" (Beauvoir 2011, 65). Woman undergoes these events in a most passive fashion, with no control or influence over most of them: "From puberty to menopause she is the principal site of a story that takes place in her and does not concern her personally" (Beauvoir 2011, 62).

Of man, on the other hand, the species does not require such alienating processes: "the male's sex life is normally integrated into his individual existence" and "his surpassing toward the species is an integral part of the subjective moment of his transcendence: he is his body" (Beauvoir 2011, 61). Man, hence, "is infinitely more privileged: his genital life does not thwart his personal existence; it unfolds seamlessly, without crises and generally without accident" (Beauvoir 2011, 66). Of course, like man, also woman is her body: but her body is something other than her (Beauvoir 2011, 63); the species requires of woman that she abdicates her individuality (Beauvoir 2011, 58).

Moreover, and in connection with her reproductive characteristics, woman "has less muscular strength, fewer red blood cells, a lesser respiratory capacity; she runs less quickly, lifts less heavy weights;" she "cannot enter into a fight with the male" and "has less firmness and perseverance in projects that she is also less able to carry out" (Beauvoir 2011, 68). Because she has a far more limited grasp on the world, woman's individual life is poorer than a man's in all spheres of experience (Beauvoir 2011, 68–69). It is crucial for woman's continued subordination that this is ratified and reinforced by customs and traditions, even when the material conditions change so as to allow for women to acquire a greater grasp on the world (e.g., with the advent of tools and machines that tend to compensate for lesser strength or resistance).

The events of woman's life, depicted so far from an external gaze, are portrayed from the perspective of woman's lived experience in volume 2 of *The Second Sex*, where Beauvoir describes in rich detail the processes in childhood and youth by which woman becomes accustomed to her "feminine destiny." She opens the chapter on childhood with the notorious sentence:

One is not born, but rather becomes, woman. No biological, psychic, or economic destiny defines the figure that the human female takes on in society; it is civilization as a whole that elaborates this intermediary product between the male and the eunuch that is called feminine. (Beauvoir 2011, 330)

Beauvoir argues that infants of both sexes equally experience the "drama of birth and weaning;" they "have the same interests and pleasures" and react similarly in the face of frustration or jealousy (2011, 330). There is no *anatomical* limitation to the experiences of the female infant; neither girls nor boys grasp themselves as sexually differentiated. In their upbringing, however, the girl and the boy discover the hierarchy of the sexes: "The more the child matures, the more his universe expands and masculine superiority asserts itself" (Beauvoir 2011, 348). The revelation that man, not woman, is the master of the world "imperiously modifies her consciousness of herself" (Beauvoir 2011, 349).[9] She increasingly learns the range of roles, plans, and desires allotted for her in a world that is shaped by, and belongs to, man.

In adulthood, the married woman lives "enclosed in her flesh, in her home," grasping "herself as passive opposite to these human-faced gods who set goals and standards" (Beauvoir 2011, 725). Beauvoir claims marriage is a perverted institution: not only does it fail to satisfy both spouses, but it also seldom does not *destroy* woman (2011, 586). Comparing the tasks of the housewife with the torment of Sisyphus, Beauvoir claims that "she does nothing; she only perpetuates the present" (2011, 539). Housework hence amounts to activities outside of time, as it were: "Washing, ironing, sweeping, routing out tufts of dust in the dark places behind the wardrobe, this is holding away death but also refusing life: for in one movement time is created and destroyed" (Beauvoir 2011, 541). Everything that lives appears to her as "a promise of decomposition demanding more endless work," so she starts to lose her *joie de vivre* and become hostile to life itself (Beauvoir 2011, 542). In her "boredom, waiting, and disappointment" (Beauvoir 2011, 583), she is mutilated, doomed to repetition and routine (Beauvoir 2011, 587), in a word: to immanence.

To be sure, woman finds social justification by administrating her home: "her job is also to oversee the food, clothing, and care of the familial society in general. Thus she too realizes herself as an activity" (Beauvoir 2011, 536–37). This activity, however, "brings her no escape from her immanence and allows her no individual affirmation of herself" (Beauvoir 2011, 537). Man, on the other hand, is a producer; he "goes beyond family interest to the interest of society" and "opens a future to her by cooperating in the construction of the collective future" (Beauvoir 2011, 506). Thus man "will act as intermediary between woman's individuality and the universe; it is he who will imbue her contingent facticity with human worth" (Beauvoir 2011, 533–34).

In motherhood, woman can again only indirectly connect her existence to the broader world:

> She can do no more than create a situation that solely the child's freedom can transcend; when she invests in his future, it is again by proxy that she transcends herself through the universe and time; that is, once again she dooms herself to dependency. (Beauvoir 2011, 645)

The older woman's days, finally, are filled with "solitude, regret, and ennui" (Beauvoir 2011, 718). She is now relieved of her duties, sure, but "she discovers this freedom when she can find nothing more to do with it" (Beauvoir 2011, 711). The wisdom achieved by woman as she grows old—contestation, accusation, refusal—is merely negative, thus sterile: the highest form of freedom she can have is "stoic defiance or skeptical irony" (Beauvoir 2011, 722). Her activities are but *pastime*:

> with needle or hook, woman sadly weaves the very nothingness of her days. Water-colors, music, or reading have the very same role; the unoccupied woman does not try to extend her grasp on the world in giving herself over to such activities, but only to relieve boredom; an activity that does not open up the future slides into the vanity of immanence. (Beauvoir 2011, 718–19)

Destiny?

As poignant as Beauvoir's depictions are of woman's passivity, the great novelty of her work lies rather in her firm assertion that women are not destined to this situation: it is a product of historical development. In contrast to most forms of domination grounded on ethnicity, however, gender-based subjugation cannot be traced back to identifiable historical events, such as wars or colonization enterprises: "as far back as history can be traced, they have always been subordinate to men; their dependence is not the consequence of an event or a becoming, it did not *happen*" (Beauvoir 2011, 28). Because "it falls outside the accidental nature of historical fact" (Beauvoir 2011, 28), woman's alterity appears as absolute. Beauvoir then analyzes different scientific discourses—biology, psychoanalysis, and historical materialism—that could explain this absolute alterity and its presumed necessity.

The givens of biology, for one, indicate no physiological fact that proves the necessity of the difference between the sexes: reproduction could be asexual or occur between individuals not differentiated by sex. Neither do they point to a necessary hierarchy that posits one sex above the other on a value scale—ethical, aesthetic, or otherwise. It is not a matter of neglecting the facticity of the human body, but of denying it has any meaning in and by itself: "nature only has reality for him insofar as it is taken on by his action: his own nature is no exception" (Beauvoir 2011, 69). As significant as woman's enslavement to the species is, "her body is not enough to define her; it has a lived reality only as taken on by consciousness through actions and within a society" (Beauvoir 2011, 71). Biological givens are therefore but one key to understanding woman's situation as the Other; they must be examined "in the light of ontological, economic, social, and psychological contexts" (Beauvoir 2011, 71).

The advancements brought about by the advent of psychoanalysis do not pass Beauvoir by. Psychoanalysis adds complexity to the understanding of woman in that it considers the body of human individuals not only as an object to be described by scientists but also as a concrete existence lived by subjects in a realm of affectivity and values (Beauvoir 2011, 73). It detects an important constant in human life: individuals both desire and fear freedom. The anguish of freedom manifests itself as an inclination toward alienation: subjects tend to project themselves into things in order to attempt an inauthentic flight. Psychoanalysts consider this tendency toward alienation as feminine and the transcendent behavior as masculine (Beauvoir 2011, 85). But the psychoanalytical viewpoint is limited to the extent that it takes up a constant as a destiny and description as Law. In its determinism, it neglects the openness of history and the freedom that inhabits human life. In addition to that, psychoanalysis takes the masculine development as a model from which woman's is derived. Combined with the mentioned determinism, this perspective does not leave much room for activity on the part of women.

Just as the givens of biology, sexuality does not carry values or meaning in itself. It does not determine how affectivity is lived by the subject in concrete relations. Like the physiology of the human body described by biologists, sexual life as depicted by psychoanalysts is but one aspect of human's quest for being (Beauvoir 2011, 80). Only in *history*, says Beauvoir, can psychoanalysis find its truth (2011, 82).

Historical materialism contributes to the analysis of human life—and thus woman's situation—precisely in this direction. It considers humanity not an animal species, but a historical reality, and, in this sense, an anti-*physis*: "it does not passively submit to the presence of nature, but rather appropriates it" (Beauvoir 2011, 87). This appropriation is carried out with the development of instruments to control the material world; and the economic structure of society indicates "the degree of technical evolution humanity has attained" (Beauvoir 2011, 87). Beauvoir points out how, for Engels, the development of tools led not only to the advent of private property and slavery but to the oppression of woman as well. Accordingly, woman's destiny would be interconnected with the destiny of the proletarian: "both must be set free by the same economic development resulting from the upheaval caused by the invention of machines" (Beauvoir 2011, 89).

Nonetheless, historical materialism too is limited to the extent that it "takes for granted facts it should explain: it posits the *interest* that attaches man to property without discussing it; but where does this interest, the source of social institutions, have its own source?" (Beauvoir 2011, 89). The invention of tools and instruments does not explain why humans desire to dominate nature:

> The discovery of bronze enabled man, tested by hard and productive work, to find himself as creator, dominating nature; no longer afraid of nature, having overcome resistance, he dares to grasp himself as autonomous activity and to accomplish himself in his singularity. But this accomplishment would never have been realized if man had not originally wanted it; the lesson of labor is not inscribed in a passive subject: the subject forged and conquered himself in forging his tools and conquering the earth. (Beauvoir 2011, 90)

Restricted to the abstraction of the *Homo oeconomicus*, historical materialism "cannot provide solutions to the problems we indicated" (Beauvoir 2011, 89). The question posed by Beauvoir in the introduction of the book thus remains open: if it is not written in the stars—inscribed in the facticity of the body, the sensuality of the psyche or the materiality of the tool—"[w]here does this submission in woman come from?" (2011, 27).

History

Beauvoir does not reject the contribution of the three examined disciplines but rather considers "that the body, sexual life, and technology exist concretely for man only insofar as he grasps them from the overall perspective of his existence," adding that "[t]he value of muscular strength, the phallus, and the tool can only be defined in a world of values: it is driven by the fundamental project of the existent transcending itself toward being" (2011, 94). In her own account of the history of humanity from nomad hordes to industrialized, capitalist societies, Beauvoir locates the origins of woman's submission to man within the particular combination of physio-, psycho-, and technological givens with what she calls the *existential infrastructure of human life* (2011, 93), meaning that human beings are not merely given but make themselves what they are (2011, 68). The "key to the whole mystery" is that "[b]y transcending Life through Existence, man guarantees the repetition of Life: by this surpassing, he creates values that deny any value to pure repetition" (Beauvoir 2011, 99). Humanity is transcendence, it "does not seek to survive as a species; its project is not stagnation: it seeks to surpass itself" (Beauvoir 2011, 97–98); it values *reasons for living* over *life itself* (2011, 100).

Correspondingly,

[e]very time transcendence lapses into immanence, there is degradation of existence into 'in-itself,' of freedom into facticity; this fall is a moral fault if the subject consents to it; if this fall is inflicted on the subject, it takes the form of frustration and oppression; in both cases it is an absolute evil. (Beauvoir 2011, 37)

That is precisely what happens to woman. Her misfortune "is to have been biologically destined to repeat Life, while in her own eyes Life in itself does not provide her reasons for being, and these reasons are more important than life itself" (Beauvoir 2011, 99). In serving the species, on the other hand, the human male "shapes the face of the earth, creates new instruments, invents and forges the future" (Beauvoir 2011, 99). This is why man has set himself as master over woman: "Male activity, creating values, has constituted existence itself as a value; it has prevailed over the indistinct forces of life; and it has subjugated Nature and Woman" (Beauvoir 2011, 100). The constellation that characterizes woman's situation is thus a paradoxical one: "being, like all humans, an autonomous freedom, she discovers and chooses herself in a world where men force her to assume herself as Other: an attempt is made to freeze her as an object and doom her to immanence" (Beauvoir 2011, 37).

Woman's situation is thus neither an original condition nor an eternal one; there is no destiny set for her by a first *or* a second—in any case an immutable—nature. Once aware of her confinement to the inessential, it is up to woman to trigger a change in her current state of subordination (Beauvoir 2011, 28).[10] *The Second Sex* is thus a praise of and a call for the independent woman—she who transcends the limits of immanence set for her. Would that mean, as it has been argued, that Beauvoir is calling for women to be more "like men," in the sense of overcoming passivity through active control of nature? In many parts of Beauvoir's book, that seems to be precisely the case. "Today," she affirms, for example, "what women claim is to be recognized as existents just like men, and not to subordinate existence to life or the man to his animality" (Beauvoir 2011, 100).

IMMANENCE *VERSUS* TRANSCENDENCE OR DILACERATION *VERSUS* AMBIGUITY?

Emancipation as Transcendence

Safeguarding women the level of freedom, autonomy, and independence—in a word: of transcendence—men already enjoy is indeed a major tenet for feminist activists and theorists. First- and second-wave feminists, for example, fought for equal rights for men and women in the public and private spheres: in politics, the workplace, and family life.[11] It is beyond doubt that *The Second Sex* played a significant role in this process with its demystification of woman's subordination to man and its call for women to surpass mere immanence.

In the wake of many formal achievements favoring women's social, political, and economic independence, many feminists have questioned the efficacy of a *de jure* equality in the face of several *de facto* inequalities that persist between men and women. Reproductive (and generally unpaid) work is still disproportionally carried out by women, for example, so that their integration in the labor market has often meant that they have had to face double, or triple, shifts. The very capacity of conceiving a child has historically meant that women tend to be seen as a liability and have thus been forced to accept less stable working conditions and lower wages when compared to men.

While many of the inequalities stemming from the unjust division of reproductive work can be mitigated by changes in public policy and cultural conceptions (e.g., maternity and paternity leave policies, sufficient offer of nurseries and kindergartens, and valorization of care work), it remains a physiological facticity that women are the ones biologically responsible for engendering the continuity of the species within their own bodies—with all the consequences this brings for them individually. With that in view, a less domesticated version of the idea of women's independence emerged in the 1960s and 1970s that sees masculine domination based on women's reproductive role as the root of all other forms of oppression, including racial and class domination. Echoing Beauvoir, radical feminists argue that women's autonomy in the social, economic, and political realms can only be achieved if they are also freed from their corporeal limitations, thus released from the fetters imposed on them by the reproduction of the species.

An early landmark in this movement is *The Dialectic of Sex*, a book deeply influenced by (and indeed dedicated to) Simone de Beauvoir, published in 1970 by Shulamith Firestone, a founder of the Women's Liberation Movement. With its outline of a cybernetic socialism, the book became a manifesto for radical feminists and is also considered a precursor of contemporary xeno- and cyberfeminism (Paasonen 2010). Firestone calls not only for a *postgendered* but also for a *postsexual technological embodiment* that would free women "from the tyranny of their sexual-reproductive roles" (1970, 31). The biological family is depicted as a "vinculum through which the psychology of power can always be smuggled" (Firestone 1970, 12), a social unit organized around reproduction which subjects women to their biological destiny (Firestone 1970, 206–207); hence the "tapeworm of exploitation" can only be annihilated by a radical sexual revolution that uproots the biological family (Firestone 1970, 12). Just as workers need to seize control of the *means of production*, in Firestone's sex-based materialism women need to seize control of the *means of reproduction*, "not only the full restoration to women of ownership of their own bodies, but also their (temporary) seizure of control of human fertility" (Firestone 1970, 11).[12]

For Firestone, and radical feminists in general, the fundamental inequality between the sexes is institutionalized by society but is originally produced by nature (Firestone 1970, 205). She develops an analysis "in which biology itself—procreation—is at the origin of the dualism" (Firestone 1970, 8); the different reproductive functions of men and women *necessitate* the development of a class system, the domination of one group by another: "[u]nlike economic class, sex class sprang directly from a biological reality" (Firestone 1970, 8). This does not mean, however, that women's fate is forever decided: "to grant that the sexual imbalance of power is biologically based is not to lose our case," because "[w]e are no longer just animals" and "the Kingdom of Nature does not reign absolute" (Firestone 1970, 9). Recent scientific developments that range from birth control to assisted reproductive technologies, including not only in vitro fertilization but also research on ectogenesis, artificial uteri, and extra-uterine gestation, now seem to announce a not too far away future where any significant distinction between the male and female bodies is abolished along with its oppressive effects on women. Only this ultimate sexual revolution—which, for Firestone, is broader than and indeed encompasses socialist revolution—would allow for humanity to finally become "the real conscious Lord of Nature" (Engels *apud* Firestone 1970, 13). Firestone hence not only radicalizes Beauvoir's insights but ultimately transforms them in a significant way: whereas Beauvoir sought to *denaturalize social domination*, Firestone seeks to *socially de-reify nature*.

With accelerationist and trans-humanist affinities, xenofeminism embodies this tendency today even more strongly. It seeks, according to the manifesto published by the Laboria Cuboniks collective, "to strategically deploy existing technologies to re-engineer the world" (2018, 17). From this perspective, control over the world in order to attain reproductive justice is both *possible* and *desirable* (Hester 2018, 22): the manifesto maintains that nothing "should be accepted as fixed, permanent, or 'given'—neither material conditions nor social forms" (Cuboniks 2018, 15); nothing "is so sacred that it cannot be re-engineered and transformed so as to widen our aperture of freedom;" there is nothing "that cannot be studied scientifically and manipulated technologically" (Cuboniks 2018, 65).[13]

This notion of nature gives rise to the peculiar combination of a *normative anti-naturalism* (where "nature" is a sacred, immutable given) and an *ontological naturalism* (where "nature" is exorcized into the rationally knowable): "To say that nothing is sacred, that nothing is transcendent or protected from the will to know, to tinker and to hack, is to say that nothing is supernatural. 'Nature'—understood here as the unbounded arena of science—is all there is" (Cuboniks 2018, 65). The manifesto thus ends with the movement's motto: "If nature is unjust, change nature!" (Cuboniks 2018, 93).

This vehement normative anti-naturalism does not imply a lack of concern toward the issues raised by environmentalists regarding the predatory exploitation of nature. Already in her foundational text, Firestone is attentive to this matter; she dedicates a whole chapter of *The Dialectic of Sex* to ecology. The particularity of this ecology is that it is not conservationist, it does not seek to *redress* natural balances, but rather to *create* new ones: "[w]hat is called for is a revolutionary ecological program that would attempt to establish a humane artificial (man-made) balance in place of the natural one, thus also realizing the original goal of empirical science: human mastery of matter" (Firestone 1970, 192). *Mastery* is a keyword here, and freedom means transcendence.

Emancipation as Immanence

Precisely this element of manipulability, this focus on mastering the given, is challenged by other feminists as being inherently masculinist. The ideal of women's emancipation through transcendence—"be it according to the more palabe version of mainstream feminism or xenofeminism's radical one—has been condemned by authors and activists that usually identify themselves as ecofeminists. They see a link between the domination of women and the domination of nature and consider the very idea of a subject unencumbered by natural constraints as fraught with a destructive masculinist ideology that demonizes both nature and the human body as symbols of passivity and enslavement.

Although Rosemary Ruether had already denounced "the male ideology of transcendent dualism" (1975, 195) by the mid-1970s, this stream gained impulse in the 1980s and especially 1990s. Ecofeminists see either a structural homology or even a causal interconnection between the oppression of women by patriarchy and the exhaustion of the Earth by colonialism and capitalism. For eminent ecofeminist advocates Vandana Shiva and Maria Mies, Western science not only epitomizes this logic but is instrumental in shaping the world accordingly: "science's whole paradigm is characteristically patriarchal, anti-nature and colonial and aims to dispossess women of their generative capacity as it does the productive capacities of nature" (Shiva and Mies 2014, 16). At the basis of these predatory phenomena would lie an engagement with the world based on dualisms—humanity/nature, mind/body, male/female, self/other, spirit/matter, subject/object, reason/emotion, and so on—which are always hierarchical to the extent that, in the words of Val Plumwood, they imply a "denied dependency on a subordinated other" (1993, 41).

Correspondingly, the liberation of women and nature would be one and the same enterprise (Gaard 1993, 1). It would involve acknowledging their intrinsic value and redressing their lost balance, which would require undermining "Earth-destroying male culture by expressing the nurturing and caring values associated with women as the basis of an alternative culture" (Mellor 1992, 51). Contrary to radical and xenofeminism, technological development is seldom seen in this context as an ally toward emancipation: because of its patriarchal and rationalist bias, technology is usually regarded with suspicion by ecofeminists.[14] Recent contributions to a feminist critique of the Anthropocene—for example, Grusin (2017) and MacCormack (2020)—point out that counting on technology to redress both environmental catastrophes and gender oppression actually mean that "scientists and engineers continue to rely on many of the same masculinist and human-centered solutions that have created the problems in the first place" (Grusin 2017, ix). The "heroic agency of geoengineering" would not do much more than reinforce the very tendencies it seeks to offset (Grusin 2017, ix).

Ecofeminists condemn the idea of emancipation as transcendence with regard to nature and immanence not only in the radical version proposed by xenofeminists, but in milder variants as well. They criticize the abstract equality whereby "[w]omen's liberation is prescribed as the masculinisation of the female" (Shiva 1988, 47). Several ecofeminists consider Beauvoir's praise of the independent woman as fitting in this category of abstract equality and heroic masculinism. For Shiva, "[t]he liberation that de Beauvoir conceives of is a world in which the masculine is accepted as superior and women are free to assume masculine values" (1988, 47). Plumwood argues, similarly, that

for Simone de Beauvoir woman is to become fully human in the same way as man, by joining him in distancing from and in transcending and controlling nature. [. . .] Woman becomes "fully human" by being absorbed in a masculine sphere of freedom and transcendence conceptualized in human-chauvinist terms. (1986, 135)

Mies agrees that Beauvoir

> maintains the dualistic and hierarchical split between life and freedom/self-
> determination, between nature and culture, between spirit and matter. She
> maintains alienation from the body, especially from the female body which,
> according to her, hinders self-determination (transcendence). Our body is our
> enemy. [. . .] She wants to be like man, like the master, and sees no other pos-
> sibility but to establish dominance of the head (master) within the female body
> (slave). (Mies 1993, 225–26)

Beauvoir thereby would hope "to reach female self-determination by following exactly the same logic, which must however mean to subject some other
Other" and, as a consequence, says Mies, "[t]hose who define autonomy,
self-determination, transcendence, and freedom in Simone de Beauvoir's
terms, cannot but agree to self-mutilation, or to the mutilation of others"
(1993, 226).

Although diametrically opposed in their assumptions, xeno- and ecofeminism
share the common intention of *dissolving the dualism of immanence and
transcendence*. In each case, however, one pole of the dualism seems to be
no more than *absorbed* by the other: against a rigid dualism, both streams
oppose an all-embracing indistinction. Transcendence absorbs immanence
in a techno-materialism that sees nature as thoroughly susceptible to human
manipulation oriented to freedom. Immanence absorbs transcendence in a
holistic interconnectedness that sees organic equilibrium as the emancipatory
horizon *par excellence*. In both cases, whereas dualism is openly rejected,
in theory it remains untouched—each time, one of the poles is abstractly
negated and turns into a sort of repressed, haunting Other.

At the beginning of this chapter, it was suggested that elements to overcome an unmediated and unproductive split between immanence and transcendence could be found in Beauvoir's own approach. The advantage of
Beauvoir is precisely that *she does not intend to dispel dualism*. Only episodi-
cally stressed in *The Second Sex*, this idea is nonetheless central to *The Ethics
of Ambiguity*, Beauvoir's essay on existentialist ethics published in 1947.

From Dilaceration to Ambiguity

The opposition between immanence and transcendence is formulated in
Beauvoir's 1947 philosophical essay as that between facticity and freedom,
one of the major themes in French existentialism (1976c).[15] Existentialists
were often reproached for supposedly adopting a quietist position toward
ethics: if there is no essential meaning in the world or human life, there is

no basis on which to justify human action in one direction or another. If the world is absurd, it is pointless to discuss what distinguishes right from wrong, good from evil, and one is hence faced with hopeless moral relativism. Beauvoir acknowledges that existentialism, as it appears to many, is "a philosophy of the absurd and of despair. It encloses man in a sterile anguish, in an empty subjectivity. It is incapable of furnishing him with any principle for making choices" (Beauvoir 1976c, 10).[16] But the horrors of World War II added an urgent complexity to the matter. Faced with the absence of universal moral values that would unequivocally orient human action in this world and, at the same time, with the impossibility of remaining neutral before the tragedy of the war—one either resists or collaborates with the Nazi occupation (and faces the ensuing consequences in each case)—Beauvoir sets out to delineate an ethics that would consistently take into account the paradox of the human condition as both freedom and facticity.

This paradox, or ambiguity, is twofold. First, life itself is at once repetition and creation, passivity and activity, perpetuation and surpassing of itself (Beauvoir 1976c, 83). To be sure, human beings share this ambiguity with every other living being. But a second paradox concerns humans as they are aware of the first, inescapable paradox: as rational animals, they can escape their natural condition, but cannot completely set themselves *free* from it. In Beauvoir's words: "[h]e is still a part of this world of which he is a consciousness. He asserts himself as a pure internality against which no external power can take hold, and he also experiences himself as a thing crushed by the dark weight of other things" (1976c, 7). These "other things" that limit our creative power and agency are not only the material world that surrounds us but other human beings as well: "This privilege, which he alone possesses, of being a sovereign and unique subject amidst a universe of objects, is what he shares with all his fellow-men. In turn an object for others, he is nothing more than an individual in the collectivity on which he depends" (Beauvoir 1976c, 7).

To consciously undergo the tragic paradox of being at once subject and object is certainly a disturbing experience, and one that grows in intensity with humanity's increasing control over nature: "[t]he more widespread their mastery of the world, the more they find themselves crushed by uncontrollable forces" (Beauvoir 1976c, 8–9). For this reason, there have been several attempts throughout history to eliminate ambiguity, or at least conceal it. Philosophers have often "striven to reduce mind to matter, or to reabsorb matter into mind, or to merge them within a single substance" (Beauvoir 1976c, 7). The goal of moral action itself would be, then, to flee the paradox "by making oneself pure inwardness or pure externality, by escaping from the sensible world or by being engulfed in it, by yielding to eternity or enclosing oneself in the pure moment" (Beauvoir 1976c, 8).

For Beauvoir, however, attempts to flee ambiguity are doomed to be revealed as illusions: "[i]n spite of so many stubborn lies, at every moment, at every opportunity, the truth comes to light, the truth of life and death, of my solitude and my bond with the world, of my freedom and my servitude" (1976c, 9). Instead of trying to dissipate the paradox, Beauvoir suggests we "try to look the truth in the face," "assume our fundamental ambiguity" (1976c, 9), and "accept the task of realizing it" (1976c, 13).[17]

Assuming or realizing one's ambiguity involves, for Beauvoir, a movement of going beyond and returning to oneself, without thereby dissolving the paradox: "[i]n order for the return to the positive to be genuine it must involve negativity, it must not conceal the antinomies between means and end, present and future; they must be lived in a permanent tension" (1976c, 133). As Beauvoir portrays it, this movement is a positive kind of *alienation*, as in the German *Entäußerung*, that is part and parcel of the human existential condition: "[h]e rejoins himself only to the extent that he agrees to remain at a distance from himself" (1976c, 13).[18]

If the tense ambiguity between facticity (immanence) and freedom (transcendence) is to be maintained and assumed, instead of done away with, how can one understand the emphasis Beauvoir gives to freedom/transcendence in *The Second Sex*? After all, a great deal of the book's more than eight hundred pages is dedicated to condemning immanent, morbid passivity and praising transcendent, lively activity. This shift does not necessarily mean, however, that Beauvoir has changed her mind about ambiguity in the two years that separate one book from the other.

To the extent that women have been historically denied the realm of transcendence, there is an emphasis on this aspect in *The Second Sex*. Both woman and man live in ambiguity, since both are indeed subject/transcendence and object/immanence, but they live it quite differently from one another, and this difference is the focal point of Beauvoir's masterpiece. Man's privilege "from childhood onward is that his vocation as a human being in no way contradicts his destiny as a male" (Beauvoir 2011, 815); he is expected, both as a human being and as a male, to surpass himself in an outward movement; he is not divided by contradictory urges. On the contrary, "for a woman to accomplish her femininity, she is required to be object and prey; that is, she must renounce her claims as a sovereign subject" (Beauvoir 2011, 815). But this renunciation can never be completed, because "one cannot willfully kill one's gaze and change one's eyes into empty pools; a body that reaches out to the world cannot be thwarted and metamorphosed into a statue animated by hidden vibrations" (Beauvoir 2011, 818); Beauvoir maintains that "no existent ever renounces his transcendence, especially when he stubbornly disavows it" (2011, 533). This includes woman, for she is also an existent: "transcendence also inhabits her and her project is not repetition but surpassing herself toward another future" (Beauvoir 2011, 99). So woman is in a rather thankless position: she is subject and activity, but "has to fit into a world that has doomed her to passivity" (Beauvoir 2011, 816). Thus, she lives her confinement to immanence as a dilaceration in her own being.[19] It is *alienation* in a negative sense, as in the German *Entfremdung*.

The situation is particularly dramatic for the woman who *knows herself to be a subject*: the active, working woman. For her, dilaceration appears more directly *as dilaceration*, since she knows that "being an autonomous activity contradicts her femininity" (Beauvoir 2011, 817) and, simultaneously, that "[r]enouncing her femininity means renouncing part of her humanity" (Beauvoir 2011, 816); in both cases, she is mutilated (Beauvoir 2011, 815). As a consequence of the fact that she "wants to live both like a man and like a woman," not only "her workload and her fatigue are multiplied" (Beauvoir 2011, 817); even more significant is that, "split between the desire to affirm herself and self-effacement, she is divided and torn" (Beauvoir 2011, 827). The independent woman faces these difficulties more explicitly "because she has chosen not resignation but combat" (Beauvoir 2011, 819), as opposed to the woman who has accepted her female destiny: "[a]ll living problems find a silent solution in death; so a woman who works at living is more torn than one who buries her will and desires" (Beauvoir 2011, 819).

INTERSUBJECTIVE BECOMING

There is indeed an insistence, in *The Second Sex*, on the need for woman to embrace transcendence, become independent, and free herself from the bounds of pure immanence. But this does not imply negating immanence, rising above it, or leaving it behind, as it were; it does not require woman to dissolve the existential ambiguity that resides in every living being that is at once subject *and* object. What is needed, rather, is for her to overcome the paralyzing dilaceration caused by her confinement to one pole of the tension between immanence and transcendence. The question then arises: how, on Beauvoir's account, can the subjugated side of a social relation of domination go from contingent, static dilaceration to existential, dynamic ambiguity? More precisely, in the case in question, how can woman attain freedom from her confinement to immanence? How can she exercise creative, transformative agency, transcending her given situation?

Had Beauvoir merely insisted that women increase control over their bodies and the world around them in order to achieve the same scope of freedom enjoyed by men, she would still fall prey to the ecofeminist criticism about abstract equality based on the masculinist ideal of human emancipation as mastery of nature. Beauvoir's *non-dualistic ontology* and her *intersubjective conception of selfhood*, however, indicate that this is not the case. This becomes clear as one traces the convergences and particularly the divergences between Beauvoir's appropriation of Hegelian philosophy and the influential reading of *The Phenomenology of Spirit* proposed by Alexandre Kojève.

Kojèvian Echoes: Agonistic Anthropogenesis

It should be noted that Beauvoir's conception of selfhood is deeply rooted in the notion of otherness. "The category of *Other* is as original as consciousness itself," she writes, adding that "[n]o group ever defines itself as One without immediately setting up the Other opposite itself" (Beauvoir 2011, 26); people from abroad are foreigners for us, "Jews are the 'others' for anti-Semites, blacks for racist Americans, indigenous people for colonists, proletarians for the propertied classes" (Beauvoir 2011, 26).

As Beauvoir's examples suggest, this intersubjective process is not peaceful and constructive, but has a basic agonistic dimension:

> These phenomena could not be understood if human reality were solely a *Mit-sein* based on solidarity and friendship. On the contrary, they become clear if, following Hegel, a fundamental hostility to any other consciousness is found in consciousness itself; the subject posits itself only in opposition; it asserts itself as the essential and sets up the other as inessential, as the object. (2011, 26–27)

To characterize this "imperialism of human consciousness" (2011, 37), the coexistence in it of "both the original category of the Other and an original claim to domination over the Other" (2011, 91), Beauvoir alludes to the relationship of lordship and bondage depicted by Hegel in *The Phenomenology of Spirit* (1952).[20]

To be sure, Beauvoir refers to Hegel through the lens of the unorthodox interpretation of Alexandre Kojève, a key figure in the Hegel renaissance that took place in post-World War II France. His lectures held on the *Phenomenology* between 1933 and 1939 at the École Pratique des Hautes Études, later published as a book (Kojève 1980), had a deep impact on a whole generation of intellectuals, in France and elsewhere. Echoing both Marx and Heidegger, Kojève idiosyncratically combined the themes of class struggle as the motor force of history and the mortality of the *Dasein*, applying both revolutionary and existential undertones to his reading of Hegel. He also places the relationship of lordship and bondage—or, in Kojève's terms, the "master-slave dialectics"[21]—as the key to understanding not only the *Phenomenology* but Hegel's *oeuvre* as a whole.

The basic features of this Hegelian motif are well known: every self-consciousness seeks to present itself as independent, not bound and shackled to life, as "fettered to no determinate *existence*" (Hegel 1952, §187); it seeks to assert its self-certainty, its being-for-itself through the exclusion from itself of all that is other than itself. When faced with another self-consciousness that has a reciprocal claim, each one seeks to negate the independence of the other; the other one exists as an unessential object. Each self-consciousness thus seeks the death of the other and, for that, is compelled to put its own life at stake (Hegel 1952, §187). As one self-consciousness surrenders to the other fearing imminent death, it becomes the other's slave. The other self-consciousness becomes the master, since it showed no fear of death and thus has not degraded itself to the level of mere physical existence (Hegel 1952, §189). In this new, unequal situation after the death struggle, the slave works for the satisfaction of the master and the master consumes and enjoys the product of the slave, who is compelled to indefinitely postpone his own gratifications (Hegel 1952, §190). The master thus depends on the slave— not only for the satisfaction of his needs but also for his recognition as an independent being (Hegel 1952, §191–192). As a consequence, the certainty of the master as an independent self-consciousness is challenged: "the *truth* of the independent consciousness is the *servile consciousness*" (Hegel 1952, §193). The slave, on the other hand, experiences work as the overcoming of his attachment to natural existence. By means of his transformative laboring on the natural and material world in order to create the products to meet the master's demands, the slave comes to develop his own capacity to create and give form to an independent object, and thus comes to see himself in the products he creates (Hegel 1952, §195). In this cultivation of himself and the natural world motivated by the fear of death, the slave "attains the consciousness that he himself exists in and for himself" (Hegel 1952, §196).

Whereas Hegel then refrains from immediately giving a clear account of how this consciousness of autonomy would play out in practice, Kojève argues that a *new struggle for recognition* is needed for the slave to assert his status as "for-itself," his independent self-consciousness vis-à-vis the master:

[t]o be sure, this work by itself does not free him. But in transforming the World by this work, the Slave transforms himself, too, and thus creates the new objective conditions that permit him to take up once more the liberating Struggle for recognition that he refused in the beginning for fear of death. (1980, 29; translation modified)

For Kojève, the proof of free, autonomous "humanness" is the willingness to risk one's biological life "for an essentially nonvital end" (1980, 7), thereby overcoming animal life. Kojève hence turns the *Phenomenology* into a work of philosophical anthropology where the slave's labor, motivated by fear of death, impels him to engage once more in a struggle with the master for the recognition of his autonomy achieved through the domination of nature; this "final Struggle for Recognition" (Kojève 1980, 231) would contain the only possibility of freedom from social domination and toward reciprocal recognition.[22]

This is a very peculiar reading of the *Phenomenology*, and Kojève admits in a letter that "it was of relatively little importance" to him "to know what Hegel himself meant to say in his book," adding that "I did a course on phenomenological anthropology using Hegelian texts, but only saying what I considered to be the truth, and dropping what seemed to me to be a mistake in Hegel" (Jarczyk and Labarrière 1996, 64; my translation).[23] One such mistake would be the "Hegelian monism" (Jarczyk and Labarrière 1996, 64; my translation) of the *Phenomenology*, which is why Kojève insists, in his seminars, commentaries, and translations of Hegel's book on *an ontological dualism between Nature and Spirit*. For Kojève, man can only become the "unique 'synthetical' or 'total' Man" once he "acts as combatant for the sake of glory alone" (1980, 231), thus showing no attachment for natural, animal life, for his physiological body. Hence, the slave has to free himself by showing to the master that he, too, is above mere immanence.

Following Kojève's Hegel, Beauvoir also considers that one consciousness always posits itself initially as the essential and the other as the inessential. Beauvoir notes that, as the second consciousness manifests an opposing reciprocal claim, throughout history a series of events—wars, agreements, treatises, and struggles—generally remove "the absolute meaning from the idea of the *Other* and bring out its relativity; whether one likes it or not, individuals and groups have no choice but to recognize the reciprocity of their relation" (Beauvoir 2011, 27). Eventual reciprocal recognition would be the expected result of both individual and collective identity formation for Beauvoir.

Up to this point, Beauvoir's considerations are in accord with the Kojèvian philosophical model of anthropogenesis through reciprocal recognition after the violent encounter between two consciousnesses. Although it cannot be denied that she was greatly influenced by Kojève's interpretation of Hegel, it would be hasty, however, to conclude that Beauvoir unreservedly adopts either his ontological dualism or his claim for a final struggle for recognition.

Distances: Non-Dualistic Ontology and Intersubjective Selfhood

In the case addressed in *The Second Sex*, man is the subject, the absolute, essential, and woman is an object, the Other, inessential (Beauvoir 2011, 26); she is an incidental (Saint Thomas) or naturally defective (Aristotle) being (Beauvoir 2011, 25). But Beauvoir contends that the relation between man and woman, differently from that between master and slave, is not mutual—not even in an agonistic, conflictual sense. Man, asserting himself as the essential, denies at the same time any *relativity* to his other, defining woman as *pure* alterity (Beauvoir 2011, 27): "[t]he relation of the two sexes is not that of two electrical poles," for while woman is the negative, the particular, man is at once the positive and the neuter, that is, the universal (2011, 25). Woman is thus an alterity without reciprocity; she is not a mere other, a *relative* other like the Kojèvian slave: she is the *absolute* Other. While the slave is *inferior* to the master, woman is purely *different* from man.

In contrast to the Kojèvian slave, for Beauvoir woman became subordinate to man without a death struggle between them: when man posits himself as for-itself, as a subject that negates woman as its other, he is not met with a reciprocal claim and challenge. Woman has not risked her life and consequently has failed to prove to man as well as to herself that she, too, has goals above mere biological survival. The Kojèvian slave surrenders his freedom to protect his life in the face of death, but at least he risks his life, and this fear, leading him to his labor, prompts him to achieve a form of self-consciousness and to see himself as for-itself too. Beauvoir's woman, by contrast, does not engage in the struggle nor risks her life in the process. Moreover, woman in her servitude does not serve man by means of the production of objects in creative intercourse with the natural, material world; thus, woman does not cultivate herself through productive work. She is, rather, identified with nature itself; she does not become analogous to the workman (Beauvoir 2011, 111), who can begin to attain the status of subject in his creative labor. The relationship between man and woman is therefore static; woman is fixed as the absolute Other in her relation to man. Hence, since for Beauvoir man and woman do not pose claims of recognition to each other in a reciprocal manner, she does not merely apply Kojève's master-slave dialectics to the relationship between man and woman. Rather, she uses it as a contrast foil to make the specificity of this relationship visible.

Similarly, the possible way out of this relation of subordination is different for Kojève and Beauvoir. For Kojève, since the slave already works on material objects, all he needs is to assert his being-for-itself by "annulling" the master:

And this annulling is what is manifested in and by the final Struggle for Recognition, which necessarily implies the Risk of life on the part of the freed Slave. This Risk, moreover, is what completes the liberation which was begun by his Work, by introducing in him the constituent-element (*Moment*) of Mastery which he lacked. (1980, 231; translation modified)

For Beauvoir, however, emancipation cannot come from this heroic final struggle for recognition, and this for two interconnected reasons. First, because she does not rely, like Kojève, on a dualistic ontology: for her, transcendence can only be attained *through*, instead of *against*, immanence. And second, because her conception of freedom is eminently intersubjective, and not merely agonistic: it requires that transcendence via immanence be directed toward the freedom of others.

The non-dualistic character of the ontology that underpins Beauvoir's writings is manifest, for example, in her treatment of the human body as a *situation* rather than a *thing*, as "our grasp on the world and the outline for our projects" (2011, 68). Biological life is not seen as merely passive matter to be surpassed:

> What is called vitality, sensitivity, and intelligence are not ready-made qualities, but a way of casting oneself into the world and of disclosing being. Doubtless, every one casts himself into it on the basis of his physiological possibilities, but the body itself is not a brute fact. It expresses our relationship to the world. (Beauvoir 1976c, 41)

If "the body is the instrument of our hold on the world" (Beauvoir 2011, 66), surpassing oneself through one's projection into the future cannot be done at the expense of one's corporeal existence. Transcendence, in short, cannot be achieved to the detriment of immanence:

> [i]n truth, all human existence is transcendence and immanence at the same time; to go beyond itself, it must maintain itself; to thrust itself toward the future, it must integrate the past into itself; and while relating to others, it must confirm itself in itself. These two moments are implied in every living movement. (Beauvoir 2011, 506)

For Beauvoir, there is not a realm of "raw" immanence which needs to be denied for transcendence to emerge. Humanity is a historical becoming defined not by how it *negates*, but rather "by the way it *assumes* natural facticity" (Beauvoir, 848; my emphasis).

Therefore, if human life—with the promise of decay and death that necessarily accompanies it—is not the enemy, woman's emancipation would look like something quite different than her proving to man that she, too, is above and beyond mere immanence. Indeed, discussing the independent woman, Beauvoir stresses that "[t]o do great things, today's woman needs above all forgetfulness of self" (2011, 834); she has to learn "from the practice of abandonment" before grasping it anew (2011, 843). Emphasizing transcendence is thus but a *moment*—though a crucial one—in woman's liberation process. A further moment would involve abandoning herself "to the contemplation of the world" and, then, creating it anew (Beauvoir 2011, 838).[24]

Hence, a final struggle for recognition, as proposed by Kojève, would not satisfy the requirements to end woman's subordination: in resolutely affirming her transcendence over her facticity, woman could achieve a position similar to man's; and yet, as sheer transcendence, man is not free either. Woman does not have to become "a subject like man": both man and woman have to live as subjects *and* objects, experiencing their ambiguity in a permanent tension, but without dilaceration. "[T]omorrow's humankind," writes Beauvoir, "will live the future in its flesh and in its freedom" (2011, 861).

For Beauvoir, moreover—and this is crucial—a dynamic and productive ambiguity cannot be a solipsistic experience; it can only be lived among, and toward, other existents themselves characterized by such ambiguity.[25] From this perspective, an existent can only affirm itself through its other—what we called *Entäußerung*, or positive alienation. Freedom, writes Beauvoir in the conclusion of *The Ethics of Ambiguity*, "can be achieved only through the freedom of others" (1976c, 156). But the existent's other is not nature, matter, or his body: it is another existent, itself made up of both immanence and transcendence. In short, for Beauvoir, a *subject* does not find its other in an *object*: a *subject-object* finds its other—allowing it to go beyond and then rejoining itself—in *another subject-object*:

> [R]ecognizing each other as subject, each will remain an *other* for the other; reciprocity in their relations will not do away with the miracles that the division of human beings into two separate categories engenders: desire, possession, love, dreams, adventure. (Beauvoir 2011, 862)

Hence, differently from how both xeno- and ecofeminism (either critically or approvingly) characterize her, Beauvoir does not equate the emancipation of women with the mere increase of their control over their bodies and the natural world surrounding them. As women become free to pursue their autonomously chosen projects, the realm of the given is not to be suppressed, but rather assumed and creatively integrated in its givenness, since immanence is not only a limit to transcendence but also its very condition of possibility. Beauvoir's perspective thus allows for a more mediated conception of the ambiguity of the human condition as subject and object at once. Instead of a prison, in this context, the body is (or can be) "the radiation of a subjectivity" (Beauvoir 2011, 330)—as long as it experiences its ambiguity among and toward other ambiguities, without dilaceration.[26]

NOTES

1. Beauvoir (1976b, 13) in the English translation: "One is not born, but rather becomes, a woman" (Beauvoir 2011, 330). The quote has become so notorious that an edited book on its biography, so to say, was recently published: *On ne naît pas femme: on le devient. The Life of a Sentence* (Mann & Ferrari 2017).

2. Although the "sex/gender system" was first coined by Gayle Rubin (1975), Beauvoir is seen as having given this approach its kick-start (e.g., Butler 1987, 128, and Haraway 1991, 131).

3. The focus here is on cis-women, as many traits of their subordination do not apply, or do so differently, to trans-women. It is noteworthy, however, that Beauvoir's work has also provided important tools for the analysis of the situation of transgendered individuals, not least the idea that one is not born but rather becomes a woman—and, conversely, a man. See, for example, Antonopoulos 2017. Judith Butler's engagement with Beauvoir also points in this direction, as noted by Ann Murphy (2012, 214); see Butler 1986; 1987; 2004, 65.

4. I will retain the singular form "woman" when referring to Beauvoir's account of the making of womanhood, and the plural form "women" to concrete female individuals; the same applies to man/men.

5. For the perspective of the man of science, see "Destiny" (volume 1, part 1); for that of the layman, see "Myths" (volume 1, part 3).

6. See "Formative years," "Situation," and "Justifications" (volume 2, parts 1, 2, and 3).

7. Besides the book's "Introduction" and "Conclusion," see "History" (volume 1, part 2); Beauvoir also frequently intervenes in the other parts of the book. Part 4 of volume 2, "Toward Liberation," is the moment woman's lived experience and Beauvoir's voice converge.

8. Beauvoir thus depicts menstruation: "This is when she feels most acutely that her body is an alienated opaque thing; it is the prey of a stubborn and foreign life that makes and unmakes a crib in her every month; every month a child is prepared to be born and is aborted in the flow of the crimson tide" (2011, 62–63).

9. This revelation is far more consequential for woman than the discovery of the penis (Beauvoir 2011, 349). Beauvoir's criticism of Freud's castration complex was an influential source for later feminist critiques of psychoanalysis.

10. This calls for a discussion of women's complicity with their own detrimental situation, an issue that concerned Beauvoir greatly.

11. To be sure, advocating for women's independence has become the face of a palatable feminism not only accepted but also promoted by mainstream media and politics; official discourses in most countries preconize equal opportunities for both sexes in almost every area of activity—to the point it has become cliché. Recent developments in many parts of the world remind us, however, that no social achievement is set in stone: conservative forces have been trying with relative success to challenge the very idea that men and women are, or should be, equal partners in interaction.

12. This seizure would be temporary because "just as the end goal of socialist revolution was not only the elimination of the economic class privilege but of the

economic class distinction itself, so the end goal of feminist revolution must be, unlike that of the first feminist movement, not just the elimination of male *privilege* but of the sex *distinction* itself: genital differences between human beings would no longer matter culturally" (Firestone 1970, 11).

13. Firestone and the proponents of xenofeminism acknowledge that technology alone will not free women: "[o]n the contrary," says Firestone, "the new technology, especially fertility control, may be used against them to reinforce the entrenched system of exploitation" (Firestone 1970, 10). It is a matter of political intervention to put technology to the service of women's emancipation: "technologies are not inherently beneficial" (Hester 2018, 9); they "need to be conceptualized as social phenomena, and therefore as available for transformation through collective struggle" (Hester 2018, 11).

14. Reproductive technologies greeted by xenofeminists, for example, are generally seen by ecofeminists as detrimental to women's control over—or, more precisely, their *connection with*—their own bodies.

15. The original French title reads *Pour une morale de l'ambiguïté* (Beauvoir 2017).

16. Although in this text Beauvoir still retains masculine terms ("man," "he") to refer to humanity in general, I will employ gender-neutral ones ("human being," "humanity," "humans").

17. To avoid the accusation of moral relativism and political quietism, Beauvoir insists that *ambiguity* does not equate to *absurdity*: "[t]o declare that existence is absurd is to deny that it can ever be given a meaning; to say that it is ambiguous is to assert that its meaning is never fixed, that it must be constantly won. [. . .] Thus, to say that action has to be lived in its truth, that is, in the consciousness of the antinomies which it involves, does not mean that one has to renounce it" (1976c, 129).

18. To be sure, to recognize that human ambiguity (that is, the fact that one never coincides immediately with oneself), is irremediable sounds like a rather pessimistic view: "[i]t is the assertion of our finiteness which doubtless gives the doctrine which we have just evoked its austerity and, in some eyes, its sadness" (Beauvoir 1976c, 158). But the finiteness of life is "open on the infinite" (Beauvoir 1976c, 159) precisely in this outward/inward movement. It is not only *despite* one's limits but also *through* them that the individual can "fulfill his existence as an absolute [. . .] in the face of the universe which crushes him" (Beauvoir 1976c, 159).

19. I explore the concept of dilaceration (*Zerrissenheit*) in its Lukácsian formulation, along with a discussion of the development by different feminist standpoint theorists, in Teixeira (2020a and 2021).

20. See chapter 4, part A in particular.

21. The translation of "*Herr*" and "*Knecht*" by "master" and "slave" ("*maître*" and "*esclave*" in French), though not uncommon, is contested today by most Hegel scholars. As I am not addressing here Hegel's text, but rather Kojève's and Beauvoir's appropriation of it, I will retain their master-slave vocabulary in the presentation of their ideas.

22. Kojève's peculiar reading can be traced back, in my view, to his conscious and unilateral privileging of the perspective of natural consciousness ("*for it*") to the

detriment of the viewpoint of philosophical consciousness (*"for us"*) in Hegel's book (Teixeira 2020b).

23. Letter from Alexandre Kojève to Tran-Duc-Thao, October 7, 1948.

24. Abandoning oneself, however, requires that one "first be solidly sure that one has already found oneself." Beauvoir continues: "[n]ewly arrived in the world of men, barely supported by them, the woman is still much too busy looking for herself" (2011, 834). So, first things first: in the case of woman, "[a]s long as she still has to fight to become a human being, she cannot be a creator" (Beauvoir 2011, 845).

25. The erotic experience, for example, appears as "one that most poignantly reveals to human beings their ambiguous condition; they experience it as flesh and as spirit, as the other and as subject" (Beauvoir 2011, 476). See also the following excerpt from the conclusion of the book: "the contradictions opposing flesh to spirit, instant to time, the vertigo of immanence to the appeal of transcendence, the absolute of pleasure to the nothingness of oblivion will never disappear; tension, suffering, joy, and the failure and triumph of existence will always be materialized in sexuality" (Beauvoir 2011, 862).

26. This chapter is a result of a project funded by the German Federal Ministry of Education and Research under the grant number 01UK2023A (the responsibility for the content of this publication lies with the author). A shortened and modified version of the text appeared in Portuguese (Teixeira 2022).

REFERENCES

Antonopoulos, Alexander A. 2017. "Who Is the Subject of *The Second Sex*? Life, Science, and Transmasculine Embodiment in Beauvoir's Chapter on Biology," in *A Companion to Simone de Beauvoir*, L. Hengehold and N. Bauer (eds.), 463–77. Hoboken: Wiley.

Beauvoir, Simone. 1976a. *Le Deuxième Sexe*, 1. Paris: Gallimard.

Beauvoir, Simone. 1976b. *Le Deuxième Sexe*, 2. Paris: Gallimard.

Beauvoir, Simone. 1976c. *The Ethics of Ambiguity*, B. Frechtman (trans.). New York: Citadel Press.

Beauvoir, Simone. 2011. *The Second Sex*, C. Borde and S. Malovany-Chevallier (trans.). New York: Vintage Books.

Beauvoir Simone. 2017. *Pour une morale de l'ambiguïté : Suivi de Pyrrhus et Cinéas*. Paris: Gallimard.

Butler, Judith. 1986. "Sex and Gender in Simone de Beauvoir's *Second Sex*," *Yale French Studies*, 72: 35–49.

Butler, Judith. 1987. "Variations on Sex and Gender: Beauvoir, Wittig, and Foucault," in *Feminism as Critique: On the Politics of Gender*, S. Benhabib and D. Cornell (eds.), 128–42. Minneapolis: University of Minnesota Press.

Cuboniks, Laboria. 2018. *The Xenofeminist Manifesto: A Politics for Alienation*. New York: Verso.

Firestone, Shulamith. 1970. *The Dialectic of Sex: The Case for Feminist Revolution.* New York: Bantam Books.

Gaard, Greta. 1993. "Living Interconnections with Animals and Nature," in *Ecofeminism: Women, Animals, Nature*, G. Gaard (ed.). Philadelphia: Temple University Press.

Grusin, Richard (ed.). 2017. *Anthropocene Feminism.* Minneapolis/London: University of Minnesota Press.

Haraway, Donna. 1991. *Simians, Cyborgs, and Women: The Reinvention of Nature.* New York: Routledge.

Hegel, Georg W. F. 1939. *La Phénoménologie de l'Esprit*, 1, J. Hyppolite (trans.). Paris: Aubier.

Hegel, Georg W. F. 1941. *La Phénoménologie de l'Esprit*, 2, J. Hyppolite (trans.). Paris: Aubier.

Hegel, Georg W. F. 1952. *Phänomenologie des Geistes.* Leipzig: Felix Meiner.

Hegel, Georg W. F. 2018. *The Phenomenology of Spirit*, T. Pinkard (ed.). Cambridge: Cambridge University Press.

Hester, Helen. 2018. *Xenofeminism.* Cambridge: Polity.

Jarczyk, Gwendoline, and Labarrière, Pierre-Jean. 1996. *De Kojève à Hegel : 150 ans de pensée hégélienne en France.* Paris: Albin Michel.

Kojève, Alexandre. 1947. *Introduction à la lecture de Hegel : Leçons sur la Phénoménologie de l'Esprit professées de 1933 à 1939 à l'École des Hautes Études réunies et publiées par Raymond Queneau.* Paris: Gallimard.

Kojève, Alexandre. 1980. *Introduction to the Reading of Hegel: Lectures on the Phenomenology of Spirit Assembled by Raymond Queneau*, A. Bloom (ed.), J. H. Nichols and Jr. Ithaca (trans.). Ithaca: Cornell University Press.

MacCormack, Patricia. 2020. *The Ahuman Manifesto: Activism for the End of the Anthropocene.* Bloomsbury Academic.

Mann, Bonnie, and Martina, Ferrari (eds.). 2017. *On ne naît pas femme : on le devient: The Life of a Sentence.* New York: Oxford University Press.

Mellor, Mary. 1992. *Breaking the Boundaries: Towards a Feminist Green Socialism.* London: Virago Press.

Mies, Maria. 2014. "Self-Determination: The End of a Utopia?," in *Ecofeminism*, V. Shiva and M. Mies (eds.), 2018–230. London/New York: Zed Books.

Murphy, Ann V. 2012. "Ambiguity and Precarious Life: Tracing Beauvoir's Legacy in the Work of Judith Butler," in *Beauvoir and Western Thought from Plato to Butler*, S. Mussett and W. Wilkerson (eds.), 211–26. New York: SUNY Press.

Paasonen, Susanna. 2010. "From Cybernation to Feminization: Firestone and Cyberfeminism," in *Further Adventures of the Dialectic of Sex: Critical Essays on Shulamith Firestone*, M. Merck and S. Sandford (eds.), 61–84. New York: Palgrave Macmillan.

Plumwood, Val. 1986. "Ecofeminism: An Overview and Discussion of Positions and Arguments," *Australasian Journal of Philosophy*, 64 (supplement): 120–38.

Plumwood, Val. 1993. *Feminism and the Mastery of Nature.* London/New York: Routledge.

Ruether, Rosemary R. 1975. *New Woman New Earth: Sexist Ideologies and Human Liberation.* New York: Seabury.

Rubin, Gayle. 1975. "The Traffic in Women: Notes on the 'Political Economy' of Sex," in *Toward an Anthropology of Women*, R. Reiter (ed.), 157–210. New York/ London: Monthly Review Press.

Shiva, Vandana. 1988. *Staying Alive: Women, Ecology and Survival in India.* New Delhi/London: Kali for Women & Zed Books.

Shiva, Vandana, and Mies, Maria. 2014. *Ecofeminism.* London/New York: Zed Books.

Teixeira, Mariana. 2020a. "The Revolutionary Subject in Lukács and Feminist Standpoint Theory: Dilaceration and Emancipatory Interest," in *Confronting Reification: Revitalizing Georg Lukács's Thought in Late Capitalism*, G. Smulewicz-Zucker (ed.), 227–51. Leiden: Brill.

Teixeira, Mariana. 2020b. "Kojève's « Dialectique du Maître et de l'Esclave »: On the *Wirkungsgeschichte* of a traitorous translation" in *Verifiche: Rivista di scienze umane*, XLIX (1–2): 159–175.

Teixeira, Mariana. 2021. "Masters, Slaves, and Us: The Ongoing Allure of the Struggle for Recognition," in *Hegel's Phenomenology of Spirit: Exposition and Critique of Contemporary Readings*, I. Boldyrev and S. Stein (eds.), 74–95. London: Routledge.

Teixeira, M. 2022. "Ambiguidade e dilaceração: Simone de Beauvoir, leitora de Hegel e Kojève," *Revista Eletrônica de Estudos Hegelianos*, 19 (33): 18–42.

Chapter 9

The Naturalist Presuppositions of the Focus on Work and Economy in Dewey's Social Philosophy

Emmanuel Renault

In which respect could it be said that Dewey's social philosophy is naturalist? If this question deserves consideration, it is because Dewey's naturalism is less apparent in his social philosophy than in his metaphysics (e.g., in *Experience and nature*) or in his logical theory (e.g., in *Logic. A theory of inquiry*). Moreover, it is worth noting that there is a strong tendency, in Dewey's scholarship, to understate the naturalist premises of his social philosophy. According to a shared line of interpretation, his naturalism would only play a methodological role in his writings about society and politics. The only implication of the Darwinian revolution for social philosophy would consist in the fact that it is no longer possible to consider that scientific methods are relevant only insofar as nature is concerned. In other words, Dewey's social philosophy would be Darwinian only in the sense that it tries to apply methods of naturalist inquiry and experimentation to the conflicts that occur in social life. It makes no doubt that Dewey's social philosophy is Darwinian in this methodological sense, as pointed out in the article "The Influence of Darwinism on Philosophy" where one reads: "Philosophy must in time become a method of locating and interpreting the more serious of the conflicts that occur in life, and a method of projecting ways for dealing with them: a method of moral and political diagnosis and prognosis" (2008, MW 10, 14). But Dewey's social philosophy is naturalist also in other senses. In what follows, I will analyze Dewey's lectures on social philosophy in order to spell out the non-methodological dimensions of his naturalism, with a special focus on his accounts of work and the economic processes. In the first step, I will distinguish three types of argumentation in Dewey's social philosophy: a socio-ontological argumentation, an anthropological argumentation, and a social theoretical argumentation. In the second step, I will analyze the naturalist premises of Dewey's definition of human being as *Homo faber* or "tool-making animal." In the third step, I will try to make sense of Dewey's definition of economic processes as the "substructure of social life."

DEWEY'S NATURALISM IN SOCIAL ONTOLOGY, PHILOSOPHICAL ANTHROPOLOGY, AND SOCIAL THEORY

To begin with, I would like to recall that it is a fact that Dewey has elaborated a naturalist account of social life. It is well known that Dewey supported a kind of non-reductionist naturalism, defined by the concept of continuity. The clearest definition of this naturalism is to be found at the beginning of his *Logic. A theory of inquiry*:

> The primary postulate of a naturalistic theory of logic is continuity of the lower (less complex) and the higher (more complex) activities and forms. The idea of continuity [. . .] excludes complete rupture on one side and mere repetition of identities on the other; it precludes reduction of the "higher" to the "lower" just as it precludes complete breaks and gaps. The growth and development of any living organism from seed to maturity illustrates the meaning of continuity. (Dewey 2008, LW 12, 31)

In his article "Social as Category" also published with the title "The Inclusive Philosophic Idea," Dewey applies this naturalism to the definition of society. He argues that it is just as wrong to conceive of society as a reality independent of nature as it is wrong to believe that social phenomena should be explained solely through mechanical and biological properties. According to Dewey's principle of continuity, on the one hand, mechanical and biological properties still play a role in social life. But, on the other hand, mechanical and biological processes are raised to a higher level of complexity and integration when they are transformed into social processes, and, at this stage, mechanical and biological entities (for instance, human organisms) take on new properties that are irreducible to mechanical or biological ones. Given that Dewey himself has highlighted that his conception of society is naturalist, one could have expected that his social philosophy would also be explicitly grounded on naturalist premises. If it is not really the case in the "Lectures on social and political philosophy" published as *Lectures in China* (Dewey 1973), it is indisputably the case in the lectures on the social philosophy of the Autumn or Winter of 1926, a collection recently published in the second volume of the *Class Lectures* with the misleading title of "Lectures on Political Philosophy" (Dewey 2016). In these lectures, Dewey starts with the themes elaborated in "The Inclusive Philosophic Idea." And, since this latter article comes from a conference given in December 1927, one year later, we shall probably find in the lectures the first version of the main argument of the article.

In these lectures, Dewey starts with these socio-ontological statements:

> Social phenomena themselves present a fuller reality in their actual concrete nature than is exemplified in either the physical, the biological, or mental realms. [. . .] Social phenomena are really inclusive of the phenomena dealt with by the above three sciences (2016, 2, 2678)

He then introduces the three types of objects of social philosophy—economic problems, political problems, and cultural problems—just as he did in the *Lectures in China*. However, here, he then highlights that economic processes manifest the continuity between the natural and the social insofar as we find in them "the closest connection with the physical and biological phenomena" (2016, 2, 2681). None of these ideas were articulated in the *Lectures in China*.

> We find three groups, phases, or aspects: (1) Economic-Industrial; (2) Political; (3) Intercourse and Communication. Culture used in the narrower sense would express (3). It is dependent upon or closely associated with language or tradition. You might call it Ideal, not as a norm or standard of perfection, but as depending upon ideas and furthering the life of ideas. Economic or Industrial phase. In this phase we find the closest connection with the physical and biological phenomena. (Dewey 2016, 2, 2680–81)

This sheds interesting light on Dewey's project of social philosophy. A striking feature of the different versions of his lectures on social philosophy from the 1920s, the *Syllabus: Social Institutions and the Study of Morals*, or the lectures I am commenting on right now, or also the still unedited lectures on social philosophy given between Autumn 1927 and Summer 1928,[1] is that they deal mostly with issues concerning work and economic processes. And even if such a focus on work and economic processes is not so apparent in the *Lectures in China*, it is worth noting they also contend that economic problems are the most important of the three subject matters of social philosophy. This focus on work and economic processes has three main explanations and concerns the three types of argumentation that are at play in Dewey's social philosophy: a socio-ontological argumentation, an anthropological argumentation, and a socio-theoretical argumentation. Let me now analyze these three explanations.

The first justification for the focus on work and economy is that the economic processes reveal the continuity between nature and society, while one of the objectives of Dewey's social philosophy is precisely to make this continuity explicit. This socio-ontological objective is crucial in the first part of the 1927 lectures where Dewey highlights the continuity of economic processes with both the physical and the biological processes. On the one hand, he points out that:

What we call industry is obviously dependent upon, is an affair of the selection and utilization of physical energy in connection with purely physical material. Everything that we have in the industrial activity of society is in the fundamental sense a reshaping of certain physical materials by the application to them of certain physical forms of energy. (Dewey 2016, 2, 2680)

On the other hand, Dewey says that:

The economic processes are the projection of biological processes upon a distinctly human plane. The biological affair reduced to its lowest terms is one of bringing about adaptations of organisms to their environment so as to maintain their life functions—maintaining and perpetuating life. The economic process is exactly the same sort of thing—gain the control over natural environment that will maintain and perpetuate the life-function. The difference in content is due to the fact that the life-function of the human being is different from that of animals. Their qualities of life are so different that the differences tend to obscure the fundamental identity in the processes. (2016, 2, 2682)

This idea was already formulated in the *Syllabus* where it is written, in very similar terms, that

Fundamentally, economic processes are continuations of biological processes upon the distinctly human plane. [. . .] While the whole economic-industrial cycle represents a continuation of the biological process, or the process of maintaining life, its continuation upon the human plane exhibits significant differences. (Dewey 2008, MW 15, 258 and 250)

The second reason why Dewey's lectures on social philosophy give so much room to economic issues is linked with a definition of human being as a tool-making animal, or as *Homo faber*. As we will see in the next section of this chapter, this definition is supported by Darwinian arguments.

The third reason why Dewey's lectures on social philosophy put economic issues to the fore is linked with a conception of economic processes as the "substructure" of the whole social life, in the words of the *Lectures in China* (Dewey 1973). This conception doesn't belong to the socio-ontological and anthropological dimensions of Dewey's social philosophy to which I have already referred, but to its socio-theoretical dimension. Indeed, this dimension is less overtly naturalist than the other ones, but it is nevertheless dependent on some implications of the naturalist social ontology and the naturalist anthropology supported by Dewey, as we will see in the last section of this chapter.

In other words, the room given to work and economic processes in Dewey's social philosophy helps to understand that one should think of Dewey's social philosophy as being naturalist not only in socio-ontological terms but also in anthropological and socio-theoretical terms. I will now focus on these two latter dimensions.

THE TOOL-MAKING ANIMAL

In at least two series of lectures on social philosophy, Dewey has supported a definition of human being as "tool-making" and "tool-using animal," or as *Homo faber*. One finds these definitions in the *Lectures in China* and in the *Lectures on social philosophy of the years 1927–1928*, as well as in *Reconstruction of Philosophy* (Dewey 2008, MW 12, 120), and in the revised edition of the *Ethics* (Dewey 2008, LW 7, 374).

> Philosophers have defined man in a number of ways: as the talking animal, or as the rational animal. Attention has even been called to the fact that the man is the only animal capable of laughing. Recently the French philosopher Henri Bergson has proffered the definition of man as the tool-making animal—a particularly apt definition, in my opinion. Bergson definition directs attention to man's ability to devise from the materials of nature instrumentalities for the satisfaction of his desire—a characteristic which lower orders of animal do not possess, and which is therefore unique to man. (Dewey 1973, 101)

Again: "Tools, instruments, appliances, machinery—those objects [are] not used or consumed for their own sake but as mechanical means for reaching command of satisfaction—man the tool making animal [,] *homo faber*" (Dewey 1927/1928, 71). For Dewey, this definition is consistent with Darwinism. In fact, from an evolutionist point of view, species should not be defined by static morphological features but by the type of interaction with the natural environment that sustain their biological processes. As Dewey says in his lectures on *Political Ethics* of the year 1898, "the only criterion that has been got for a species is the particular way in which those special forms get their living," and it represents, in each species, "the industrial aspects," so that "the organization of the particular type of industrial work," in each society, "and the organization of the structure of a particular type of fishes has to be conceived essentially on the same basis" (Dewey 2016, 1, 1769). The specificity of humanity as a species is that work, that is, the use of tools in order to satisfy one's needs, has been selected as the main means of interaction with nature.

> It is hardly possible to avoid the conclusion that after giving up the old static definition of species, the point of view of conceiving species is from the side of morphology and genetic descent. The only criterion that has been got for a species is the particular way in which those special forms get their living. They represent the industrial aspects, and the morphological side, the structure side, is secondary, that is, the particular instruments which enable it to perform its particular form of the life process. The organization of the particular type of industrial work and the organization of the structure of a particular type of fishes has [*sic*] to be conceived essentially on the same basis. (Dewey 2016, 1, 1769)

These quotes lead to the conclusion that Dewey believed that the definition of human beings as a tool-making animal or *Homo faber* is the best definition of human nature. Indeed, this conclusion is not in tune with what is usually considered as Dewey's main contribution to philosophical anthropology, namely the definition of human being as a being of habits as elaborated in *Human Nature and Conduct* (2008, MW 14, 19). Still, far from being in competition with one another, these two anthropological definitions are mutually complementary. It could even be argued that his habit-based definition of human nature presupposes the definition of human being as a tool-making animal.

It is well known that in *Human Nature and Conduct* Dewey explains that impulses and habits are the two main explanatory factors of human conduct. It is less known that this contention is based on Darwinian premises. Dewey follows former attempts to elaborate a Darwinian psychology. Morgan, notably, had already pointed out that natural evolution is not only selecting capacities that are adapted to the environment as a whole (instincts) but also capacities to adapt to changing environments (in Deweyan terms, impulses that are liable to be transformed into habits) (1896).[2] From a Darwinian point of view, the reason why instincts are not the best way to regulate interactions with human environments is that these environments are artificial rather than natural, and artificial environments are capable of transforming themselves faster than natural environments. The crucial fact is that the pace of natural selection is not fast enough to select instincts adjusted to constantly changing social environments. As a result, natural selection has to select flexible impulses that may be adapted to artificial environments once transformed into habits, rather than rigid instincts. Now, work is precisely the activity that is responsible for the transformation of nature into an artificial environment, let alone for the possibility of constant transformation of this environment. To put it in the words of *Human Nature and Conduct*: "The eternal dignity of labor and art lies in their effecting that permanent reshaping of environment which is the substantial foundation of future security and progress" (Dewey 2008, MW 14, 19).

There is also another reason why the definition of human being as *Homo faber* and as a being of habits should not be contrasted one with another. This second reason does not relate to processes that turn biological instincts into human impulses but to processes that turn human impulses into actual habits. In fact, Dewey seems to believe that working activities have stronger formative effects on habits than any other activities. As said in the *Ethics* of 1932, for example: "Every occupation leaves its impress on individual character and modifies the outlook on life of those who carry it on" (Dewey 2008, LW 5, 117).

The definition of human beings as tool-making animals then appears as an integrative anthropological definition. It does not only explain that human adaptation to natural environment is effectuated by work. Since work is the origin of a transformation of a natural environment into artificial environments, this definition also explains why human beings are naturally endowed with impulses rather than instincts, and why these impulses get transformed into habits. Moreover, this definition also captures the fact that work also plays a central role in the transformation of impulses into habits. Finally, Dewey's account explains why social life has a specific cooperative dimension: according to Dewey, the division of labor implies cooperation, and the fact that cooperation is rooted in human nature explains the altruist dimension of human nature. In the 1927–1928 lectures, Dewey says that "This interdependence [that of the division of labor] [is] the reality of altruism. I am my brother's keeper" (1927/1928, 73).[3]

Just as biological life has an organic structure, the division of labor defines something similar to an organic complementarity of functions. This complementarity is the origin of the cooperative dimension of social life. This point was already made in the lectures on *Political Ethics* of the year 1898, where it is said that "individuals are primarily held together on the basis of their relations to nature" and that social division of labor constitutes "the primitive bond of union":

> The point is that individuals are primarily held together on the basis of their relations to nature. Of course that is never the whole bond of unity, and in later and more complex societies it is very difficult to find even that primitive bond of union; but the immediate conjunction, the immediate connections I think, are always found, even in the more developed societies, in the common relation of attack, so to speak, upon nature, the control and utilization of nature, and certainly in the primitive forms that bond constitutes a very large part of the whole social bond. (Dewey 2016, 1, 1788)

A similar idea is to be found in all the series of lectures on social philosophy of the 1920s. For instance, in the 1926 *Lectures on Political Philosophy*,

Dewey highlights the fact that division of labor is "the determining fact in social organization" and that it involves cooperation, even if societies could be more or less cooperative, not only because the division of labor can be more or less developed but also because the relation between social groups can be more or less cooperative:

> [Division of labor] is the determining fact in social organization and the deter-
> mination of individuals to the social whole. Involves cooperation. Physical
> cooperation is not coincident with social or moral cooperation. Social interde-
> pendence is established but may not take the form of cooperation, that is, not
> necessarily, for it may take the form of repressing certain occupations and also
> subjecting peoples. (2016, 2, 2684)

The fact that the division of labor is the origin of the cooperative dimension of social life plays a role from a socio-theoretical point of view, as we will see in the next section—as it is suggested here where Dewey says that division of labor "is the determining fact in social organization." For the time being, it is from a socio-ontological point of view that I would like to draw attention to the implications of such facts. According to Dewey, what defines social activities is that they are not only interdependent activities, as all organic activities, but also involve participation and shared interests, that is, they are *joint* activities. To put it in the words of *The Public and its Problems*:

> While associated behavior is, as we have already noted, a universal law, the fact
> of association does not of itself make a society. This demands, as we have also
> seen, perception of the consequences of a joint activity and of the distinctive
> share of each element in producing it. Such perception creates a common inter-
> est; that is concern on the part of each in the joint action and in the contribution
> of each of its members to it. (Dewey 2008, LW 2, 288–89)

Now, the cooperative dimension of social life is also at the origin of the very possibility of partaking of common values and transforming associated behavior into social arrangements in the truest sense of the term. And, since the social division of labor is the origin of the cooperative dimension of social life, it is also the origin of one of the specific traits of social reality. This point is remarked in the following two quotes. In the first, coming from the 1926 *Lectures on Political Philosophy*, Dewey highlights that the very possibility of participation in joint action depends not on psychological processes, such as imitation, but on the division of labor:

> Participation is not a process or operation, not anything which could be defined
> in terms of imitation. It is rather the consequent of certain processes. Those pro-
> cesses are not themselves psychological, the division of labor, e.g., which may

bring about an actual share in the purposes and sentiments which may animate the entire group. (2016, 2, 2689)

In the second quote, coming from the 1923 *Syllabus*, Dewey points out the source of the moral significance of one's occupation:

> The moral significance of a career, calling, occupation, depends upon, first, the fact that it evokes energy, creates skill and knowledge, liberates and consolidates individualized capacities, and secondly, upon the fact that it makes possible participation in the consequences of other occupations to the enrichment of the significant content of life. (Dewey 2008, MW 15, 253)

As a conclusion of the second section of this chapter, let me recall that, in the first section, the reason why Dewey focused on economic processes in his social philosophy appeared to be that these processes manifest the ontological continuity between nature and society. Now, we have seen that work is much more than a mere illustration of this continuity. It defines human beings from a naturalist point of view. Moreover, this definition of human beings helps to make sense, also from a naturalist point of view, of a series of other specificities of human nature, such as the role of habits and altruistic feelings. We have also seen that the definition of human being as *Homo faber* is decisive for socio-ontological principles other than Dewey's principle of continuity. Society is not only a more complex and integrated set of processes than natural processes, it is also an artificial environment, produced by work; moreover, it is not only defined by a higher degree of interdependence than biological or organic interdependence, but also by the possibility of joint action regulated by shared meanings, values, and ideals, a possibility grounded in the fact that the division of labor is the "primitive bond of union."

THE ECONOMIC SUBSTRUCTURE

I have already pointed out that the division of labor is not only "the primitive bond of union," since it is also "the determining fact in social organization." Similarly, in the *Lectures in China*, Dewey says that the economic processes are the "substructure" of society. In the last section of this chapter, I would like to try to make sense of these formulations ("determining fact," "substructure") that belong to the argumentative level of social theory and economics rather than of social ontology and philosophical anthropology.

A first point to note is there is no doubt that one of the reasons why Dewey focused on economic issues in his various series of lectures on social philosophy is that he wanted to struggle against the philosophical dualism of the spiritual and the material, as well as against the subsequent tendency of social and political philosophers to understate the role of the economic dimensions of social life. In the *Lectures in China*, for instance, one reads that:

> The most dangerous luxury in which social and political philosophers can indulge—and one in which a number of such philosophers have indulged—is to deprecate economics, to suppose that because its subject matter is no more than the mundane business of production and distribution of good it does not call for philosophic examination. [. . .] [There is a] futility of trying to understand political problems and intellectual problems without first exploring the economic substructure upon which other social institutions are erected. (Dewey 1973, 99–100)

However, one sees here that the concept of "economic substructure" is not only meant to criticize some spiritualist prejudices widely shared among philosophers. It also defines a social theoretical principle according to which one should pay due attention to the economic substructure in order to analyze accurately the other dimensions of social life. Just before this quote, Dewey has distinguished three types of problems social philosophy has to deal with—namely economic, political, and cultural problems—adding that economic problems must come first because the "economic problems determine" the rest of the social life. "I take it as axiomatic that the ways in which a people meet their economic problems determine in a large degree what they do about their other social problems" (1973, 99).

Indeed, the idea that economic processes determine the rest of social life, together with the idea of an economic substructure, sounds more Marxian than Deweyan. Marx conceived of work as the "metabolism between nature and society," just as Dewey; and Marx too stressed the fact that there is a reciprocal action between the economic and non-economic dimensions of social life. Nevertheless, there is something specific in Dewey's version of the idea of an economic substructure determining the rest of social life. What is specific to Dewey is that this idea is elaborated from the point of view of a theory of action. In Dewey, one can find three justifications for the economic determinism thesis, and all of them are grounded in his theory of action.

The first justification for this thesis is that all actions are conditioned by instrumentalities at their disposal. Now, the instruments of human action are mainly artifacts, as they result from work as a transformation of nature into artifacts. Given that economic processes are dynamic processes, implying the transformation of the ways in which working activities produce artifacts, and given that social practices are conditioned by artifacts, it follows that economic processes condition social practices. As said in the 1926 *Lectures on Political Philosophy*, the truth of economic determinism is that the means determine the ends, and it is for this very reason that social control on the economic substructure of social life is required. Instead of promoting such control, the materialist determinism professed by political economy rules it out, assuming that economic processes are subjected to inflexible laws that are rational laws:

> Ideals and purposes that can be effected must have under their control means of existence. [. . .] An ideal without any means is nothing, but means separated from ideals are still there. They are powers, causal conditions, and they do operate to bring about consequences, whether those consequences are themselves rationally desirable or not. [. . .] Materialistic determinism and this particular type of ethical idealism really suffer from the same fallacy, namely, the separation of means from ends, only each takes the separation from opposite poles. The economic theory makes the separation in that, while it is correct in holding that economic processes do determine the purposes and ends of human beings that become operative, they hold also that these ends are essentially what they ought to be, that there is no need of any rational control over and above that which is found in actual deliberation incident to the existing of the economic situation. (Dewey 2016, 2, 2707)

A second justification for economic determinism is linked to the fact that social practices are controlled by habits. The relation with economy comes from the fact that working activities, when they take the form of occupations, that is, of enduring specialized participation in the social division of labor, exert powerful formative effects on habits and character. Given that working activities are determined by economic processes, and given that working activities control the formation of habits and habits control social practices, it follows that the economic substructure controls the rest of social life. To put it in the words used in the article "Interpretation of the Savage Mind": "If we search in any social group for the special functions to which mind is relative, occupations at once suggest themselves. Occupations determine the fundamental modes of activity, and hence control the formation and use of habits" (Dewey 2008, MW 2, 41). It is probably with reference to this second justification of the economic determinism thesis that the *Lectures in China* state that "the ways in which a people meet their economic problems determine in a large degree what they do about their other social problems" (Dewey 1973, 99).

A third justification for Dewey's idiosyncratic economic determinism relates to the abovementioned fact that what defines social activities is that they are not only interdependent activities but also joint activities involving shared goals and values. I have already mentioned that the division of labor is the origin of the possibility of partaking of common values. Now, given that economic processes are dynamic factors that transform the division of labor, they can make it possible to partake of new values, and, therefore, they are causative factors of new types of participation in social life. This is the gist of the argument elaborated in this excerpt from the 1926 *Lectures on Political Philosophy*:

> The economic process is the kinetic process in social phenomena. The economic processes are the causative factors bringing about the participation in the values produced by the interaction of wants and efforts. It is the mechanism by which the result is brought about, that there is a production which utilizes the energies of others and a consumption which is what it is because it shares in the values which are produced by others. [. . .] Individuals in society are capable of and do participate in the consequences of the activities of the others, and that participation is not a mechanical fact, but is significant of the fact that there is a real partaking of the values or goods. From this standpoint, the idea that the economic is the causative factor in social phenomena is a platitude rather than a discovery. Social changes ultimately depend upon arousing of wants or demands for changes in the manner of living. (Dewey 2016, 2, 2689–90)

A similar idea is expressed later in these lectures, in a discussion concerning the relations between economic values (values that should organize economic processes) and non-economic values (human or moral values that should organize the rest of the society). Dewey rejects the Aristotelian position according to which there is no economic value, and that economic processes should be subordinated to external human or moral values. Dewey rejects also the opposite view, that of eighteenth-century political economy according to which economic values and human or moral values are identical. Dewey contends, on the contrary, that there are immanent criteria for working activities and economic processes, and that they are distinct from the normative criteria for the other spheres of social life. He adds: "They [the values] do overlap, impinge, or coincide on many points, but instead of human values determining economic values, the economic values largely determine the moral or human values" (Dewey 2016, 2, 2701).

It is not so easy to understand in which sense "the economic values largely determine the moral or human values." Dewey probably suggests that when the social division of labor is not organized according to its immanent criteria, criteria that are mainly norms of cooperation (when, for instance, social division of labor takes the form of a slavery system such as in ancient Greece), then the possibility of social communication is restricted, and the social definition of moral or human values is altered. Hence the way economic values regulate economic processes determines the ways human values are conceived and exert in their turn their regulative function.

To conclude, I would like to draw attention to the fact that these three justifications of the primacy given to economic factors in social theory are not directly grounded on naturalist premises. They are directly dependent on Dewey's instrumentalism, on his dispositional theory of action, and on his conception of communication and participation as being distinctive features of society—yet not on his theory of economic processes as the transformation of biological processes. On the other hand, we have seen that each of these justifications has naturalist assumptions insofar as the socio-ontological and anthropological significance of work plays a role in them. Work is the origin of artificial instrumentalities and as such also contributes to the formation of habits and character, and division of labor is the origin of the possibility of participation in joint action. Defining naturalism by continuity implies, on the one hand, that there is no gap between natural arguments and social theory, on the other hand, that naturalist arguments cannot be applied to social theory but with theoretical mediation, namely with socio-ontological and anthropological mediations.

NOTES

1. Morris Library, Box 65—Folder 7: Social Philosophy, 131, September 29, 1927–January 9, 1928, 39 pages—Folder 9: Social Philosophy, January 9–May 15, 1928, 41 pages (quoted 1927/1928).

2. On Morgan's theory, see Hogdson (2004), 110–15.

3. In other words, the definition of human nature as based on work also integrates a definition of humans as social animals. Dewey sometimes refers to this correlation: "We repeat over and over that man is a social animal, and then confine the significance of this statement to the sphere in which sociality usually seems least evident, politics. The heart of the sociality of man is in education" (Dewey 2008, MW 12, 185).

REFERENCES

Dewey, John. 1973. *Lectures in China*. Honolulu: University Press of Hawaii.

Dewey, John. 2008. *The Collected Works of John Dewey 1882–1953 (Early Works, Middle Works, and Late Works)*, J. A. Boydston (ed.). Carbondale: Southern Illinois University Press.

Dewey, John. 2016. *Lectures. Electronic Edition*. Charlottesville: InteLex Corporation.

Hodgson, Geoffry M. 2004. *The Evolution of Institutional Economics: Agency, Structure and Darwinism in American Institutionalism*. London: Routledge.

Morgan, Conwy L. 1896. *Habit and Instinct*. London: Arnold.

Part III

NATURALISM AND SOCIAL CRITICISM

SOCIAL PATHOLOGY AND PHILOSOPHICAL THERAPY

Chapter 10

The (Meta)Physician of Culture

Early Nietzsche's Disclosing
Critique of Forms of Life

Arvi Särkelä

Denn die einen sind im Dunkeln
Und die andern sind im Licht
Und man siehet die im Lichte
Die im Dunkeln sieht man nicht

—Bertolt Brecht, *Moritat von*
Mackie Messer (19, 320)

INTRODUCTION

Social philosophers, in particular Critical Theorists, have for a long time been interested in the socio-critical potential of Friedrich Nietzsche's philosophy (see, e.g., Deleuze 1962; Foucault 1971; Butler 1997; Owen 2002; Saar 2002; 2008).[1] In their varying attempts to enrich our understanding of philosophical social critique by interpreting Nietzsche, they have focused strongly on his later writings, predominantly *On the Genealogy of Morality*. Without in any way intending to deny the great value and accomplishments of the very diverse perspectives that have emerged from these studies, I will instead turn to the young Nietzsche, from whose works I will excavate a thus far neglected conception of philosophical social critique, a conception importantly different from, yet no less valuable than, genealogical critique.

My primary intention is to unearth a form of philosophical social critique from Nietzsche's *Untimely Meditations*: a disclosing critique of forms of social life. However, this task is linked, through the figure of "the physician of culture," to a broad spectrum of issues in contemporary social philosophy:

199

the idea of social pathology, the question of the embodiment of domination and critique, the relation of first and second nature, the role of metaphysical speculation in social criticism, and, more generally, the shape of naturalism in social philosophy.

Nietzsche's second and third *Untimely Meditations* touch upon one of social philosophy's central debates today, the discourse on social pathologies (see Honneth 2007; 2009; 2014; Freyenhagen 2015; Hirvonen 2018; Laitinen 2015; Laitinen and Särkelä 2018; 2019; Neuhouser 2016; Särkelä 2017; Särkelä and Laitinen 2019; Zurn 2011). This discourse is central not only because it revolves around the questions of what social philosophy is and how it should be distinguished from neighboring disciplines such as moral and political philosophy but also because it asks how social philosophy's critical claim is to be understood. As to the first set of issues, two ways to distinguish social philosophy from moral and political philosophy have been suggested. The first one is methodological: social philosophy is defined by its way of proceeding; it has a different method of normative assessment than moral or political philosophy (Jaeggi and Celikates 2018; Fischbach 2009; Renault 2017). The second one is ontological: social philosophy is defined by its peculiar object, namely social pathologies (Honneth 2007; 2009; Neuhouser 2016); here much rests upon what ontology of this object is presupposed (Hirvonen 2018; Särkelä 2018; Laitinen and Särkelä 2019).

In early Nietzsche, one finds both methodological and ontological reflections on a kind of inclusive perspective on our social life that is in many ways similar to the enterprises that we today would call "social philosophy." On the one hand, there is Nietzsche's conception of the philosopher as a "physician of culture." Methodologically then, the work of the philosopher can be described in analogy to the physician's diagnoses and cures. On the other hand, there is his strongly naturalistic vocabulary of "malady" and "degeneration" as well as "health" and "growth" of entities we would classify as social or cultural. Ontologically then, the social philosopher's object is taken as the kind of entity that can either degenerate or grow, fall ill or get well. To get early Nietzsche's critical social philosophy right, much hangs on how to correctly understand the ontological implications of this vocabulary.

However, with regard to the second set of issues—how to understand social philosophy's critical claim—Nietzsche takes a further step rarely given explicit consideration today: he understands the evaluative force of social philosophy in terms of its *disclosing effects*. It is this aspect of his early work I wish to inquire about in this contribution. I will investigate his early reflections on the critique of forms of life in his *Untimely Meditations* as an exemplary expression of what has sometimes been called "a disclosing critique of society" (Honneth 2000; see also Särkelä 2020), a form of philosophical social criticism that claims less to pass a normative judgment on social life than to shift its horizon of meaning and to help transform it.

In the *Untimely Meditations*, Nietzsche includes an extravagant cosmological reflection in support of his diagnosis of a degeneration of social life. While I do not think that this cosmology of "plastic power" is correct or particularly supportive of the important tasks of social criticism today, I will indeed claim that Nietzsche's inclusion of metaphysical speculation into his practice of philosophical social criticism is something we can still learn from. Challenging for us today is not so much what he says but how he says it, that is, the *way* in which he sets up the praxis of a physician of culture. Indeed, the way in which Nietzsche sets up his inquiry will bolster a better and richer understanding of the practice of a *disclosing* critique of society. His metaphysical speculation thus enables a form of educative recalcitrance which is both *immanent* to and *disclosing* of forms of social life.

THE MALADY OF HISTORY

As a "physician of culture," young Nietzsche *diagnoses* a social pathology, from which we all as members of a form of life suffer.[2] In his second *Untimely Meditation* on the "Uses and Disadvantages of History for Life," he calls this pathology "the malady of history" and he conceptualizes it as a "degeneration of life": "we are all suffering from a consuming fever of history and ought at least to recognize that we are suffering from it" (Nietzsche 2007, 246). Correspondingly, in the third *Untimely Meditation* on "Schopenhauer as Educator" (2007), Nietzsche *prognosticates* his age to be a "time that really will be killed," and this killing he then specifies as meaning to become "struck out of the history of the true liberation of life" (2007, 338). The qualification that his time will "really" be killed and the specification that this means a lack of the "liberation of life" point to Nietzsche's serious take on naturalistic vocabulary and ascribes evaluative force to it. He suggests that in its crystallization into a form of life, the process of social life can literally become pathological: there is a way in which a "people" or a "culture" can degenerate (Nietzsche 2007, 250). In both works, Nietzsche refers to the philosopher dealing with these pathologies as a "physician" (Nietzsche 2007, 264 and 345f, 366f, 400); her task is to offer diagnoses and prognoses in order to help cure and heal the forms of social life.

By "malady of history," Nietzsche does not refer to a merely scholarly phenomenon. Nietzsche's critique of "history" is not only directed against the homonymous science and not even specifically against the role this science has come to play in public discourse. Already on the first pages of the second *Untimely Meditation*, it becomes clear that Nietzsche presents "history" as a *cosmological* category (2007): it says something about something's place in the cosmos, namely about human social practices as part of "life." He contrasts such paradigmatically human social life activity with that of animals by noting humans' inability to forget (Nietzsche 2007, § 1). History operates through a specific adaptive mechanism: memory. Memory adapts the individual to the environment by the fact that the environment becomes operative through the individual: the environment imprints itself on the individual and thereby preforms its future interactions. "History" is the way in which a life-process, by means of the mechanism of memory, relates back upon its past so as to redirect its movement toward a specific future. It is a particular mode of life's directedness, a mode that we would associate with processes that we characterize as distinctively social, such as a "people" or a "culture." Therefore, Nietzsche's critique of "history" qualifies as a *social critique*.

The historicity of life comes in degrees. Though humans do display a certain inability to forget, there is no clear discontinuity between the relatively unhistorical animal life and the relatively historical human life. The historicity that is characteristic of our social form of life comes, as it were, creeping: following Leibniz, Nietzsche seems to suggest that some minimal amount of memory must be given even in the most primitive forms of life.[3] On the other hand, he emphasizes that forgetting is absolutely necessary for all living beings. Without the ability to forget, memory would trap the living being in a vicious circle of constantly reinforcing the same environmental conditions: the individual's "memory revolves unwearyingly in a circle and yet is too weak and weary to take even a single leap out of this circle" (Nietzsche 2007, 253).

"History" is an aspect of the life-process, of the living being's way to constitutively relate back upon itself so as to redirect its ongoing movement, but the processes of life are also driven to *break* with their past and, as it were, act forward—a drive which Nietzsche calls "the unhistorical" (2007, § 1). "This, precisely, is the proposition the reader is invited to meditate upon: *the unhistorical and the historical are necessary in equal measure for the health of an individual, of a people and of a culture*" (emphasis in original) (Nietzsche 2007, 252). Life-processes need to be both historical and unhistorical, and they must exercise both memory and forgetfulness. Individual living beings have to both *adapt* to their environment and *adjust* to it. It follows that there can be an "excess of history," an "oversaturation of an age with history," which leads to a collective "sleeplessness" and "rumination," that is, the "fever of history" (Nietzsche 2007, 253 and 279, 250, 246).

To open up these metaphors, let's take a closer look at early Nietzsche's conception of life.

THE COSMOLOGY OF PLASTIC POWER

The degree to which a form of life can use history without degenerating is relative to its "plastic power" (Nietzsche 2007, 251). Nietzsche claims that all life possesses some degree of plastic power.

What is "plastic power"? It is (a) plastic (πλαστικός), which means that it has been shaped and designed to be directed toward something; (b) power (*Kraft*), which means that it is itself further shaping the thing toward which it is plastic; (c) both shaped and shaping.

Both the thing that shapes it and the thing that it shapes are *life*. The shaping arises from life and works on life, that is, the living environment to which the individual living being relates itself. Life's plastic power is the capacity of a living being to redesign, to reshape, and to transform itself by modifying its environment. Or as Nietzsche himself puts it:

> I mean by plastic power the capacity to develop out of oneself in one's own way, to transform and incorporate [*einzuverleiben*] into oneself what is past and foreign, to heal wounds, to replace what has been lost, to recreate broken moulds. (2007, 251)

The plastic power of a living being or a form of life is then its capacity to use its *adaptation* to its environment for the benefit of an active *adjustment* of that environment. By "plastic power," Nietzsche articulates something like Spinoza's *natura naturans* and *natura naturata* (Spinoza 2003, 1p29): at every instance, nature is creating and receiving at the same time.

Plastic power comes in degrees. All living beings and forms of life have it to some degree: they all are always plastic toward some ends, have evolved, but also creatively mold their environment and themselves, redirecting the process of life's evolution. Yet they do this with differing intensity. Nietzsche is a metaphysical naturalist in construing, as it were, a continuity between the "amoebae and us" (Rorty 1998, 295f). The criterion of continuity is the degree of plastic power.

Early Nietzsche's cosmology of plastic power can be understood as relying on a combination of two metaphysical commitments: ontological monism and modal pluralism. This idea can be traced back to the metaphysics of Spinoza. Ontological monism is the idea that all existence can be explained as expressing one principle; in Spinoza, this is famously *Deus sive natura* (*God or nature*) expressed as *potentia* (*power*) (Spinoza 2003, 1p11). Similarly, in early Nietzsche, the principle is nature expressed as plastic power. Modal pluralism, moreover, is the idea that there are several ways to express this principle; there is a plurality of *modes* of being the one thing. Spinoza famously claimed that there is an infinite number of modes of the one substance, which can be gradually ordered according to their degree of complexity along the two parallel attributes of extension and thinking, or body and mind, and individuated by their particular way to endeavor to persist in their own being (*conatus*) (Spinoza 2003, 1p10; 2p13; 3p7). Similarly, in early Nietzsche, there is a plurality of modes of plastic power, which can be ordered gradually according to the degree of their transformative capacity, each with its particular way to develop out of itself in its own way.

These two commitments allow Nietzsche to distinguish between higher and lower forms of life according to the plastic power they exhibit, that is, according to the degree to which their current shape allows them to shape their further life-processes. On the bottom end, we have forms of life whose activity predominantly serves their *self-maintenance*, whereas the *growth* they display is arbitrary and minimal. For these forms of life, death means a collapse of this activity of self-maintenance and the dissolution of the plastic power that kept that unit of activity intact. On the top, we have forms of life whose activity is a creative quest for self-transformation, an expansion of the concept of what they are. Their activity not only serves the maintenance of the form but also strives to transform it. This self-transformative mode of life Nietzsche calls "culture" (2007, 257 and 272f). Culture is the mode of life-process that strives to transform itself.

Because forms of life are *modes*, and not substances, they can move up and down this ladder of plastic power: They can ascend to a "higher life" and gain creative freedom by a higher degree of plastic power, but they can also "degenerate," lose intensity by a lower degree of plastic power (Nietzsche 2007, 268). Such degeneration is the cultural physician's model for social pathology. Correspondingly, this ascendency is her model for health, growth, and the "liberation of life."

The operation of plastic power then puts two requirements on any form of life: first, it has to *sustain its shape*, otherwise it would lose *its* plastic power and dissolve into a manifold of elements developing their own plastic powers. Any form of life must be constantly reproduced in order to persist. Its plastic power must to some extent be exercised by its operating components to maintain its shape. Let's call this the requirement of *self-maintenance*. Second, any form of life has to *modify its shape*, otherwise, it would not display plastic *power* but merely degenerate into a minimal intensity uncharacteristic of a living process. Life must evolve. Its plastic power must, to some extent, be exercised by its operating components varying, deviating, and acting toward a modification of the current shape. Let's call this the requirement of *self-transformation.*

Both operations, the self-maintaining and the self-transforming, are necessary for Nietzsche (Stiegler 2021; Thomä 2015). But they can also conflict. The greater the plastic power of a form of life, the more effort its elements must invest into negotiating the extent to which their activity aims at maintaining or transforming its shape.[4]

HISTORY AS INITIATION INTO A FORM OF LIFE

"Plastic power" denotes something shaped that is further shaping, something designed that is further designing, the process of life's evolutionary yet active redesigning its self-maintaining and self-transformative operations. This implies that, at any given point in time, any form of life must involve something *innate* as well as something *acquired*. In this context, Nietzsche takes up an Aristotelian conceptual pair, "first nature" and "second nature."[5]

Like Aristotle, Nietzsche initially understands "first nature" as something innate, original; and "second nature" as something acquired, learned by *initiation* into a form of life. What is innate, first nature, Nietzsche associates with our "instincts" (2007, 270); what is acquired, second nature, he associates with our "habits" and "customs" (*Sitten*) (2007, 299); and the process of initiation he understands as that of "habituation" (*Gewöhnung*) (2007, 272). To continue, a form of life must involve activities on the part of its elementary members to bring individuals in line with its shape, to initiate younger members to its ways. What Nietzsche calls "history" thus involves the instruction and education of the individual living members of a form of life so that the individual acquires their own past.

However, Nietzsche makes a crucial update with the intention to transform the Aristotelian picture: He says that "[every] first nature was once a second nature and that every victorious second nature will become a first" (2007, 270). First and second nature are in Nietzsche neither different "logical spaces," as in McDowell (1994), nor metaphors for ontological stages of nature. They are *interchangeable placeholder concepts* for describing *phases* of an evolutionary and active process of life, of the operation of plastic power.[6]

Now, as "plastic power," the ongoing redesigning of life operates by expressing, acquiring, and making traits innate. It constitutes a spiral-like movement of second and first nature: the customs of the form of life, the individual's social environment, find embodiment in the habits of the individual, which "inplant [sic!]" a "new instinct" that is then expressed again in the social environment (Nietzsche 2007, 270). *History* is a medium of this organic interaction: the individual acquires the past shape of the social environment, which makes itself inhere to that shape and becomes expressed through its activity as environment again. Whereas a minimum of history would hold us below the intensity of social life and hinder us from raising above the animal inside us, an excess of history would degenerate life toward mere self-maintenance of the form. The spiral of plastic power would stagnate into a vicious circle of second to first nature and back.

Therefore, Nietzsche argues, we need history "in the service of life": that is, relating back upon ourselves in order to reshape ourselves, an activity by the individual to transform itself and its form of life through its social environment (2007, 257f and 269ff). It relates back to the past to account for what has been acquired in order to give the first nature of the members of the form of life a specific shape; it habituates them to channeling their instincts according to prevailing or desirable customs. Therefore, history operates through *educational* practices directed at the living members of the form of life: "This path, however, leads through human brains! Through the brains of timorous and shortlived animals" (Nietzsche 2007, 259).

Such practices are always *socially asymmetrical*: They involve power differences between the instructors and those to be instructed, the educators and those to be educated, typically between the old and the young. Thus, in any life from maintaining itself through "history," one can distinguish an instructing and educating *core* from its *margins*. The core consists of those second-natural customary and institutional arrangements that enable the established members to initiate less established members to act in accordance with a desirable continuation of the form of life. To emphasize the educational and socially asymmetrical character of the historical reproduction of the form of life, Nietzsche calls the core "old-age" and the margins "youth" (2007, 322f).

Nietzsche famously distinguishes three ways in which individuals can realize these relationships, or, as he calls them, three "species of history" (2007, § 2f): "monumental," "antiquarian," and "critical history." History in this sense is ontologically constitutive of *social* life.

Social life needs, first, to maintain itself in order to go on, to continue as a life-process; for this, it must relate back upon itself in the *antiquarian* mode to *preserve what is good*. This is established in ordinary life by adapting individual living beings to what their social environment values as desirable for the continuation of their form of life. The initiation, which this mode of a life form's relation back upon itself results in, Wittgenstein calls "training" [*Abrichtung*]: established partakers of a form of life bring less adapted members into line with that form by disciplining, telling, and showing them what must be done in order for it, or all that is valuable in it, to go on (Wittgenstein 1978, § 22 and § 46; see also Hampe 2018, 72–80). In the second *Untimely Meditation*, Nietzsche too uses the concept of *Abrichtung* to characterize how the "old-age" pulls the "youth" toward the core of the form of life (2007, 299 and 323).[7] First nature is then adapted to second nature, the individual living being molded into the form of life by habituation implanting socially desirable instincts in it: "The history of his city becomes for him the history of himself" (Nietzsche 2007, 265). Thus, the antiquarian species of history responds to plastic power's requirement of self-maintenance.

But social life also needs, second, to grow in order to exhibit the kind of intensity that qualifies it as a characteristically social form of life; therefore, from time to time, every society, every organization of the social life-process must reflect its movement in the *monumental* mode so as to *inspire* its members to mold not only themselves but also their social environment; they must not only *adapt to* it but also *adjust* it. Importantly, this shaping process of the social environment operates by the re-appropriation of examples from the history of the form of life itself. It uses its *own* past to inspire members to work toward a certain future movement. Here individual living beings look back at the past of their own form of life, to something once acquired that now seems lost. They then *repair* their second nature by, as it were, assembling a jigsaw puzzle: in their past, they find the pieces that are missing in their current second nature. This reminds of the picture of Neurath's boat self-repairing in open sea (see McDowell 1994, 4, § 7; Lovibond 2002, 7, § 1). Monumental history adapts the second nature to itself without any external reference, laying out the puzzle one piece at a time. Michael Walzer (1987), John McDowell (1994), Sabina Lovibond (2002), and others have called this type of self-repair "internal criticism." Monumentalist educators therefore go beyond their antiquarian colleagues: whereas "training" [*Abrichtung*] works to bring the individual first nature in line with the social second nature, internal criticism implies a more *educational* project in the sense of turning the attention of the individual living beings from just adapting themselves to adjusting their common second nature according to internal demands and by means of its internal historical normative resources, such as the exemplary great deeds of the past. It adapts, as it were, second nature to itself. Thus, monumental history responds to plastic power's requirement of growth.

However, taken alone, each of these modes of social life relates back upon its movement to reshape itself and its members tend to stagnate social life or even to degenerate it below the level of its characteristic plastic power. By simply one-sidedly adapting the individual living beings to their social second nature, the form of life will lose plastic power; without active individual living beings reconstructing their social environment and challenging their second nature, the form of life will stagnate to a minimum of growth (see Stiegler's critique of adaptionism in Chapter 4 of this volume). And by simply solving the jigsaw puzzle of the already acquired, the form of life will only grow on its own account but never "out of itself"; even if monumentalist education can achieve growth, it cannot really *transform*. Nietzsche remarks that the form of life thereby does injustice to its very own past: those exemplary great deeds of the past were not the deeds of the form of life itself, but of individual members challenging it by deviating from it. The only difference between antiquarian training and monumentalist education is that, in the former case, the living beings work on adapting the individual beings' first nature to the second, while, in the latter, they work to adapt the current second nature to its own past. Both species of history therefore constitute educational projects that enforce a *self-perpetuating circle of second and first nature*.

The third species is critical history. In the critical mode, individual partakers of a form of life relate back upon the past in order to break away from it. They observe that the current form is not growing anymore, it is stagnating. Whereas antiquarian and monumental histories make the past present, *critical history makes the present past*. It kills what is already dead, and thereby seeks to enliven the form of life. Critical history is the attempt to *disclose* the self-perpetuating circle of second and first nature. It does this by creating a break between the social second nature and the individual first nature and envisioning an alternative second nature that would give life new form:

> We . . . confront our inherited and hereditary nature with our knowledge, and through a new, stern discipline combat our inborn heritage and inplant [*sic*] in ourselves a new habit, a new instinct, a second nature, so that our first nature withers away. (Nietzsche 2007, 270)

It initiates a new way of initiating individual beings to the form of life, a new education.

However, for making the present past, critical history must seek inspiration outside the prevailing form of life. It cannot rely simply on the exemplarity of what it once was nor on its elites of instruction and institutional core. It can also not simply invoke its individual members' first nature, because that is essentially the first nature of its second nature. What does it then feed on?

DE-CENTERING AND RE-CENTERING
THE FORM OF LIFE

I suggest that the following *Untimely Meditation* answers the question of what an education that makes the present past would look like. My claim is that Nietzsche, in his third *Untimely Meditation*, articulates the practice of *critical disclosure as the creative deviation of individual living beings challenging the social environment that instructs them*. Paraphrasing Lovibond, I shall call the stance of such individuals toward their social environment "speculative recalcitrance" (2002). I understand it as a kind of intentional deviation from a form of life that discloses its limitations and possibilities.

In the third *Untimely Meditation*, Nietzsche returns to critical history as a peculiarly *philosophical* task:

If occupation with the history of past or foreign nations is of any value, it is of most value to the philosopher who wants to arrive at a just verdict . . . on the highest fate that can befall individual men or entire nations. (2007, 361)

It is indeed *critical* history, with which the philosopher engages: she seeks namely to make the present past, to disclose the self-perpetuating circle of second and first nature: "the philosopher must deliberately under-assess [his own age] and, by overcoming the present in himself, also overcome it in the picture he gives of life, that is to say render it unremarkable and as it were *paint it over*" (2007, 361; my emphasis). The critical philosopher paints over the self-perpetuating circle of the current form of life. This is a paraphrasis of Hegel's statement in his infamous preface to the *Philosophy of Right* that philosophy grasps only a "shape of life grown old" and "paints its grey in grey" (Hegel 2008, 16). By contrast, Nietzsche's turn of the phrase makes it the very task of the philosophical critic to *render* the current shape of life old, and then to paint *over* it a picture of life—not in grey but, presumably, in multicolor!

Starting from this remark, one can distinguish two phases of critical disclosure: first, it has the *negative* task of representing the present as a self-perpetuating circle. As a physician of culture, the philosopher *diagnoses* it as a degenerated form of life, a shape grown old, and intentionally *exaggerates* it as being, in fact, already dead. Or as Nietzsche puts it:

A historical phenomenon, known clearly and completely and resolved into a phenomenon of knowledge, is, for him who has perceived it, *dead*: for he has recognized in it the delusion, the injustice, the blind passion, and in general the whole earthly and darkening *horizon* of this phenomenon, and has thereby also understood its power in history. This power has now lost its hold over him insofar as he is knowing: but perhaps not insofar as he is living. (2007, 257; translation amended; my emphasis)

The disclosing critic must grasp the dead shape of the present life. This is a *de-centering* movement of disclosure: she portrays her form of life from an alienating perspective, presenting it as *not livable anymore*. She aims at a disclosing effect by hauling her addresses from the "darkening horizon," the enclosed circle, toward her own alienated position, in order to jolt its core. But Nietzsche also remarks that, if nothing living takes its place, what is dead can still persist by petrifaction; the individuals might go on living under the power of the old shape, if the critic does not point to *new* life.

Representing the present as old and exaggerating the old as dead is not enough.

Therefore, the second phase of critical disclosure consists in the *positive* task of disclosing a new life. As we have seen in the preceding quote, the critic must also paint a picture of life over the old circle. In addition to the rather scientific job of grasping the old shape, the disclosing critic must take on the more poetic task of articulating a new life:

> History become pure, sovereign science would be for mankind a sort of conclusion of life [*Lebens-Abschluss*] and a settling of accounts with it. Historical education is something salutary and fruitful for the future only as the attendant of a mighty new current of life [*Lebensströmung*], of an evolving culture. (Nietzsche 2007, 257; translation amended)

Taken alone, history even in its critical mode of relating back on itself to make the present past is, in Nietzsche's view, degenerating for life, because healing demands new life, something to affirm. It is not enough for the physician of culture to present a *diagnosis*: she must also participate in the *curing process*. This is a *re-centering* movement of disclosure: from an alienating perspective, the critic points to an alternative to her form of life as *something livable*. She aims at a disclosing effect by showing her addressees what their life could be.

It is easy to see that both tasks present the critic with a vital problem that applies to every form of external critique. For both de- and re-centering the form of life, the disclosing critic needs a perspective from the outside. The physician must speak without the degenerating body. Yet, if she speaks from the outside, how can her critique be disclosing on the inside? Ideally, social criticism should be compelling even to those who do not enter into discourse with the same individual commitments and worries as the critic. It appeals to the life form's members' willingness to consider arguments that come with no positional preconditions. However, if it is the expression of an external standpoint that the addressees cannot be expected to share, it cannot meet that requirement. Why should then our physician's death certificate for the old form of life be valid for those enclosed in it, and why should her alternative be persuasive for them?

Let us start to trace Nietzsche's way of responding to this challenge by taking a step backward. The physician of culture draws a circle of given second and first nature so as to break it, and paints a picture of life over it. To do this, she must place herself at least partly "outside" or "over" that circle. She must *dissociate* herself from the form of life she is about to disclose. Nietzsche is far from insensitive to the philosophical difficulty here. In fact, he notes that this necessary dissociation is "a difficult, indeed hardly achievable task" (Nietzsche 2007, 361). What is interesting, however, is Nietzsche's description of where exactly the difficulty lies. The dissociation demanded by critical disclosure is so intricate because "everything contemporary is importunate; it affects and directs the eye even when the philosopher does not want it to; and in the total accounting it will involuntarily be appraised too high" (Nietzsche, 361f). Rather than normative or epistemological, the problem is for Nietzsche pragmatic through and thorough: given the self-perpetuating circularity of the current form of life, how could *any* form of social criticism be expected to come across as compelling and promising of practical success? The question turns then into: what exactly must the philosopher dissociate herself from and where can she withdraw to in order for the critique to succeed?

She must find a position outside the self-perpetuating circle of second and first nature. This position, as we have seen, Nietzsche already in the second *Untimely Meditation* terms "culture." In the third one, Nietzsche's term for the circle from which the physician must dissociate herself is "the state":

> I am concerned here with a species of man whose teleology extends somewhat beyond the welfare of a state, with philosophers, and with these only in relation to a world which is again fairly independent of the welfare of a state, that of culture. (2007, 365)

Somehow beyond the core societal organization of the form of life, from which the philosophical social critic needs to dissociate herself, there is according to Nietzsche the "fairly independent" "world" of "culture." This world, out of which the disclosing critic shall paint over the self-perpetuating circle of second and first nature, is, however, jeopardized by that very circle: "Now, how does the philosopher view the culture of our time? [H]e almost thinks that what he is seeing are the symptoms of a total extermination and uprooting of culture" (Nietzsche 2007, 366). The condition that the philosopher seeks to criticize, that is, the degeneration of social life to mere maintenance of its form, threatens the very possibility of critique. The social environment tends to reduce even educated individuals to organs, mere means, of society's self-maintenance: "The cultured man [*der Gebildete*] has degenerated [*abgeartet*] to the greatest enemy of culture [*Bildung*], for he wants lyingly to deny the existence of the universal sickness and thus obstructs the physicians" (Nietzsche 2007, 366). The self-perpetuating circle of second and first nature is the dystopian vision projected into the present of a sickness of social life, which affects not only individual components but its very *form*, a universal disease, a pathology affecting not only individual living beings but their species. It is a *social* pathology, since it hinders the characteristic plastic power of social life operating through transformative critique from culture. It prevents the cultural physicians from operating from within by denying them their operating theater:

In the times when physicians are required the most, in times of great plagues, they are also most in peril. For where are the physicians for modern mankind who themselves stand so firmly and soundly on their feet that they are able to support others and lead them by the hand? (Nietzsche 2007, 345f)

This is what Adorno later calls "*Bannkreis*," the vicious circle of a social second nature that continues into our individual first nature, thereby dismantling critique (Adorno 1965; see also Blili-Hamelin and Särkelä 2020; Särkelä 2020). "*Bann*" is Adorno's concept for those conditions that shape individuals into reinforcing a social environment that is hostile to their freedom and critical capacities. "*Bannkreis*" is his concept for the vicious circle by which those conditions are reproduced. Nietzsche is well aware of the problem of *Bann*: in fact, he even uses this very word when he, in the second *Untimely Meditation*, tells his reader that the "supreme commandment" is to "become mature and to flee from that paralyzing upbringing [*Erziehungsbann*] of the present age which sees its advantage in preventing your growth so as to rule and exploit you to the full while you are still immature" (2007, 295).

Not only the outside but also the inside is problematic: if our form of life reproduces itself as a vicious circle, how can efficient critical consciousness ever arise in it? How can a form of life, which continues into the innermost pre-intentional habitual and drive the structure of the individual be criticized from within?

Nietzsche's answer is that it cannot. At least not from within its institutional and educational core, the "state" and the "old-age." The critic needs a world of "culture" *beyond* the self-perpetuating circle of the state. Therefore, Nietzsche anchors *culture* in a world beyond any form of life claiming universality—in *nature*.[8]

CRITICAL COSMOLOGY

To map the place of culture in nature, Nietzsche turns in his third *Untimely Meditation* again to cosmological speculation and, indeed, he here further develops the conception of social life arising from the preceding *Meditation*. Again, Nietzsche stresses that a disclosing critique demands the "belief in a metaphysical significance of culture" (2007, 401; see also 372, 377f, 382, 399). Disclosure of the vicious circle requires metaphysics on behalf of critique, a *critical cosmology*.

In the third *Untimely Meditation*, Nietzsche's concept of self-perpetuating circularity is "animality." And he claims that we are yet to become "men," yet to raise ourselves above the animal. The self-perpetuating circle of second and first nature, enforced by antiquarian and monumental history, degenerates culture to merely self-maintaining animal life. Such a form of human social life is *culturally* dead: it means death to culture as the self-transformative mode of social life, because the individuals who are instructed and educated to adapt to their society as their social environment habitually reinforce it in its given shape.

Yet why should culture evolve in the first place? Nietzsche's metaphysical assumption is that the plastic power of nature itself seeks redemption from self-perpetuating circularity in recalcitrant individuals who strive to transform their environment:

> if all nature presses towards man, it thereby intimates that man is necessary for the redemption of nature from the curse of the life of the animal, and that in him existence at last holds up before itself a *mirror* in which life appears no longer senseless but in its metaphysical significance. Yet let us reflect: where does the animal cease, where does man begin?—man, who is nature's sole concern! As long as anyone desires life as he desires happiness he has not yet raised his eyes above the horizon of the animal, for he only desires more consciously what the animal seeks through blind impulse. But that is what we all do for the greater part of our lives: usually we fail to emerge out of animality, we ourselves are the animals whose suffering seems to be senseless. (Nietzsche 2007, 378; my emphasis)

That "animality" is an expression of the self-perpetuating circle becomes clear in the expression "horizon of the animal." Antiquarian and monumental history do exercise plastic power consciously, but they still do it within the form of a merely animal life, working to continue the form of life. The universal social sickness of the self-perpetuating circle makes individuals' relation to their form of life a mere continuation of animals' relation to their species. Like animals, the members of a thus degenerated form of human social life reduce themselves to instruments of the senseless continuation of the current form of life, now as an overpowering society that maintains itself through its individual members.

What explains this bizarre proposition that all nature presses toward man is the idea of plastic power and that Nietzsche associates our truly becoming "men" with the idea of culture, that is, the self-transformative mode of life: plastic power presses toward the achievement of the self-transformative mode. It is nature operating as plastic power directing itself toward itself and doing this not only *negatively* in the mode of critical history, but also *affirmatively, giving itself a positive form from what had been deviating content.*

Nietzsche's robust claim is that culture is the culmination of nature: "Culture [*Bildung*] is liberation" (2007, 341).

In the deviating individual of culture, "existence . . . holds up before itself a mirror," nature comes reflectively to itself. Nietzsche, the philologist, is utilizing the mirror—*speculum* in Latin—as the metaphor for the speculative character that the deviating practice of culture takes. Culture is nature's coming to itself in a speculative mode. Culture is therefore not alien to nature, but nature itself gives itself a determinate conceptual shape.

This might seem like a very dubious metaphysical claim. However, we do not need to commit ourselves to a vitalistic reading of plastic power as a life force causing nature to behave in certain ways; instead, we can read it in terms of a *critical cosmology*, a descriptive metaphysics sketched for the very purpose of critical disclosure. It is a metaphysics sketched in the course of critical practice for mapping the place of critical practice in nature. The cosmology of plastic power situates social critique within the realm of nature as the disclosure of a natural process for itself.

In fact, one could make the case that Nietzsche's claim that nature presses toward culture turns out rather Darwinian. If the animality of the state reduced individuals to mere means of its reproduction, then culture intensifies life's plastic power by taking control of its selective mechanism. This, I suggest, is Nietzsche's claim in the perhaps most provocative passage of the entire *Untimely Mediations*:

> How much one would like to apply to society and its goals something that can be learned from observation of any species of the animal or plant world: that *its only concern is the individual higher exemplar, the more uncommon, more powerful, more complex, more fruitful*—how much one would like to do this *if inculcated fancies as to the goal of society did not offer such tough resistance*! We ought really to have no difficulty in seeing that, *when a species has arrived at its limits and is about to go over into a higher species, the goal of its evolution lies... in those apparently scattered and chance existences which favourable conditions have here and there produced*; and it ought to be just as easy to understand the demand that, *because it can arrive at a conscious awareness of its goal, mankind ought to seek out and create the favourable conditions under which those great redemptive men can come into existence.* (2007, 384; my emphasis)

The challenge to the self-perpetuating circle of the form of life, the locus of its potential critical disclosure, lies in its *margins*, where favorable conditions produce deviations that might present legitimate challenges to the normative expectations embodied in its second nature. Now, Nietzsche's solution to the vicious circle that silences critique from within, and forbids it from the outside, starts from the observation that even the organic continuation of the

species, and thus also the self-maintenance of a form of social life degenerated to "animality," inevitably produces "scattered and chance existences" in
its margins. Every form of life relies on the *selection of arbitrary variations*
as a condition and consequence of its own reproduction.[9] Therefore, it is a
mistake to think of forms of life as having clear boundaries defining what is
inside and what remains outside. Rather, their limits are fluid. Their boundaries are potential thresholds of "go[ing] over into a higher species." They
are *margins* inhabited by scattered and chance existences with a distanced
perspective on the *core*.

Critical disclosure does then not need to assume a position in a clearly
defined "outside," or to remain in the supposedly unproblematic "inside" of
the criticized form of life. The form of life itself requires margins for its own
reproduction, and from these borderlands there is a distanced perspective
on the home state and a privileged view into foreign lands.[10] The horizon is
broadened from the margins.

Culture is a mode of social life that supports the overcoming of its own
form by favoring conditions in its margins. A form of social life with culture is one that fosters a second nature plastic and is powerful enough to
identify, take on, and support those borderland challenges. This Nietzsche
calls the promotion of "an evolving culture and the procreation of genius"
(2007, 358).

Nietzsche stresses that *every* individual living being is a unique variation, a
deviation from the form of life. Every individual has this potential for speculative recalcitrance. But realizing that potential demands a tremendous effort,
because the form of life itself tends to put it in *chains* (a circle!):

> Each of us bears a productive uniqueness within him as the core of his being;
> and when he becomes aware of it, there appears around him a strange penumbra
> which is the mark of his singularity. Most find this something unendurable,
> because . . . a chain of toil and burdens is suspended from this uniqueness [*weil
> an jener Einzigkeit eine Kette von Mühen und Lasten hängt*]. (Nietzsche 2007,
> 359)

The potential of each of us to present a challenge to the current form of life
is socially repressed: it is put in chains, that is, bound in the cold lifeless circle
of society which continues deep into the individual's relation to itself. This
is what Adorno in his sociological tracing of *Bannkreis* calls "concretism."
By "concretism," Adorno conceptualizes the socially caused inability of individuals "to resist their immediate interests" (Adorno 2019, 40), which averts
them from socially transformative action (see also Blili-Hamelin and Särkelä
2020). In a metaphoric vocabulary reminding of Nietzsche's *Untimely
Mediations*, Adorno describes concretism as the everyday social phenomenon

that the people who are given the burden, and consequently walk bent over with their heads bowed, that it has always been very hard for them to hold those heads up high [. . .] and see more than their immediate interests. (Adorno 2019, 41)

The consciousness of individuals is tied so firmly to the immediately given conditions that any critical reflection on them or attempt to reshape them becomes nearly unimaginable—it is put in chains. Adorno thinks that these chains are so hard to resist, because they alleviate the individuals' pain of experiencing their own impotence every day, finding themselves confronted with overwhelming social powers. Adorno calls this the "affective power" of *Bannkreis* (2019, 35). Adaptive pressure from the social environment affects the individuals with a "feeling of powerlessness" [*Gefühl der Ohnmacht*] (Adorno 1957, 213).

Similarly, Nietzsche describes the affect of being enclosed in the vicious circle as "suffocation" or "drowning,"[11] and disclosure as raising one's head above the surface to observe the stream:

we feel at the same time that we are too weak to endure those moments of profoundest contemplation for very long and that we are not the mankind towards which all nature presses for its redemption: it is already much that we should raise our head above the water at all, even if only a little, and observe what stream it is in which we are so deeply immersed. And even this momentary emerging and awakening is not achieved through our own power, we have to be lifted up—and who are they who lift us? (2007, 380)

Although each of us is a unique variation, not everyone has the plastic power to take on these affects of one's form of life and to turn them into a picture of a higher life: to be a physician of culture is an *art*. Her practice requires not only the methods and knowledge of a critical historian, which are necessary for the correct diagnosis, it also demands a certain sensibility for social suffering[12] and specific skills of turning knowledge into painting through that sensibility.

SPECULATIVE RECALCITRANCE: JUDGING, FEELING, PAINTING

The vicious circle can be broken by disclosing exemplarity coming from speculative recalcitrance at the margins of the form of life. Yet what is speculative recalcitrance? Clearly, not all deviations from the normative expectations embodied in the life form's second nature are critical and disclosing. Most of them are meaningless, futile, or downright wrongful. And, as we have seen, the intention to give them transformative power is mostly put in chains by concretism.

Nietzsche does, however, deliver criteria for conditions that speculative recalcitrance must meet in order to count as critical rather than just criminal. The critical exemplarity, which can truly challenge the allegedly universal form of present second nature and disclose its self-perpetuating circle, must thus include the *negativity of critical history*, making the present past, the *positivity of delivering a new picture of life*, modifying the social environment to something that can be freely affirmed, and a *sensibility for social suffering*, directing the negative and the positive tasks.

Speculative recalcitrance is then critical by virtue of its location in a certain conjunction of judgment, feeling, and speculation:

> there is a kind of denying and destroying that is the discharge of [a] mighty longing for sanctification and salvation [. . .] *All that exists that can be denied deserves to be denied*; and being truthful means: to believe in an existence that can in no way be denied and which is itself true and without falsehood. That is why the truthful man *feels* that the meaning of his activity is *metaphysical*, explicable through the *laws of another and higher life*, and in the profoundest sense *affirmative*: however much all that he does may appear to be destructive of the laws of this life and a crime against them. (Nietzsche 2007, 372; my emphasis)

Here, again, the practice of the disclosing critic looks much like some sort of *external critique*, a critique that judges the form of life on external criteria (Honneth 2009b; Stahl 2013, 26–30; Jaeggi 2018, 177f). After all, its meaning is expressed in "the laws of another and higher life." Note, however, that the laws of the higher life are not the basis of a judgment upon current life: the present form of life is "denied" on *its own terms*, whereas the laws of the other life are instead "in the profoundest sense affirmative." The disclosed higher life is therefore not a normative standard for the negative judgment of the current form of life. On the contrary, it presents a speculative hypothesis of a life worth affirming derived from "feeling" and "denying" current life.

Not only would it be misleading to represent the cultural physician's disclosing critique as an external judgment on the current form of life, but it would also be wrong to reduce her practice of critique to judgment as such. Following the negative judgment on the current form of life then comes *speculation*. Nietzsche describes the speculative task as being *felt*: as a *meta*physician, the physician of culture lets herself be *affected* by the plastic power in the form of life and channels that affect into a transformative practice. Remember that Nietzsche described the affirmative task as "painting." Metaphysical speculation thus presents a kind of poetic re-description of life following the scientific, critical-historical refutation of the form of life. A physician is both a scientist and an artist.

Speculation *grows out of* the refutation with the task of expressing a higher life to be affirmed. Because speculative recalcitrance arises from the felt suffering and immanent negation of the current form of life, the physician of culture is a disclosing critic in both negating the present form of life and affirming new life *in one and the same circular expression*. Her refutation of the present is accompanied by the expression of a higher form of life already present yet repressed, shoveled to the margins, as it were. This involves metaphysical speculation as an artistic enterprise. Disclosing critique *involves* judgment but cannot be *reduced* to it: it must include also feeling and speculation.

The critic, Nietzsche stresses, suffers in order to overcome the suffering of the present (2007, 373f). This is her immense plastic power: she lets herself be affected by the current social environment and channels those affects into something higher. Instead of devastation, her plastic power turns her suffering into a "longing for a stronger nature, for a healthier and simpler humanity" (Nietzsche 2007, 362f). She turns undergoing into doing, re-shapes what is shaping her: "That heroism of truthfulness consists in one day ceasing to be the toy [the eternal becoming] plays with" (Nietzsche 2007, 374).

Speculative recalcitrance is then a *specific type* of individual deviation from the normative expectations crystallized in the second nature of the form of life. It requires (a) becoming aware of one's uniqueness, the extent to which one deviates from the second nature to which the antiquarians seek to "train" us; (b) expressing this deviation in a way that truly challenges the current self-perpetuating circle of second and first nature; and (c) doing so as the member of a specific kind of community, which Nietzsche calls a "circle of culture." Let's call the first condition "self-reflexivity," the second "critical creativity," and the third "antiauthoritarian community." Becoming reflexive of one's deviation is part of dissociating oneself from the self-perpetuating circle and participating in its de-centering (*diagnosis*). Expressing this deviation is part of delivering something positive to affirm and participating in the re-centering movement (*cure*).

CIRCLES OF CULTURE: EDUCATION
FROM THE MARGINS

Disclosing critique does not, at least not necessarily, operate by universal normative standards. Therefore, it does also not rely on "external standards," as it is sometimes assumed (Honneth 2007). Instead, it is defined pragmatically: disclosing critique is defined by its *disclosing effects*. It can approach rationality by means of an immanent negation that leads up to the expression of a *particular* experience from the life form's margins, an expression of life; this refutation, and the speculation to which it gives rise, challenges the alleged universality of a form of life enclosed in a self-perpetuating circle. In other words, instead of external universal standards, disclosing critique can operate by *marginal exemplarity*. However, to fulfill the requirement of being compelling as a form of criticism, disclosing critique relies on its disclosing effects. Eventually, this reliance makes it constitutively dependent on its reception, that is, on the capacity of its expression to become effective in the practice of the addressees. It achieves, as it were, its rationality in execution.

Because of the reliance on reception, disclosing critique cannot be practiced alone. This makes it an *educational* project. Practicing disclosing critique in this educational sense presupposes recalcitrant individuals who are willing to grow beyond themselves by learning from examples. Disclosing critique requires that these scattered chance existences in the borderlands organize themselves as *antiauthoritarian communities*. Such communities constitute what Nietzsche calls "circles of culture."[13]

Like antiquarian training and monumentalist internal criticism, such communities exhibit power asymmetries between educators and disciples. But Nietzsche is confident that this time around the purpose of education is not just to adapt individuals to the environment nor merely to adjust it. Rather, it is to transform oneself by transforming the form of life: "your educators can be only your liberators [*Befreier*]" (Nietzsche 2007, 341). Disclosing critique of the form of life is an educational project that focuses not on the concrete universal, as do antiquarian training and monumentalist internal criticism. By provocation and exaggeration, it instead seeks to initiate a learning process among the members of the form of life to let themselves be compelled by the picture of life emerging from the margins. It focuses our attention toward those among us who do not conform and, more precisely, who do not conform in the specific mode of self-reflexivity and critical creativity characteristic of speculative recalcitrance.

The power asymmetries in these communities cannot resemble those of antiquarian training and monumentalist internal criticism. Nietzsche emphasizes that in these communities the asymmetries must be shaped such that education becomes an issue of helping the recipients to elevate themselves to "culture," because "they long for a culture, for a transfigured *physis*" (2007, 361f). He also underlines that this tendency to the capacity to be educated is something we all already possess: "we [already] know what culture is" (Nietzsche 2007, 383). The disclosing critic then avoids making the recipient "malicious and envious" and instead helps him to "turn his soul in another direction so that it shall not consume itself in vain longing" (Nietzsche 2007, 381). When she has helped the recipient to turn his soul, "he will *discover* a new circle" (Nietzsche 2007, 381). The discovery of what has been disclosed must be undertaken by the *recipients themselves*.

Nietzsche identifies three phases of the reception of disclosure, three "consecrations to culture": "love," "judgment," and "deed" (2007, 385f). "[L]ove alone," he writes, "can bestow on the soul, not only a clear, discriminating and self-contemptuous view of itself, but also the desire to look beyond itself and to seek with all its might for a higher self as yet still concealed from it" (Nietzsche 2007, 385). The disclosure of one's higher self proceeds through "attach[ing]" one's "heart" to an educator and "hat[ing] one's own narrowness" (Nietzsche 2007, 385). Love corresponds then to the first condition for speculative recalcitrance I dubbed above "self-reflexivity": becoming aware of one's uniqueness, one's deviation from the expectations of the antiquarian trainers.[14]

"Judgment" marks the "rediscover[y]" of the "great world of action"; one applies one's newly discovered longing for culture as "the alphabet by means · of which [one] can now read off the aspirations of mankind as a whole" (Nietzsche 2007, 386). One passes, in other words, a critical judgment on the form of life, diagnoses it as ill, and exaggerates it as already dead. "Deed," finally, means the "struggle on behalf of culture and hostility towards those influences, habits, laws, institutions in which [one] fails to recognize [one's] goal" (Nietzsche 2007, 386). The educated goes on to actively modify the social environment as part of her own education and social transformation as part of self-transformation. Judgment and deed then correspond to the second condition of speculative recalcitrance, "critical creativity," expressing one's deviation in a way that challenges the current self-perpetuating circle of second and first nature.

The recipients then perform the disclosure *themselves* in becoming speculatively recalcitrant. Note that, similarly to the initiation by which the form of life maintains itself (training and internal criticism), the disclosing initiation to culture is a *circle*. In fact, this initiation *is* the "circle of culture." Through love, the individual molds her first nature, re-shapes her impulses, and re-directs her instincts by new habituation, a modification of her individual second nature. Through judgment and deed, she then returns to a new social environment, that of an antiauthoritarian community. It is, however, not the old kind of initiation that pulls the margins toward the core, but a new kind that *de-centers* the form of life.

In the initiation into a "circle of culture," the de-centering movement of critical disclosure is completed. Yet, how is the re-centering movement of disclosure to be understood? Wherein does the affirmative aspect of disclosing recalcitrance lie? What shape shall the philosopher *cum* artist paint over the gray old shape of life in multicolor? What does her "picture of life" represent?

Nietzsche recognizes the urgency of these issues and seeks to respond to them:

The hardest task still remains: to say how a new circle of duties may be derived from this ideal and how one can proceed towards so *extravagant* a goal through a practical activity [*regelmässige Tätigkeit*]—in short, to demonstrate that this ideal *educates*. (2007, 376; my emphasis)

What the philosopher paints over the vicious circle is *another circle*. "The hardest task" for a disclosing critique of forms of life is to be not merely destructive and speculative, but also educative. In other words, disclosing critique must go beyond the refutation of the current form of life and the painting of higher life to actually participating in the establishment of a new *form* of life, that is, a new crystallization of normative expectations in a social second nature. Like the instruction it opposes, it too involves *formation*, the initiation of individuals into the second nature of a form of life. It must complete the de-centering education of the marginal "circle of culture" with a re-centering education.[15]

That the speculative painting must amount to a "new circle of duties" means at least two things: first, the transformative must also be reproducible. The re-centering result must be a new *circle*, that is, a social second nature shaping our individual first nature with greater plastic power. The difficulty is to establish this new mode of habitual and customary practice according to an *extravagant* goal, something disclosed beyond the path that social life has so far traversed (*extra* + *vagari*). The danger is namely that the critic's "dignity and loftiness can only turn our heads and thereby exclude us from any participation in the world of action; coherent duties, the even flow of life are gone" (Nietzsche 2007, 376). Nietzsche's disclosing critic stumbles on a robust demand for immanence. Critique has to hit its target. But this relation of immanence between the critic and the object is not so much a question of normative criteria as of the practicality of critique: it is a predominantly pragmatic issue. The disclosed new path, as extravagant as it may seem, must be *traversable*. It must express a "new circle of duties," which are fulfillable for the higher selves that this formation is to disclose in us. Disclosure has to materialize in a new *form* of life, that is to say in new habits, customs, and institutions.

Second, that new circle must establish a new normativity of antiquarian and monumental education. This is why Nietzsche describes the result of disclosure as a new circle of *duties* and emphasizes it as a "*regelmässige Tätigkeit*," a customary activity, an action shaped and stabilized by modified habits. This requires that "from that ideal image it is possible to fasten upon ourselves a chain of fulfillable duties, and that some of us already feel the weight of this chain" (Nietzsche 2007, 377). The painting must actually be *affirmable*. The affirmability of the painting includes that the duties must be fulfillable by the higher selves of current living human beings. The disclosed form of life must be felt by some members of the current form of life, the "duties" it implies must be fulfillable by those who would be its partakers, and some of those of the current form of life must be receptive to the philosopher's disclosing education.

However, even if the new form of life includes moments of antiquarian training and monumentalist internal criticism, it cannot present a self-perpetuating circle of second and first nature. Instead, the new picture of life, which the physician of culture paints over the old circle, presents a form of life that is plastic and powerful enough to embrace the creative social recalcitrance coming from such antiauthoritarian communities; a life in which individual living beings are plastic and powerful enough to hang their hearts on critical educators and challenge their form of life, that is, to enter antiauthoritarian communities.

In the meantime, the antiauthoritarian community at the margin of the old form can itself serve as a lab for that new form of life. In that community, not only the negativity of the self-perpetuating circularity is *felt* but also the already new positivity. The margin operates as a mediator between the old and the new center of the form of life. The community, the circle of culture, channels the negative affect of the old form of life into the positive affect of a higher life, which can be expressed in speculation and established through the formation. The margin then presents to the core a picture of life that claims exemplary force for the formation of social life. The circle turns into a circle of circles that shifts it toward a spiral movement.

Three pragmatic demands of immanence of re-centering disclosure can then be identified: (a) the new duties must be fulfillable for (the higher selves of) current actors; (b) the coming form of life must be already felt by some (marginal) participants of the current form of life; and (c) some members of the current form of life must be receptive to disclosing education.

EXCAVATING THE (META)PHYSICIAN OF CULTURE

In the second *Untimely Meditation*, Nietzsche presents life as a process that must both maintain a form and transform. A form of life must both reproduce itself and grow out of itself. Life can fail at both tasks. Then it would either stagnate or die. To grow, in particular, the life-process, furthermore, must both relate to its past and break away from it. The operation of plastic power, that is, the way in which a form of life relates back upon itself so as to grow out of itself and into its new, higher "self," essentially both requires and repels "history." It must both dwell on its past and let it go. It must make the past present by adapting individuals to the environment and adjusting the environment through the individuals, but also make the present past by letting individuals transform the environment in the course of their self-transformation. History is the specific way a social life-process relates back upon itself to design, shape itself. Because social life evolves by such a mechanism of self-design, social criticism has a primarily aesthetic character. Nietzschean social criticism is then *not* a type of judgment. Although it certainly involves judgments, it cannot be reduced to judgment. Instead, it is a kind of design, an artistic practice. But there is also room for science, namely in killing the old form of life by demonstrating its suffocating circularity. In the figure of the physician, the scientist and the artist merge.

In the third *Untimely Meditation*, Nietzsche presents the extravagant cosmology of the (meta)physician of culture as emerging from a specific type of individual deviation, namely what I have, paraphrasing Lovibond, termed "speculative recalcitrance," as an attempt to disclose the suffocating form that social life has come to take under a self-perpetuating circle of second and first nature. This circle presents a "universal sickness." It is the alleged universal form of life itself that has become pathological. The task of the physician of culture is to diagnose and cure the life enclosed in that form. The cure demands pre-existing receptivity for disclosure in the guise of antiauthoritarian communities. Like any physician, she can only help individuals to help themselves. By drawing the current circle in the mode of critical history and painting a new circle over it in a speculative mode, she helps her recipients to lift themselves up: they eventually have to perform the disclosure themselves as active participants of formation in antiauthoritarian communities.

Toward the end of the second *Untimely Meditation*, Nietzsche says: "Only give me life, then I will create a culture for you out of it" (2007, 119f). Nietzsche here paraphrases Archimedes: "δῶς μοι πᾶ στῶ καὶ τὰν γᾶν κινάσω" (*Give me the place to stand, and I shall turn the world*). That makes Nietzsche say: "give me a position outside our form of life, and I shall transform it." This is Ralph Waldo Emerson's idea of "drawing a new circle," which Nietzsche refers to later in the third *Meditation*. The artist takes a position outside our horizon so as to expand our horizon. However, part of the metaphysical baggage with which early Nietzsche's example of disclosing critique comes is intended for showing that the limits of a form of life are always fluid like those of natural species—as we understand them at least since Darwin. Rather than clear boundaries, forms of life have margins and borderlands inhabited by recalcitrant individuals. When these individuals in antiauthoritarian communities help each other to help themselves to lift themselves up, the form of life has been de-centered and the re-centering formation can begin. From the margins, one sees beyond the center's horizon. And the higher one rises, the further it will span.

Let me conclude by rephrasing four points. First, the cosmology of plastic power is nothing separate from the early Nietzsche's social criticism. In fact, it is this cosmology that allows his project of social criticism to proceed as the "praxis" of a physician of culture, diagnosing and curing social pathologies. Second, such speculatively recalcitrant social criticism is part and parcel of its own object, "social life." Social life is namely the kind of life that refers to critical disclosure as one of its three ways to modify its form. Third, the critical practice of the physician of culture is *immanent* in the sense of speaking from within life, that is, with the authority of life, responding to the requirements of plastic power; and yet it is *disclosing* too, in the sense of speaking from without the form of life, at least from outside its core, that is, from an "Archimedean point" in its margins in order to expand the concept of what we are. Fourth, as such an operator of plastic power, of life's activity of redesigning itself, social criticism has a primarily aesthetic character. It aims not at the judgment but mobilizes judgment as a phase of redesign. The physician is simultaneously a scientist and an artist. Therefore, Nietzsche develops an aesthetic metaphysics for critical purposes—a critical cosmology. "Critical" does not, however, mean negative. In contrast to his later minimalist metaphysics of the will to power (see Miyasaki 2013), the cosmology of plastic power has positive content: It develops a performative theory of nature that explains how the physician of culture, the disclosing critic, can operate from within and outside her form of life.

NOTES

1. For helpful comments and criticisms I am grateful to Amy Allen, Borhane Blili-Hamelin, Robin Celikates, Martin Hartmann, Federica Gregoratto, Arto Laitinen, Otto Linderborg, Italo Testa, Thomas Wallgren, and to the many commentators, who shall go unnamed, at the Power 2018 Conference at Tampere University, in the von Wright-Wittgenstein Research Seminar at the University of Helsinki, and at the conference "Social Critique and the Concept of Nature" at the University of Lucerne, where I had the pleasure of discussing earlier drafts of this chapter.
2. On Nietzsche's diagnosis of social pathologies in his later works, see Neuhouser (2014).
3. Leibniz maintains that not all beings have souls but that those that do have memory: "on appelle *Ames* seulement celles dont le perception est plus distincte et accompagnée de memoire" (Leibniz 1965, § 19).
4. Yet where does life's plastic power come from? Is plastic power some kind of a vitalistic life force, a power-causing growth, as it were, from behind the life process? Or is it merely a form of life process that has been selected? Often Nietzsche is read as a vitalist (see Danto 1965; Deleuze 1962; Richardson 1996; Schacht 1983): life is then characterized by a particular kind of force driving its development and

growth. Plastic power would be a kind of Bergsonian *élan vital*, the principle of a basic ontology of life. It has been suggested that the later Nietzsche's notion of "will to power" ought to be read as such a cosmic life force (Deuleuze 1962; Richardson 1996). This is a highly problematic conception: first, today, we know that we can explain evolutionary processes without postulating any vital forces pushing life processes forward. This explanation relies on the mechanism of a natural selection of arbitrary variation in individuals. Second, as Donovan Miyasaki puts it, the vitalistic reading "clearly oversteps the boundaries of Nietzsche's naturalism by treating the will to power as a metaphysical substance: a force that is self-identical and underlies all changeable, sensible properties" (Miyasaki 2013). It is also possible not to read Nietzsche's "plastic power" in the vitalistic sense of a "life-force" lurking behind and causing the movement of the life-process. The advantage of early Nietzsche's aesthetic metaphysics of plastic power is that its rather poetic expression allows for a less vitalistic reading too. Plastic power could thus be something itself designed by the process of life's evolution. In this reading, *plastic power has evolved*. It presents a characteristic of life that has been selected. Its concept describes the way in which a process, which is living, relates back upon itself so as to maintain itself by growing. It describes a mode of process in the world that constantly deals with the contrasting drives to both maintain its form and transform. For this reason, Nietzsche qualifies plastic power as a "develop[ing] out of oneself" (2007, 251). The important thing to note is that "plastic power" would then be *ontologically* basic for life, yet *genetically* secondary to natural selection. John Richardson has developed both readings with regards to the "will to power," that is, as a basic ontological (Richardson 1996) and as a selected trait (Richardson 2004). A question is whether the selectionist view could accommodate the basic ontological view. Then the kind of growth that "plastic power" describes would be something selected as basic for life; its selection would not make it ontologically less basic. Whereas interpreters from both camps tend to ascribe some sort of vitalism to Nietzsche at the outset and only disagree as to the extent to which this can be amended to Darwinism, Barbara Stiegler (2021) instead reads Nietzsche here as struggling with a topic that later becomes pivotal *within* Darwinian evolutionary theory itself, as scholars such as Richard Lewontin and Stephen Jay Gould come to stress the activity of organisms, that is, the power of individual living beings to construct their environment. In fact, this became rather quickly an issue within Darwinian philosophy: already John Dewey developed a thorough reading of Darwin stressing the need both to get rid of original forces and to conceive of individual living beings as creative with regard to their environments (Dewey 1907; 1917; see also Särkelä 2015). A similar conception of Darwinian evolution was later developed by Whitehead (1971).

5. On the significance of "first" and "second nature" for contemporary social philosophy, see Lovibond 2002 and Testa 2007.

6. For a helpful articulation of the idea of "first" and "second nature" as interchangeable placeholder concepts in Dewey, see Testa 2017. James Conant has attempted a socio-philosophical extension of Nietzsche's moral perfectionism that also works with the concepts of first and second nature. Surprisingly, Conant, who in his impressive reading of Nietzsche's moral perfectionism focuses on the third *Untimely*

Meditation, completely ignores Nietzsche's conception of first and second nature in the second *Untimely Meditation* and disregards the processual placeholding character of "first" and "second nature." Instead, Conant's socio-philosophical extension of Nietzsche's perfectionism starts with the idea that Nietzsche not only asks about the possible perfection of individual persons but also that of entire forms of life (Conant 2014, 337f). This overlooks, however, the disclosing intent in early Nietzsche's social philosophy: The cultural physician's task is less to perfect a given form of life than to help the individuals to challenge and eventually transform their own form of life.

7. Hollingdale translates this as "train[ing] up" and, somewhat confusingly, as "adjustment."

8. Somewhat similarly in the contemporary debate, Luc Boltanski distinguishes between "reality" and "world"; whereas "reality" exhibits a more or less determinate order, which social critique might ontologically challenge, the "world" is more or less chaotic and indeterminate. Social criticism can ontologically challenge social reality by assembling elements from the "world" (Boltanski 2011, 57–61).

9. See also Stiegler's contribution to this volume. She writes: "Without the mal-adapted, who take the risk of experimenting with other ways of living, there would never be evolution."

10. The de-centering disclosure liberates from what David Owen (2002) has termed "restricted consciousness" by the example of a marginal perspective. However, by virtue of including re-centering disclosure, disclosing critique is a more encompassing critical project than Owen's account of genealogy as a criticism of restricted consciousness.

11. On asphyxiation as a metaphorical net of social critique, see Särkelä 2018, part 3.

12. For the role that the category of social suffering can play in social critique, see Renault (2017).

13. In her criticism of both Rawls' and Cavell' interpretations of the third *Untimely Meditation*, Vanessa Lemm has emphasized this critical and agonistic character of (the circles of) culture: "The aim of culture is to criticize given institutionalized forms of social and political life and eventually to overcome them, fostering freer forms of life, both on the level of the individual and on the level of social and political organization" (Lemm 2007, 14).

14. On Nietzschean perfectionism about love, see Gregoratto (Forthcoming), chapters 2 and 6, in particular.

15. An ongoing example for a turn from de- to re-centering disclosure could be Greta Thunberg and the Fridays for Future movement. Thunberg's example helps to disclose an enclosure in our current form of life, to elevate others to participate in the movement that tends to function as an educative antiauthoritarian community. It remains to see whether she will succeed in re-centering our form of life.

REFERENCES

Adorno, Theodor W. 1957. "Die menschliche Gesellschaft heute" in *Nachgelassene Schriften: Abteilung V. Band I.*, M. Schwarz (ed.). Frankfurt a. M.: Suhrkamp.

Adorno, Theodor W. 1969. "Society," *Salmagundi*, 10 (11): 144–53.

Adorno, Theodor W. 2006. *History and Freedom: Lectures 1964–1965*. Cambridge: Polity Press.

Adorno, Theodor W. 2019. *Philosophical Elements of a Theory of Society*, W. Hoban (trans.). Cambridge: Polity Press.

Blili-Hamelin, Borhane, and Särkelä, Arvi. 2020. "Unsocial Society: Adorno, Hegel, and Social Antagonisms," in *Hegel and the Frankfurt School*, P. Giladi (ed.). London: Routledge.

Boltanski, Luc. 2011. *On Critique: A Sociology of Emancipation*. Cambridge: Polity Press.

Butler, Judith. 1997. *The Psychic Life of Power: Theories in Subjection*. Stanford: Stanford University Press.

Conant, James. 2014. *Friedrich Nietzsche: Perfektionismus & Perspektivismus*. Konstanz: Konstanz University Press.

Danto, Arthur. 1965. *Nietzsche as Philosopher*. New York: Columbia University Press.

Deleuze, Gilles. 1983. *Nietzsche and Philosophy*. New York: Columbia University Press.

Dewey, John. 1917. "The Need for a Recovery of Philosophy," in *The Collected Works of John Dewey 1882–1953 (Early Works, Middle Works, and Late Works)*, J. A. Boydston (ed.), MW 10. Carbondale: Southern Illinois University Press.

Dewey, John. 2008. "The Influence of Darwinism on Philosophy," in *The Collected Works of John Dewey 1882–1953 (Early Works, Middle Works, and Late Works)*, J. A. Boydston (ed.), MW 4. Carbondale: Southern Illinois University Press.

Emerson, Ralph W. 1983a. "Self-Reliance," in *Essays and Lectures*, 257–82. New York: Library of America.

Emerson, Ralph W. 1983b. "Circles," in *Essays and lectures*, 401–14. New York: Library of America.

Fischbach, Franck. 2009. *Manifeste pour une philosophie sociale*. Paris: La Découverte.

Foucault, Michel. 2001. "Nietzsche, Genealogy, History," in *Nietzsche*, J. Richardson, and B. Leiter (eds.), 139–64. Oxford: Oxford University Press.

Freyenhagen, Fabian. 2015. "Honneth on Social Pathologies: A critique," *Critical Horizons*, 16 (2): 131–52.

Gregoratto, Federica. (Forthcoming). *Love Troubles: A Social Philosophy of Eros*.

Hampe, Michael. 2018. *What Philosophy Is for*. Chicago: University of Chicago Press.

Hegel, Georg W. F. 2008. *Outlines of the Philosophy of Right*, T. M. Knox (trans.), S. Houlgate (ed.). Oxford: Oxford University Press.

Hirvonen, Onni. 2018. "On the Ontology of Social Pathologies," *Studies in Social and Political Thought*, 28: 9–14.

Honneth, Axel. 2007a. "The Possibility of a Disclosing Critique of Society: The Dialectic of Enlightenment in Light of Current Debates in Social Criticism," in *Disrespect: The Normative Foundations of Critical Theory*, 49–62. Cambridge: Polity Press.

Honneth, Axel. 2007b. "Pathologies of the Social: The Past and Present of Social Philosophy," in *Disrespect: The Normative Foundations of Critical Theory*, J. Ganahl (trans.). Cambridge: Polity Press.

Honneth, Axel. 2009a. "A Social Pathology of Reason: On the Intellectual Legacy of Critical Theory," in *Pathologies of Reason: On the Legacy of Critical Theory*, J. Hebbeler (trans.). New York: Columbia University Press.

Honneth, Axel. 2009b. "Reconstructive Social Criticism with a Genealogical Proviso: On the Idea of Critique in the Frankfurt School," in *Pathologies of Reason: On the Legacy of Critical Theory*, J. Ingram (trans.), 43–53. New York: Columbia University Press.

Honneth, Axel. 2014. "The Diseases of Society: Approaching a Nearly Impossible Concept," A. Särkelä (trans.), *Social Research*, 81 (3): 683–703.

Jaeggi, Rahel. 2018. *Critique of Forms of Life*. Cambridge, MA: Belknap Press.

Jaeggi, Rahel, and Celikates, Robin. 2017. *Sozialphilosophie: Eine Einführung*. Munich: Beck.

Laitinen, Arto. 2015. "Social Pathologies, Reflexive Pathologies, and the Idea of Higher-Order Disorders," *Studies in Social and Political Thought*, 25: 44–65.

Laitinen, Arto, and Särkelä, Arvi. 2018. "Analyzing Conceptions of Social Pathology: Eight Questions," *Studies in Social and Political Thought*, 28: 21–30.

Laitinen, Arto, and Särkelä, Arvi. 2019. "Four Conceptions of Social Pathology," *European Journal of Social Theory*, 22 (1): 80–102.

Leibniz, Gottfried. 1965. "Monadology" in *Monadology and Other Philosophical Essays*. Indianapolis: Bobbs-Merrill Company.

Lemm, Vanessa. 2007. "Is Nietzsche a Perfectionist? Rawls, Cavell, and the Politics of Culture in Nietzsche's 'Schopenhauer as Educator,'" *Journal of Nietzsche Studies*, 34: 5–27.

Lovibond, Sabina. 2002. *Ethical Formation*. Cambridge, MA: Harvard University Press.

McDowell, John. 1994. *Mind and World*. Cambridge, MA: Harvard University Press.

Miyasaki, Donovan. 2013. "The Will to Power as Naturalist Critical Ontology," *History of Philosophy Quarterly*, 30 (3): 251–69.

Neuhouser, Frederick. 2014. "Nietzsche on Spiritual Illness and Its Promise," *Journal of Nietzsche Studies*, 45 (3): 293–314.

Neuhouser, Frederick. 2016. "Hegel on Social Ontology and the Possibility of Pathology," in *I that Is We, We that Is I. Pespectives on Contemporary Hegel*, I. Testa, and L. Ruggiu (eds.). Leiden: Brill.

Nietzsche, Friedrich. 2007. *Untimely Meditations*, D. Breazeale (ed.), R. J. Hollingdale (trans.). Cambridge: Cambridge University Press.

Owen, David. 2002. "Criticism and Captivity: On Genealogy and Critical Theory," *European Journal of Philosophy*, 10 (2): 216–30.

Renault, Emmanuel. 2017. *Social Suffering: Sociology, Psychology, Politics*. London: Rowman and Littlefield.

Richardson, John. 1996. *Nietzsche's System*. Oxford: Oxford University Press.

Richardson, John. 2004. *Nietzsche's New Darwinism*. Oxford: Oxford University Press.

Rorty, Richard. 1998. "Dewey between Hegel and Darwin," in *Truth and Progress*. Cambridge: Cambridge University Press.

Saar, Martin. 2002. "Genealogy and Subjectivity," *European Journal of Philosophy*, 10 (2): 231–45.

Saar, Martin. 2008. "Understanding Genealogy: History, Power, and the Self," *Journal of the Philosophy of History*, 2 (3): 295–314.

Särkelä, Arvi. 2015. "Der Einfluss des Darwinismus auf Dewey: Metaphysik als Hypothese," *Deutsche Zeitschrift für Philosophie*, 63 (6): 1099–123.

Särkelä, Arvi. 2017. "Degeneration of Associated Life: Dewey's Naturalism about Social Criticism," *Transactions of the Charles S. Peirce Society*, 53: 107–26.

Särkelä, Arvi. 2018. *Immanente Kritik und soziales Leben: Selbsttransformative Praxis nach Hegel und Dewey*. Frankfurt a. M.: Klostermann.

Särkelä, Arvi. 2020. "Negative Organicism: Adorno, Emerson, and the Idea of a Disclosing Critique of Society," *Critical Horizons*, 21 (3): 222–39.

Särkelä, Arvi, and Laitinen, Arto. 2019. "Between Normativism and Naturalism: Honneth on Social Pathology," *Constellations*, 26 (2): 286–300.

Schacht, Richard. 1983. *Nietzsche*. New York: Routledge.

Spinoza, Baruch. 2003. *Ethics*, in *Complete Works*, M. L. Morgan (ed.), S. Shirley (trans.), Indianapolis: Hackett Publishing.

Stahl, Titus. 2013. *Immanente Kritik: Elemente einer Theorie sozialer Praktiken*. Frankfurt a. M.: Campus Verlag.

Stiegler, Barbara. 2001. *Nietzsche et la biologie*. Paris: Presses Universitaires de France.

Stiegler, Barbara. 2021. "1880: First Philosophical Critique of Adaptationism: Nietzsche, Reader of Herbert Spencer," in this volume.

Testa, Italo. 2007. "Criticism from within Nature: The Dialectic between First and Second Nature from McDowell to Adorno," *Philosophy and Social Criticism*, 33 (4): 473–97.

Testa, Italo. 2017. "Dewey, Second Nature, Social Criticism, and the Hegelian Heritage," *European Journal of Pragmatism and American Philosophy*, 9 (1): 1–23.

Thomä, Dieter. 2015. "'Falling in Love with Becoming: Remarks on Nietzsche and Emerson," in *Nietzsche and the Becoming of Life*, Vanessa Lemm (ed.), 265–79. New York: Fordham University Press.

Walzer, Michael. 1987. *Interpretation and Social Criticism*. Cambridge, MA: Harvard University Press.

Whitehead, Alfred N. 1971. *The Function of Reason*. Boston: Beacon Press.

Wittgenstein, Ludwig. 1978. *Remarks on the Foundations of Mathematics*. G. E. M. Anscombe (ed. and trans.). Cambridge, MA: MIT Press.

Zurn, Christopher. 2011. "Social Pathologies as Second-Order Disorders," in *Axel Honneth: Critical essays. With a reply by Axel Honneth*, D. Petherbridge (ed.), 345–70. Leiden: Brill.

Chapter 11

"The Sickness of a Time"

Social Pathology and Therapeutic Philosophy

Sabina Lovibond

In a passage dating from the late 1930s, Wittgenstein writes:

> The sickness of a time is cured by an alteration in the mode of life of human beings, and it was possible for the sickness of philosophical problems to get cured only through a changed mode of thought and of life, not through a medicine invented by an individual. Think of the use of the motor-car producing or encouraging certain sicknesses, and mankind being plagued by such sickness until, from some cause or other, as a result of some development or other, it abandons the habit of driving. (Wittgenstein 1978, § 23)[1]

The medical analogy deployed here is obviously in keeping with Wittgenstein's conception of his (later) philosophical method as therapeutic. But the relevant notions of sickness, health, and therapy are not altogether easy to pin down. My aim in the present discussion will be to clarify these and also to get clearer about the "changed mode of thought and of life" which Wittgenstein has in mind for himself—and presumably for his implied reader.

The phrase just quoted may not be what we expect to hear from the writer who also, and famously, said that philosophy "leaves everything as it is" (Wittgenstein 1967, § 124). Surely (we may think) if philosophy made us aware of the need for an alteration in our mode of thought and life, it would *not* leave everything as it is, but induce some kind of conversion experience.

But before proceeding further, we need to put the *Investigations* passage into context. "Leaving everything as it is" is opposed, on one hand, to "interfering with the actual use of language"; on the other, to "giving it (i.e., the actual use of language) a foundation." What we are to understand is that philosophy leaves everything as it is with respect to the legitimacy, or normative "groundedness," of the language-game. And this thought is not meant to be in any way at variance with the therapeutic conception of philosophy, which does of course turn on the idea that philosophy can make a difference to the various localized pathologies—the various forms of "bewitchment of our intelligence by means of language" (Wittgenstein 1967, § 109)—that give rise to philosophical problems. If such inquiries work as therapy, then they must indeed be making a difference—not leaving our "bewitched" *mental condition* as it is.

The therapeutic intention of the *Philosophical Investigations* is to replace the bewitched condition with one in which we "*command a clear view* of the use of our words," or arrive at a "perspicuous representation" (Wittgenstein 1967, § 122) of familiar linguistic phenomena. The method works by "assembling reminders for a particular purpose" (Wittgenstein 1967, § 127)—for instance, at § 503, which seeks to dissuade us from thoughts on the lines of "this is only words, and I have got to get behind the words," and where the aim is to reinstate our ordinary "contentment" with the communicative powers of the words at our disposal. This is the kind of contentment coordinated with Wittgensteinian "quietism," properly understood. However, it would seem that in the view of Wittgenstein we *fail* to be content where we *ought* to be content. And, if this failure gives rise, in a systematic way, to a range of philosophical problems, it can plausibly be regarded as a pathological symptom—that symptom with which it is the business of a therapeutic philosophy to concern itself.

But surely we will be taking a wrong turn if we attribute to Wittgenstein the thought that there is one *underlying* pathology, which gives rise to the problems in a *systematic* way. Won't this make it impossible to give due weight to his conviction that "what is hidden [. . .] is of no interest to us" (Wittgenstein 1967, § 126), or to the self-conscious pluralism of his later method, as captured in the words from *King Lear*: "I'll teach you differences," which he was thinking of using as a motto for the *Investigations* (Rhees 1984, 157)?[2]

The question of the degree of generality or systematicity displayed by Wittgenstein's later writings is an awkward one, always liable to lead to a stand-off between the well-meaning commentator and some quick-witted person in the audience who will say: "'Meaning as use,' yes, by all means— but if you treat that as a master-key, aren't you making him out to be just another kind of linguistic essentialist?"

There is unlikely to be a warm welcome for the suggestion that we should refrain from any general reflection on language, for fear of being drawn into some harmful form of metaphysical speculation. Here, though, it may be helpful to revisit the important declaration of principle at § 133:

[T]he clarity that we are aiming at in indeed *complete* clarity. But this simply means that the philosophical problems should *completely* disappear.
The real discovery is the one that makes me capable of stopping doing philosophy when I want to.—The one that gives philosophy peace, so that it is no longer tormented by questions which bring *itself* in question.—Instead, we now demonstrate a method, by examples; and the series of examples can be broken off.—Problems are solved (difficulties eliminated), not a *single* problem.
There is not *a* philosophical method, though there are indeed methods, like different therapies. (Wittgenstein 1967, § 133)

"There is not *a* philosophical method"—that is, no single one that would be mandatory for anybody wanting to think about a philosophical problem. But still, Wittgenstein has just said that he himself is demonstrating—or will proceed to demonstrate—*a* method (singular), by *examples* (plural, and indefinite in number). So, he does apparently take his own current method to possess some unity. And this seems to harmonize with the idea in the *Remarks on the Foundations of Mathematics* that *the sickness* (singular) of philosophical problems might be cured by *a* changed mode of thought and life (singular) (Wittgenstein 1978). It suggests that, despite the avowed pluralism or "differentism" of Wittgenstein's intellectual project, there may for all that be *a* change of attitude (singular, again) which he is seeking to bring about—a change in default of which we will not respond in the right (non-judgmental) way to the surface linguistic phenomena. So, even though there is no single method to which philosophy is committed a priori, it may be that Wittgenstein can still regard his own work in the *Investigations* as methodologically distinctive and can acknowledge certain characteristics of that work as being elicited by a certain pervasive form of intellectual malfunction—a "bewitchment of our intelligence by means of language" (Wittgenstein 1967, § 109)—which he hopes to remedy.

The question now arises: can we give a naturalistic interpretation to the words just quoted? That is: would it be appropriate to take "bewitchment" as a metaphorical way of referring to some putative breakdown in the *natural* or *normal* mode of self-understanding of language users—a breakdown which we could even approach in historical terms, as the "sickness of a time" passage appears to hint?
The immediate context of the remark about bewitchment does not look particularly favorable to this idea. Wittgenstein has just said that philosophical problems—in contrast to empirical ones—are solved by

looking into the workings of language [. . .] in such a way as to make us recognize those workings: *in despite of* an urge to misunderstand them [. . .]

Philosophy [he continues] is a battle against the bewitchment of our intelligence by means of language [. . .] The problems [. . .] arising through a misinterpretation of our forms of language have the character of *depth*. They are deep disquietudes; their roots are as deep in us as the forms of our language and their significance is as great as the importance of our language. (1967, § 111)

Here we seem to be told that the "urge to misunderstand," far from being an artifact of our own cultural moment, expresses a *timeless* susceptibility—one with "roots [. . .] as deep in us as the forms of our language." This account of the matter is certainly not apt to suggest a historicist picture of philosophical problems or of the therapy they require. I would like, however, to suspend judgment for the time being about the merits of that picture—I mean, not to dismiss it but to keep it in view as a possible factor in our reception of Wittgenstein.

A naturalistic account of the pathological condition, or conditions, to be addressed by the philosophical therapist might well be attractive in principle. Such an account would presumably involve positing a normal—or by analogy, "healthy"—state of affairs in our relation to the language we use and, by contrast, a problematic or troubled state of affairs.

There are elements in Wittgenstein's later thought to which such an account would appear congenial. Broadly, the elements in question are those where the practical aspect of language use—its integration with activity, especially physical activity—is highlighted, as with the builders of the *Philosophical Investigations* (Wittgenstein 1967, § 2); or where the origins of intelligent language use in processes of drill or (mere) training are pointed out; or where linguistic mastery is compared or equated to mastery of a technique (Wittgenstein 1967, § 199; see also 1978, 208–209). This aspect of the language-game is a candidate to be regarded as something of which we might or might not "command a clear view." It is a plausible candidate, in part, because of our pre-existing familiarity (through the Marxist tradition) with the idea that physical labor in general is subject to repression within mainstream ("idealist") philosophy; and this is a tradition that we know to have had some impact on Wittgenstein, through his exchanges with the economist Piero Sraffa at Cambridge.[3]

The condition of failure, or inability, to command a clear view of the engagement of language (in general) with the physical side of life can be identified as pathological in a certain kind of philosophical context. That identification is made, for example, when the self-understanding of a society is described as "alienated" in a Marxist (or related) sense. The vocabulary of "alienation" is of course normative in that it proposes a transition to a possible non-alienated state—the relevant normative apparatus being, in effect, Aristotelian: there is a way human society ought to be, in virtue of what-it-is-to-be-human; and there are also any number of deviant or defective realizations of the natural norm. Wittgenstein himself professed not to have read a word of Aristotle (Rhees 1984, 158), but Marx certainly did so in the course of his early intellectual formation (Prawer 1976, 26)[4] and is no doubt thinking in self-consciously Aristotelian terms when he uses the language of "species-being" (*Gattungswesen*)—a concept that belongs de facto to the same universe of discourse as the Wittgensteinian *Lebensform*, though the connection is particularly evident at those moments when Wittgenstein steps back to a distance from which he can consider the human "form of life" in a global or totalizing fashion.[5]

There certainly seems to be *something* in the later thought of Wittgenstein that is meant to address this specific intellectual pathology—that is, the condition of bourgeois squeamishness about our physicality or animal being— and to promote lucidity about the dependence of our lives on material labor, our own or that of others, to sustain them.[6] And the hint from the *Remarks on the Foundations of Mathematics* about a "changed mode of thought and of life"—in conjunction with what we know of the personal asceticism of Wittgenstein—might suggest an exhortation (to himself or to the world at large) to live in a way that *acknowledges* material labor, or expresses a serious attitude toward it; at any rate, a readiness to treat one's everyday comforts as though they were luxuries; not to relate to them frivolously or take them for granted.

Admittedly the asceticism of Wittgenstein has multiple sources, some of them of a more metaphysical nature, in keeping with the Tractarian idea of value as located "outside the world." It would be pointless, for example, to look for Marxist inspiration for his words in *Notebooks* 13.8.16: "The only life that is happy is the life that can renounce the amenities of the world. To it the amenities of the world are so many graces of fate" (Wittgenstein 1979). Yet it may be that in Wittgenstein's later philosophy this quasi-instinctual ascetic tendency is brought into connection with a fresh kind of intellectual imperative, namely, to "command a clear view" of the *use* of our words—the way language functions when it is not "on holiday," not "idling," but "doing work" (1967, § 38 and § 132). Somewhere in the background here, there seems to be a change of attitude (relative, say, to the *Tractatus*) which turns on the idea, if not exactly of the *dignity* of labor, then at least of its *significance* or *hermeneutic authority*. And at the risk of overdoing the appeal to anecdotal evidence, the "dignity of labor" motif was in fact probably not far removed from Wittgenstein's thinking in the 1930s, the period when he visited the USSR and even briefly considered settling there: the important thing, he holds at that time, is that people should have regular work, and while a class-ridden society is terrible, *"tyranny* [. . .] doesn't make [him] feel indignant" (Rhees 1984, 205). In any event it is not, I think, fanciful to find in the text of the *Investigations* the idea that when we lose sight of the practical, or work-orientated, aspect of language we succumb to a form of alienation and that in order to overcome such alienation a "changed mode of thought and of life," a *metanoia* at once cognitive and ethical, is needed.

But this leaves unresolved the question of the historicity (or otherwise) of our problems. And here Wittgenstein is undeniably rather reticent. True, a reader who perceived his later writings as offering some kind of rebuke to the dominant culture would not be mistaken: some explicit support for that reading is to be found, for example, in *Culture and Value*, where his 1930 "Sketch for a Foreword" (to the work later published as *Philosophical Remarks*) states that he "[has] no sympathy for the current of European civilization, and [does] not understand its goals, if it has any" (Wittgenstein 1980, 6). However, the nature of the rebuke is veiled. What would it be like to achieve that "complete clarity" which would result in the complete disappearance of philosophical problems? What would be the enabling conditions for this complete clarity—the required change in our "mode of thought and of life"? And is it possible to name any specific steps we could take toward the *"unbewitching"* of our intelligence?

A first response to these questions might be to admit the attractions of a style of therapy that would enlist the resources of cultural critique. For example, take the "private language argument" (PLA) in the *Philosophical Investigations* (say, from § 243 to § 326—though these famous sections are closely integrated with the surrounding text). The purpose of this discussion is to interrogate the idea of a language that would be (permanently, or in principle) limited to one person, so that no one else could understand it (Wittgenstein 1967, § 243). Wittgenstein proceeds by criticizing the conviction—which he takes to form part of a widely shared "common-sense" metaphysics—that one can define a term by associating it with some determinate introspectable datum, such as a particular type of sensation that one can be confident of recognizing when it recurs. Now, the PLA may strike us as being addressed, therapeutically, to a certain pathology which we can regard as "idealist" in a fairly literal sense: that is, shaped by the characteristic early-modern conception of "ideas" as mental representations, and by the more recent (but functionally analogous) conception of sense-data as the foundation of empirical knowledge. Persisting with the medical metaphor, we may in that case be inclined to say we have arrived, with Wittgenstein, at a *diagnosis* of the relevant problem—the relevant (localized) "urge to misunderstand the workings of our language" (Wittgenstein 1967, § 109)—and may hope to move on to various interesting proposals about the genesis of the pathology in question. And why shouldn't such proposals make reference to what is arguably pathological in the complexion of our own historical moment—that is, to the *social* genesis of the picture which, in this respect, "holds us captive" (see Wittgenstein 1967, § 115)?

For an instance of this kind of proposal, we can turn to the American philosopher Naomi Scheman, who is an attentive reader of the later Wittgenstein, though she does not claim him as a supporter of her own egalitarian political project—indeed, she brackets him with another celebrated anti-foundational naturalist, W. v. O. Quine, as a thinker to whom that project would be uncongenial.

Scheman argues in a wide-ranging essay that the post-Cartesian philosophical problem—that is, the region of discourse comprising "notably, the mind-body problem, problems of reference and truth, the problem of other minds, and skepticism about knowledge of the external world" (1993, 96)[7]—is the artifact of a specific (though prolonged) period in the cultural history of the West: an artifact about which, from the standpoint of our familiar "emancipatory metanarrative," both positive and negative stories can be told. On the positive side, "The Cartesian [self-constituting] subject was revolutionary" in relation to early modernity, manifesting itself variously as "the bourgeois bearer of rights, the self-made capitalist, the citizen of the nation state, and the Protestant bound by conscience and a personal relationship to God" (Scheman 1993, 86). Yet while the ideal of Cartesian subjecthood was in principle universally available, argues Scheman, it relied (or relies) in practice on structures of oppression by which the fully realized or "enfranchised" subject exploits the necessary menial labor of subordinate social groups—and, equally important, engages in an imaginary withdrawal from the existential condition of such groups by projecting on to them (in a Freudian sense) those "aspects of embodied humanness" (Scheman 1993, 87) which the sovereign subject is required to deny within himself: the all-too-human failings of unregimented emotion, credulity, immaturity, prejudice, and so forth.

Scheman's central claim is that the canonical (modern) "problems of philosophy" have a common psycho-social genesis: namely, they "all concern the subject's ability or inability to connect with the split off parts of itself—its physicality, its sociability" (1993, 96). "Such problems," she continues "are literally and unsurprisingly unsolvable so long as the subject's very identity is constituted by these estrangements [. . .] Philosophers' problems are the neuroses of privilege."

We may or may not be inclined to greet Scheman's complex discussion (of which I have given no more than the briefest summary) with the "Yes, of course!" response elicited by successful hermeneutic efforts. For my own part I find it very persuasive, but my immediate concern is simply to point to it as a spectacular foray into the kind of therapeutic philosophy whose object of interest is the "sickness *of a time*," meaning one phase of human experience in contrast to others.

To what extent, though, can we really think of such moves as having a Wittgensteinian pedigree? For it seems clear enough that Wittgenstein is not drawn to a treatment of our intellectual "bewitchment" in the idiom of twentieth-century social criticism—which was readily accessible to him if he had cared to make use of it—but rather to a predominantly *ethical* encounter with that tendency: an encounter through which we might rectify what is wrong in our view of the workings of ordinary language. It is as though he envisages an ethically innocent (post-philosophical) state in which we "command a clear view of the use of our words" (Wittgenstein 1967, § 122)—where the *use* consists in, or involves, some (genuine, non-bogus) form of activity.

What would count as a *non-bogus* form of activity? It is not difficult to think of things on which we spend a good deal of time (and linguistic ingenuity) that would be likely to fail this test in the eyes of the historical Wittgenstein. But this kind of social commentary—and the identification of specific social pathologies that would tend to corrupt the (authentic, lucid) relation to language use envisaged in the *Philosophical Investigations*—is not Wittgenstein's concern; indeed, to engage with it might well be to risk straying into the unworthy genre of "chatter about ethics" (Waismann 1965, 13).

Wittgenstein has a strong sense of *privacy* with respect to the detail of his experience of being-out-of-sympathy with the "current of European civilization." This attitude could itself be described as one of estrangement or "alienation." But the "alienation" targeted by Wittgensteinian philosophical therapy is of a different order. It is a matter not of subjective, individual experience but of objective, structural "bewitchment" or "captivity" of the intellect. And this objective or structural character is indifferent, in principle, to whether we take the "urge to misunderstand" (the workings of our language) as something timeless (see Wittgenstein 1967, § 111, discussed above) or as historically distinctive. The subjective alienation of Wittgenstein *qua* self-identified cultural exile expresses a fitting or rational—but not on the whole discursive—response to the objectively alienated character he attributes to the ambient "form of life." (Compare Nietzsche: "Our true experiences are not garrulous"—1968, § 82.) *Culture and Value* is a powerful source of insight into the aloof or solitary aspect of Wittgenstein's mentality, but it does not represent an intervention in any public process of cultural critique.

Nevertheless, it does seem significant that he finds even a fleeting or transitory use for the implicitly naturalistic notion of the *sickness* of a time—suggesting a contrast between sickness and health. And, in fact, this gesture is not entirely isolated. Thus, he appears to be thinking, in a broad sense, naturalistically in paragraphs 107 and 108 of the *Investigations*, where a contrast is drawn between (i) the (illusory) requirement that logic should exhibit "crystalline purity" and (ii) the *real* need for "friction" ("Back to the rough ground!"), a need met by the conditions of use of "actual language." "We are talking about the spatial and temporal phenomenon of language, not about some non-spatial, non-temporal phantasm," he continues (Wittgenstein 1967, § 108): in particular, we are talking about the kind of exchange in which some work is to be done; in which the wheels are engaged with the mechanism, not just spinning in a void (Wittgenstein 1967, § 271).

Wittgenstein's method is intended to rotate the "axis of reference of our examination" around the "fixed point of our real need" (1967, § 108). "Real need"—as contrasted with illusory need—pertains to the idea of a normal or natural mode of activity, which can be disrupted by a certain bad state of mind: the state of mind in which one loses sight of the distinction between what one *needs* (i.e., what one would be damaged in some way by the lack of) and what one would *like to have* (but could forgo without damage—luxuries, velleities, and the like). Wittgenstein applies this distinction at the cognitive (here, the philosophically reflective) level: he thinks that in philosophy there are real needs, or perhaps even *a* real need (singular), and also false or imaginary needs such as the "need" for a logic purged of the impurities of actual (spatio-temporally situated) linguistic behavior. To be estranged from one's real needs could plausibly be represented as a pathological condition, a "sickness," for which therapy is indicated.

In the remainder of this chapter, I want to return to the question of where we might locate Wittgenstein within the larger field of naturalistic social thought and, more specifically, whether his later writings have anything to contribute to the discourse of "social pathology" as a medium of critique.

On the latter point, there are some tantalizing hints that an affirmative answer might be possible. Consider for example the idea of a "naturalism of second nature" developed by John McDowell in *Mind and World*, a position very much in the spirit of the later Wittgenstein (1994, 98). Now to project this idea back on to Wittgenstein's own texts comes surprisingly close to reading him as a historical materialist. The "materialist" element enters through the fact that in the later philosophy he takes the human language-game as an expression of our "species-being," as discussed above: "as it were, something animal" (Wittgenstein 1980, § 359).[8] But a "historical" element is also present in that the relevant naturalism, being one of *second* nature, is affiliated not to reductive or positivistic views but to a conception of the language-game (with its intrinsic normative constraints) as evolving over time. Particular (local) language-games come into existence, persist for a while, and eventually become obsolete (Wittgenstein 1967, § 23); in this perception of their historicity, Wittgenstein seems close to the view of Marx and Engels that "language *is* practical consciousness that exists also for other men [. . .] like consciousness, [it] only arises from the need, the necessity, of intercourse with [others]" (1974, 51)—whereas, among non-human, not-yet-historical species of animal, the relation (as we might put it) of one individual to others does not exist *for that individual* under the aspect of a "relation." (Compare Wittgenstein's observation in the *Investigations* that a dog can't simulate pain—but *not* because he is "too honest" (Wittgenstein 1967, § 250).[9] Rather, life as a dog does not rise to that level of social complexity.)

Yet, despite these echoes or resonances, the "historical-materialist" label does not really fit the thought of Wittgenstein. What makes itself felt there is at most a "resonance" which never issues in the articulation of any lesson such as a Marxist (or similar) reader might be hoping for—this outcome being, no doubt, excluded in advance by Wittgenstein's conviction that "we may not advance any kind of theory" (1967, § 109).

Some light is shed on the situation by John B. Davis' carefully nuanced assessment of the historical-materialist moment in Wittgenstein as an effect of contact with the Marxist tradition (2002). This contact, he says—albeit contingent and rather indirect—marks Wittgenstein as a representative of European "critical theory," the genre inaugurated by Hegel and often to be credited with "revealing a hidden 'historicist' dimension to systems of ideas which claimed to be timeless and universal in their abstraction" (Davis 2002, 141). Davis is not primarily interested in the personal influence of Sraffa on Wittgenstein (and still less in any part that may have been played in this relationship by Sraffa's views on economics), but in the way Wittgenstein's later writings presuppose "the same philosophical posture of critique" adopted by Sraffa and Gramsci (Davis 2002, 142).

All this may well be on the right track, but one has to admit that the critical-theoretic contribution to Wittgenstein's later thought remains *abstract*. That is, while receptive, now, to the general idea of the historic (as opposed to timeless) character of the language-game—of *our* language-game, the totality of our linguistic practice *qua* spatio-temporal phenomenon—Wittgenstein hardly ever shows interest in the *particular* historic factors which might tend to maintain in being *particular* types of linguistic practice ("language-games" in the plural or local sense), or which might cause these to "become obsolete and get forgotten" (1967, § 23). In his capacity as a therapeutic philosopher, the condition he undertakes to treat is that of estrangement from the materiality or spatio-temporal character of language use *as such* (as if the desired therapeutic effect could be accomplished by attending to this spatio-temporal character or "reminding" oneself of it; see Wittgenstein 1967, § 127): despite the intriguing hint contained in the "sickness of a time" passage, he does not engage with any putative *social* cause of that estrangement, as for instance Scheman does with the "paranoid" tendency of liberal-individualist epistemology (discussed above). (And after all, how could one establish that any proposed account of such social causality was right? To put forward such an account would be to violate the principle that "[t]here must not be anything hypothetical in our considerations"—Wittgenstein 1967, § 109.)

These negative remarks seem to leave us with not much to show on Wittgenstein's behalf in support of his transitory reflections on the "sickness of a time." They suggest that his involvement in the "philosophical posture of critique" remains primarily melancholic rather than activist in character. Or as Gavin Kitching has put it (possibly with a touch of hyperbole, but the claim deserves a hearing): the question of the *historical and social preconditions* of one's own intellectual (or other) activity is one to which "Wittgenstein himself—and despite Sraffa's best efforts—was completely purblind. And that blindness is one respect (perhaps the only respect) in which Wittgenstein was a completely conventional 'abstracting' and 'abstracted' philosopher in the liberal tradition" (Kitching and Pleasants 2002, 16).

And yet, it's worth remembering that the psychoanalytic and, more broadly, hermeneutic methods also have a place within the European tradition of Critical Theory. Their findings are supposed to commend themselves to the inquirer in the same way as the results of Platonic recollection, namely, by prompting the response "Yes, that's it"—a gesture of recognition of what was implicitly part of one's cognitive equipment or experience all along, yet not previously accessible to consciousness. And this response is also recognized by Wittgenstein as an expression—sometimes objectively justified—of the conviction of *having got it*: for example, having remembered or understood something. Thus, paragraph 635 of the *Philosophical Investigations* on remembering what one was going to say: discrete items of "evidence" don't help—they are no more use than isolated scraps of a lost picture—but then all of a sudden "it is as if we knew quite certainly what the whole picture represented. As if I could read the darkness."[10]

So this discussion can end, after all, on a note of (qualified) optimism. If it is the role of philosophy to assemble "reminders" for particular purposes—to offer suggestions that, when successful, produce the reaction "Yes, that's it"—then we may still want to press the question: could not such "reminders" be assembled in the service of local (concrete) projects of social criticism? That exercise might display the radical potential of a naturalistic approach to linguistic phenomena—a potential which, for one reason or another, remains muted in the philosophy of Wittgenstein.

Although his method is descriptive, Wittgenstein is not a sociologist. Instead, the subject matter he selects for description opens up perspectives that transcend the (merely) sociological: when we are invited, for example, to *find it surprising*[11] that the phenomenon of normativity relies upon a material basis in practices of guidance and correction, an emancipatory ambition is at work that is arguably as big as anything in philosophy. And to the extent that this example (I mean the case of the rule following considerations) is typical, it will be true to say that the insights to be drawn from his work are not historically specific. But there may nevertheless be historically specific reasons why these insights *escape us*. And this is where a more socially engaged genre of Critical Theory, however tangential to the concerns of Wittgenstein himself, can once again lay claim to our attention.[12]

NOTES

1. In the analytical table of contents that accompanies the published text, this passage stands alone, no connection being made with what precedes or follows it.

2. Drury, one of the contributors to Wittgenstein's biography, has just recalled him saying that he did not think he would get on with Hegel because that philosopher "seems to me to be always wanting to say that things which look different are really the same. Whereas my interest is in showing that things which look the same are really different."

3. Wittgenstein writes in the Preface to the *Investigations* (viii) that he is indebted to the stimulus of Sraffa's criticism, "for many years unceasingly practised on [his] thoughts," for "the most consequential ideas of this book." Some well-reasoned, though inevitably speculative, discussion of Sraffa's influence is to be found in the contributions of Sharpe et al. 2002. See further below.

4. Marx's doctoral thesis, which concerned the post-Aristotelian phase of ancient philosophy (especially the atomists), "accepts as a truism the biological-organic scheme of history which had proved congenial to so many historians of ideas," but "censures this scheme [. . .] as too vague and general, as one in which everything can be accommodated and through which nothing can be really understood." See however Ste Croix (1981, 24) for evidence of Marx's enduring admiration for Aristotle, whom he calls "a giant thinker," "the greatest thinker of antiquity."

5. Thus Wittgenstein 1969, § 559: "[The language-game] is not based on grounds. It is not reasonable (or unreasonable). It is there—like our life."

6. Marxist influences aside, the present section is not meant to encourage a narrowly productivist conception of our "species-being." Such a conception would be foreign to Wittgenstein, who is equally interested in non-"productive" activities (chatting, playing, and the like: see 1967, § 23 and § 25)—not to mention aspects of

lived experience (such as pain, fear, or surprise) which exceed the notion of *activity* altogether. Thanks to Stella Villarmea for drawing attention to this important point.

7. For the disclaimer with regard to Wittgenstein and Quine, see Scheman 1993, p. 78. For Scheman as Wittgenstein scholar, see, for example, Scheman (1996).

8. See also § 475.

9. See also Wittgenstein (1978, 229): "A dog cannot be a hypocrite, but neither can he be sincere."

10. Compare also Wittgenstein 1978, 218: "How do I find the 'right' word? [. . .] I am dissatisfied, I go on looking. At last a word comes: '*That's* it!' *Sometimes* I can say why. This is simply what searching, this is what finding, is like here."

11. Compare Wittgenstein 1967, § 524.

12. I am grateful for comments received on earlier drafts of this chapter at conferences in Lucerne (April 2018) and Oxford (August 2019).

REFERENCES

Davis, John B. 2002. "A Marxist Influence on Wittgenstein via Sraffa," in Marx and Wittgenstein: Knowledge, Morality and Politics, G. N. Kitching, and N. Pleasants (eds.), 35–131. London: Routledge.

Kitching, Gavin, and Pleasants, Nigel (eds.). 2002. *Marx and Wittgenstein: Knowledge, Morality and Politics*. London: Routledge.

Marx, Karl, and Engels, Friedrich. 1974. *The German Ideology*, C. J. Arthur (ed.). London: Lawrence & Wishart.

McDowell, John. 1994. *Mind and World*. Cambridge, MA: Harvard University Press.

Nietzsche, Friedrich. 1968. *Twilight of the Idols*, R. J. Hollingdale (trans.). Harmondsworth: Penguin.

Prawer, Siegbert S. 1976. *Karl Marx and World Literature*. Oxford: Oxford University Press.

Rhees, Rush et al. (eds.). 1984. *Recollections of Wittgenstein*. Oxford: Oxford University Press.

Scheman, Naomi. 1993. "Though This Be Method, Yet There Is Madness in It: Paranoia and Liberal Epistemology," in *Engenderings: Constructions of Knowledge, Authority, and Privilege*, 75–105. New York/London: Routledge.

Scheman, Naomi. 1996. "Forms of Life: Mapping the Rough Ground," in *The Cambridge Companion to Wittgenstein*, H. D. Sluga, and D. G. Stern (eds.). Cambridge. Cambridge University Press.

Sharpe, Kieran et al. (eds.). 2002. *Marx and Wittgenstein: Knowledge, Morality and Politics*. London: Routledge.

Ste Croix, Geoffrey E. M. 1981. *The Class Struggle in the Ancient Greek World*. London: Duckworth.

Waismann, Friedrich. 1965. "Notes on Talks with Wittgenstein," *Philosophical Review*, 74: 12–16.

Wittgenstein, Ludwig. 1967. *Philosophical Investigations*. G. E. M. Anscombe (ed. and trans.). Oxford: Basil Blackwell.

Wittgenstein, Ludwig. 1969. *On Certainty*, G. E. M. Anscombe, and G. H. von Wright (eds.), D. Paul, and G. E. M. Anscombe (trans.). Oxford: Basil Blackwell.
Wittgenstein, Ludwig. 1978. *Remarks on the Foundations of Mathematics*, G. H. von Wright, R. Rhees, and G. E. M. Anscombe (eds.), G. E. M. Anscombe (trans.), 2. Oxford: Basil Blackwell.
Wittgenstein, Ludwig. 1979. *Notebooks 1914–1916*, G. H. von Wright, and G. E. M. Anscombe (eds.), G. E. M. Anscombe (trans.). Oxford: Basil Blackwell.
Wittgenstein, Ludwig. 1980. *Culture and Value*, G. H. von Wright (ed.), P. Winch (trans.).

Chapter 12

Objective Reason, Ethical Naturalism, and Social Pathology

The Case of Horkheimer and Adorno

Fabian Freyenhagen

In this chapter, I excavate an underappreciated resource in Horkheimer's—and by extension, Adorno's—Critical Theory of society (as their social philosophy is known). The resource in question is (their conception of) objective reason. It needs excavating because Horkheimer's exposition of it is insufficiently worked out (and Adorno's uptake of it adds little to change this). It is underappreciated not just because of this need for excavating, but in good part because the dominant reading of their work is that their own theory leaves no more room for objective reason to be socially operative—that, to put it in Habermas' words, "in the darkest years of the Second World War [. . .] the last sparks of reason were being extinguished from this reality and had left the ruins of a civilisation in collapse without any hope" (Habermas 1987, 116f).[1]

Once the resource is in full view, Horkheimer and Adorno's social philosophy is more defensible—or at least so I suggest. Specifically, I suggest (a) that a kind of "linguistic turn" already occurred with Horkheimer and Adorno's work prior to and different from Habermas' own (later) one and (b) that uncovering this hitherto overlooked "linguistic turn" enables us to see why objective reason is, in a sense, inextinguishable for Horkheimer and Adorno.

Part of my overall strategy is (c) to draw parallels to the thought of (later)[2] Wittgenstein. Importantly for the context of this volume, this allows me to comment on the sense in which Horkheimer and Adorno's social philosophy can be characterized as naturalistic. Indeed, the unearthed resources can help us to make sense of the account of social pathology operative in Horkheimer and Adorno's work—and, thereby, of a central idea of naturalistically minded social philosophy.

Let me note two preliminaries. First, let me clarify what I mean by "linguistic turn." This term is widely used in contemporary philosophy, but there is a danger that different authors mean different things by it. So, let me be clear about what I mean. This turn minimally includes accepting two key tenets:

1) *All philosophy has to be (also) philosophy of language.* There is no standpoint outside of language to grasp the world, and philosophical reflection is no different. It is mediated by language and one of its central tasks is to reflect on that mediation and the nature of language from within that medium.
2) *There is no private language.* Intersubjectivity is unavoidably inscribed into language and thereby philosophy (both of language and more generally).

As should be obvious, the linguistic turn, so conceived, owes a lot to the philosophy of (later) Wittgenstein, although others (like, I suggest, Horkheimer and Adorno) might have come to the same conclusions by other routes and expressed them differently. Also, there can be various versions of what I just described as a "linguistic turn." For example, Habermas has a specific version of it—a "communications-theoretic turn" (1984, 397)—that includes, in addition, transcendentalism (or quasi-transcendentalism) and universal pragmatics, but other philosophical theories that accept a version of the linguistic turn may not include these further commitments or they may even explicitly reject them (Horkheimer and Adorno's version is, as we shall see below, one example of the latter view).

As a second preliminary, I note that I ignore here any differences between the theories of Adorno and Horkheimer that may exist. Treating their works as a common *corpus*, I present what I take to be their shared position, whether expressed in coauthored or individually authored pieces. Relatedly, what I am presenting as their position is the result of sometimes quite considerable reconstruction. I do not pretend that position was ever explicitly stated as such by them or even that it was clearly before their minds.

I begin by attending to a neglected or maligned text, Horkheimer's 1947 book *Eclipse of Reason* (first section). While this book is problematic in certain ways, it also contains overlooked resources. I, then (in the second section), briefly introduce some key features of (later) Wittgenstein's picture of language, including its naturalism. I bring out that a similar picture of language is operative in Horkheimer and Adorno's social philosophy, making it more defensible and linking it to their account of social pathology.

ECLIPSE OF REASON—PROBLEMATIC BUT PROMISING

A good starting point for my inquiry is Marx. In a letter to Arnold Ruge, Marx wrote in 1843: "Reason has always existed, but not always in a rational form" (Schiller 2018, 143).[3] This claim could serve as a motto for Horkheimer and Adorno—or almost could do so: they would not accept that reason has always existed, but instead suggest that ever since reason has existed it has not been reasonable. The doubling of reason implied in this claim—of reason and whether or not it is reasonable—already suggests a complex, multifaceted conception of it, rather than a mere reduction of it to instrumental rationality.

Formulations reminiscent of Marx's can be found all over the works of Horkheimer and Adorno—perhaps most explicitly in Horkheimer's *Eclipse of Reason*: "Reason can realize its reasonableness only through reflecting on the disease of the world as produced and reproduced by human beings" (2013, 125). Before explicating the complex conception of reason at work here, let me note already the use of the language of social pathology in this passage. Horkheimer speaks of the social world as "diseased" here. In the paragraph preceding this passage from *Eclipse of Reason*, he also speaks of reason as affected by the disease (presumably the disease of the social world), and of the "collective madness that rages today" (2013, 124–25). There is much more to say about the idea of social pathology and its role in the Frankfurt School Critical Theory,[4] but it shall suffice to say here that Horkheimer is willing to use medical or biological language in relation to society as a whole.[5] This is not an isolated incident—Horkheimer, for example, uses similar language around the same time when speaking about anti-semitism—and Adorno also operates with that idea, although he tends to use medical or biological language less than Horkheimer does.

Let me now return to the complex conception of the reason I alluded to. It relies, centrally, on a distinction Horkheimer draws between subjective and objective reason, most notably in *Eclipse of Reason*.[6]

Subjective reason is characterized as a capacity of individual subjects (Horkheimer 2013, 1)—or rather a set of capacities: means-end reasoning, following logical laws, classifying, and distinguishing. It is "subjective" in the sense of referring to the subject's reason (its reasoning abilities). It is formal insofar as it does not rely on any specific material ends—subjects can use their reasoning abilities to choose the most effective ways to make others happy or to make them miserable; they can use their abilities to protect people from harm or to harm them; and so forth. Depending on whatever ends subjects happen to have, subjective reason can then help them to enact and connect them. As far as subjective reason is concerned, there need not be any universal human ends.

Objective reason is understood as being a characteristic of the world (or, at least, the social world).[7] It is not formal and subject-dependent, but substantive and object-dependent, and as such connected to a notion of "objective truth." Object here is understood more broadly than simply medium-sized material objects like tables and chairs. Indeed, Horkheimer, importantly, makes use of the language of "situations" to explicate the specific kind of normativity built at stake in objective reason: seeing a drowning child or animal requires those who pass by (and can swim) that they rescue it; someone's being ill requires treating them as best as we can; something beautiful requires that we appreciate it; and so on (Horkheimer 2013, 7; 1985ff, 7, 24f). Each of these situations "speaks a language of itself" (Horkheimer 2013, 7); there is "a silent appeal by the situation itself" (Horkheimer 2013, 21).

According to Horkheimer, these two forms of reason were originally connected—they are understood as aspects of the same concept. For a long time, objective reason—by being connected to various metaphysical and religious systems—was the predominant socially operative form of reason, but progressively over the course of human (natural) history this has been reversed and subjective reason has become dominant. Indeed, its dominance is the hallmark of modernity as we know it. Not just that: subjective reason increasingly threatens to nullify all remaining traces of objective reason—it *threatens* to eclipse these traces totally (but, if my argument in this chapter is correct, it can never actually extinguish them). And, in so doing, subjective reason too undermines itself (Horkheimer 2013, 37–38; 1985ff, 7, 25).

Let me expand on how this is so (according to Horkheimer). Subjective reason has been an instrument of Enlightenment—whereby "Enlightenment" is understood in Adorno and Horkheimer's sense of the long-drawn process of disenchantment of the world, not simply the more circumscribed period roughly equivalent to the eighteenth century—by allowing human beings to challenge the various magical, metaphysical, and religious approaches they faced in their respective historical situations, revealing these approaches to lack sufficient justification (notably Horkheimer 2013, 44). However, this increasingly accelerating and far-reaching process has undercut not just problematic worldviews and problematic notions of "objective truth," but any notion of objective truth. If this process succeeded in erasing any traces of objective truth altogether, then its engine, subjective reason, would thereby erase itself too: for it cannot stand on its own. And here is why: without the substantiality of objective reason, concepts are only "empty shells" (Horkheimer 1985ff, 7, 25; my translation) and thereby any "reasonable justification" becomes impossible. Without the connection to concrete—that is substantial, object-dependent—judgments, reason withers. In particular, it loses its essential element of enabling those who wield it to be able to do more than reproduce facts or apply stereotypes, with the ironical consequence that subjective reason, in its eclipse of objective reason, "loses its very subjectivity" (Horkheimer 2013, 38). It is thus unsurprising, Horkheimer claims, that subjective reason has been pliable to reigning interests and forms of domination, and co-opted by them (1985ff, 7, 26 and 28), no longer able to condemn them as irrational (2013, 12 and 20–21; 1985ff, 7, 30f). By itself, subjective reason is neutral as to humanity and inhumanity, and silent on whether despotism, cruelty, or oppression are bad in themselves or not (Horkheimer 2013, 20–21). In its triumph, subjective reason cuts us off from situational demands and undermines us as subjects and thereby itself.

It is important to note that Horkheimer does not propose—as a remedy to the "crisis of reason" (Horkheimer 2013, 4, 91)—to abandon subjective reason altogether. The idea of abandoning subjective reason is something Horkheimer ascribes to Huxley but rejects as naïve and as leading to rest on blind violence, cynicism, and contempt for the masses—and thereby contributing to domination, rather than ending it (2013, 38–39).

There is, also, no proposal to go back to previous arrangements where objective reason had priority. This is neither possible nor desirable (Horkheimer 2013, 43–44 and 103–104, 116). It is not desirable in good part because past arrangements were not free from domination either and characterized by thought systems we can and should not accept—subjective reason correctly unveiled them as problematically dogmatic. In particular, the force of the systems of objective reason had its origin in myths, taboos, and the like. These, in turn, had their origin in the (justified) fear of being overwhelmed by a hostile environment and the attempts to control this environment (Horkheimer 2013, 23–24). That fear was justified does not mean that the resulting myths, taboos, and so on were. For one thing, social domination always went hand in hand with them (Horkheimer 2013, 66 and 74). And, for another, they involved distorted and distorting projections. Indeed, according to Horkheimer, modern forms of racism or anti-semitism preserve an element of that archaic fear: the cave-dwellers' fear of strangers (2013, 61). Moreover, past ideas were in contradiction with each other and in flux (Horkheimer 2013, 44)—there is no fixed point to which we could simply return (and proper fidelity to these ideas would not be to ossify them and accept them dogmatically). Finally, Horkheimer even goes as far as claiming that the disease affecting reason is inseparable from reason and civilization as we know them (Horkheimer 2013, 124)—there is no "golden past of reason," but it has always been intertwined with the domination of nature and society.[8]

Instead, the remedy would be to reconcile subjective and objective reasons. Overcoming the rupture within the concept of reason is not merely a philosophical task, but a sociopolitical one (Horkheimer 2013, 129–30 and 131; 1985ff, 7, 34f): The "task of philosophy" is "to *prepare* in the intellectual realm the reconciliation of the two in reality" (Horkheimer 2013, 123;

my emphasis). Philosophy has a role to play in reconciliation, but it cannot accomplish reconciliation on its own.

In the absence of the required sociopolitical changes, the question arises how critical endeavors, including Critical Theory, can continue. What is it to prepare in the intellectual realm for the reconciliation in reality? What enables the self-reflection of reason and the critique of its reigning form as unreasonable? Unfortunately, on that point Horkheimer's text is not sufficiently clear, containing a number of seemingly different strategies, none of which is well worked out.

One such strategy seems to be to rely on the residual elements of objective reason still available to us. Specifically, the claim is that language still harbors such residues:

> Philosophy must become more sensitive to the muted testimonies of language and plumb the layers of experience preserved in it. Each language carries a meaning embodying the thought forms and belief patterns rooted in the evolution of the people who speak it. It is the repository of the variegated perspectives of prince and pauper, poet and peasant. (Horkheimer 2013, 117–18; see also 126–27; and 1985ff, 7, 30).

In this way, we have to rely on something from the past, like feudal attitudes or long-forgotten forms of worship and superstition:

> These old forms of life smouldering under the surface of modern civilization still provide, in many cases, the warmth inherent in any delight, in any love of a thing for its own sake rather than that of another thing. The pleasure of keeping a garden goes back to ancient times when gardens belonged to the gods and were cultivated for them. (Horkheimer 2013, 23; see also 1985ff, 7, 31)

Even the idea of human dignity feeds off the awe for the gods and rulers (Horkheimer 2013, 126; 1985ff, 7, 31f), and would become an "empty phrase" without an—however buried—experience of this awe (see also Horkheimer 2013, 21).

What is perplexing, even problematic, about this move is how such memory or experience is meant to help. It seems to rely on the idea of a golden past of which we feed—despite, as seen, having ruled out such an idea. The awe of gods and rulers might have led people to develop the idea of ends in themselves, but this does not mean that there genuinely were such ends, rather than a domination-induced illusion thereof. Moreover, Horkheimer— and similarly Adorno—suggests that the ability to experience the archaic origins is withering and with it the ability to wield objective reason. With the decline of the individual—sketched in chapter 4 of *Eclipse of Reason*—the force of resistance is in decline too. As Adorno puts it at one point in *Negative*

Dialectics, those who will see through the apologia of a total society "are certain to die out" (Adorno 1973, 268).[9]

Sometimes, Horkheimer speaks not of the awe of gods, but of the experience of past injustices. Such memories are required, he suggests, in order that value concepts like freedom, equality, justice, and humanity retain some substance with which to criticize the hypostatized subjective reason and social reality (2013, 24 and 126; 1985ff, 7, 32). Here the appeal is not to a golden past but to "dreadful origins" (Horkheimer 2013, 24), the "traces of oppression" and the experience of "barbarian forms of domination" (Horkheimer 2013, 126). If "language reflects the longings of the oppressed and the plight of nature" (Horkheimer 2013, 126), then this would present negative manifestations of objective reason and Critical Theory's role would then be to mobilize these resources by way of reminders—disclosing concrete bad and how they are interconnected and entwined with a social system that cannot but generate them.

This seems more promising an avenue—not least because it would be compatible with negativism, to which Horkheimer and Adorno are deeply committed (Freyenhagen 2012; 2013). Negativism can take at least four forms: it can be methodological, epistemic, substantive, and metaethical. The relevant notions of negativism here are epistemic and metaethical. According to *epistemic* negativism, we can—at least in our wrong current social world—only know the wrong, the bad, illness, the abnormal, and so on; we cannot know the good, the right, what health or the normal is. It is, thus, a claim about the limitations of our knowledge—or at least, it is a claim about the limitations of knowledge in specific circumstances (our wrong current social world). This qualification of epistemic negativism is important in the context of Adorno's and Horkheimer's work: both are epistemic negativists, but only within a certain historical circumstance. Specifically, they (like Hegel) think that we cannot know what the good life is prior to the realization of its social conditions. These conditions are given neither in any pre-modern society nor (contra Hegel) in our modern social world. Seeking the residues of objective reason in concrete evils and the history of resistance to them would fit well with epistemic negativism: as objective reason has never been positively realized, we cannot find any residues of such a positive realization and cannot (yet) know what it consists in; what we can know, however, are the ways in which objective reason has been negatively instantiated.[10] In other words, we can know "barbarian forms of domination" but not a "humane organization of society" (Horkheimer 2013, 126). This would also fit well with *metaethical* negativism—here the thesis is that knowledge of evil (or parts thereof) is sufficient to account for the normativity of claims based on it. Put differently, we can account for value judgments or rational criteria even in the absence of knowing the good, the right, or any positive value. On any justifiable sense of account of normativity, the bad (or wrong or ill) is normatively sufficient on its own (at least sometimes, for example, when great evils are at stake). Thus, in this context, concrete evils and the experience of them throughout history are negative manifestations for the objective reason that suffice for giving us practical orientation—their occurrence in particular situations demand by themselves certain responses, notably resistance to the wrong world that produces them (with Critical Theory as part of this resistance). This way, there would not be—and would not have to be—an appeal to a golden past.

However, serious obstacles remain. Here I want to concentrate on one such obstacle in particular: If the ruling ideas are those of the ruling classes (as Marx and Engels famously claimed) and if history is written by the victors, then why should we have any confidence that objective reason—even in its negative manifestation—has left any traces in language? Why think that language is (also) the repository of paupers and peasants, rather than just a repository of princes? *Eclipse* begins, after all, with an account of how hopeless it is to ask "ordinary men" to explain what reason is (Horkheimer 2013, 1; see also 118)—hopeless for Critical Theory because they would just reproduce in their answer what is socially dominant (i.e., formalized subjective reason). How then can and does language reflect "the longings of the oppressed and the plight of nature" (Horkheimer 2013, 126)? How can it reflect this, especially now that language is becoming (in Horkheimer's own words) "a mere tool in the omnipresent production apparatus of modern society" (1985ff, 7, 30; my translation)? Isn't it too fully saturated with ideology (in the Marxian sense of false consciousness) to be a repository of objective reason from which a Critical Theory of society can draw?

Horkheimer says relatively little about language in *Eclipse* (or, indeed, elsewhere), but one thing he does say might provide a clue for answering these questions. He writes: "Philosophy helps man to allay his fears by helping language to fulfil its genuine mimetic function, its mission of mirroring the natural tendencies" (Horkheimer 2013, 127). This is a curious statement. What could Horkheimer mean when speaking of language's "mimetic function" and of "its mission of mirroring the natural tendencies"? I propose that drawing a comparison to the work of (later) Wittgenstein can help here.[11]

A LITTLE HELP FROM (LATER) WITTGENSTEIN

Let me start with the following preliminary remark: I am not saying that Horkheimer and Adorno's view of language was influenced by (later) Wittgenstein. For one thing, that would get the chronology wrong (some of the key insights by Wittgenstein were, for example, not yet publicly available when *Eclipse of Reason* was published). For another, there is no evidence

I know of that either Horkheimer or Adorno was familiar with the work of later Wittgenstein when it became available. It is unclear how much they engaged even with his earlier work. There is mention of the *Tractatus* in some of their writings, but the way it is discussed suggests that Horkheimer and, explicitly, Adorno are nothing but critical of it, seeing it as a prime example of positivism and, thus, of a view they deeply reject. Similarly, I am not aware of any engagement of Wittgenstein with the writings of the Frankfurt School. In sum, what I am claiming is not that there was any positive influence between (later) Wittgenstein and Adorno and Horkheimer (in whichever direction). Instead, the parallel I go on to suggest is one of a similar picture of language that they, for all we know, developed independently of each other.

Naturalism is a good starting point—particularly in the context of this volume—for disclosing this parallel. As Fink (2006) suggests, Wittgenstein and Adorno (and, by extension, we can add Horkheimer) share a special kind of naturalist perspective—not one in which the natural is simply coextensive with the domain of the natural sciences, not even one in which it also includes the capacities and practices into which we become so habituated that they are a "second nature" to us, but an even more unrestricted naturalism. It understands nature as "all-inclusive" such that the cultural, aesthetics, ethical, and even logic "are not somehow based on nature or supervening on it either; rather, they simply are nature in some of its manifest operations" (Fink 2006, 217).

If there is such a shared naturalism, then one pertinent follow-up question is what kind of ethical upshot for social critique it might have. In which sense, if any, are both Wittgenstein and Adorno and Horkheimer *ethical* naturalists? This is too far-reaching a question to answer here conclusively, but I explore one such sense in what follows. As we see below, a nuanced perspective emerges, in which ethics (in the broad sense to include social philosophy and social critique) is indexed, in virtue of a certain picture of language, to the human life form, but not in a way that we can simply deduce ethical premises from what we know about human nature (and also not in a way that human nature is the normative foundation of social critique, for nothing is or can be such foundation, according to this view).

Fink is not alone to suggest that the work of (later) Wittgenstein contains a naturalism of an unrestricted kind. For (later) Wittgenstein, there is—as Garver puts it—"no metaphysical reality other than the natural world" (1994, 272), but scientific approaches to the natural world do not and can never exhaust what the natural world consists in. In particular, "something other than scientific methodology is necessary to describe the variety of human language-games" (Garver 1994, 272). What is required for the latter is not (natural) scientific explanation, but a certain kind of description.[12]

Key to this is the fact that, for (later) Wittgenstein, "to imagine a language means to imagine a form of life" ([1953], §19). As interpreted by Garver, this is to say that meaning cannot be captured simply "in terms of words and syntax," but instead we need to look at how we use language, how it is "integrated into the activities of some sort of living being" (1994, 246).

This can, among other things, be seen from the way we would have to proceed in order to learn an unknown language. In order to do so, Wittgenstein tells us, one would have to ask "what circumstances would you say that the people gave orders, understood them, obeyed them, rebelled against them, and so on?" (2001, § 206). One would have to turn to the "common behavior of mankind" as one's "system of reference" (Wittgenstein 2001, § 206). Language is and functions in the particular ways it is and does, because of this commonality in behavior, whereby behavior is broadly understood to include capacities. For example, human beings are typically capable of learning basic algebra, but they typically do not have perfect pitch; this is reflected in the language(s) they operate with.

The common behavior that we can use as a system of reference is natural, but not something we know by way of scientific methodologies. It concerns certainties (as different from scientific knowledge), that is, it concerns that which "lies beyond being justified or unjustified; as it were, something animal" (Wittgenstein 1969, § 359). In good part, this is—as Crary puts it—because "there is no such thing as a standpoint outside language from which to characterize the relationship between language and the world" (2018, 26). Indeed, there *could not* be such a standpoint outside of language (hence, the first key tenant included in accepting the "linguistic turn"). Offering justification is part of what we use language for and perhaps there are even specific justification language-games, but these uses and games presuppose the human life form and cannot ground it in their turn. Moreover, it is also not the case that human life—or the "world" more generally—does or could ground language. In Winch's words: "Reality is not what gives language sense. What is real and what is unreal shows itself *in* the sense language has" (1972, 12).

What I want to suggest is that a similar picture of language (and, thereby, the first key tenet constitutive of the linguistic turn in philosophy) is at work in Horkheimer's (and Adorno's) theory. Let me provide my first piece of evidence for this: intriguingly, we can find in Horkheimer the very thought that the human life form is something like a system of reference with which we always make sense of specific formulations, concepts, or theories (including scientific ones), but which only shows itself in the sense language has, rather than being something we can explicitly speak about and delineate. In a neglected text from 1946 (*Trust in History* [*Vertrauen auf die Geschichte*]), Horkheimer writes that what it is to be human "cannot be captured by any concept" but "Unnamed, it is at the basis of language and its concepts" (1985ff, 12, 127; my translation).

I introduce more evidence for my ascription below (including passages from Adorno's work), but for now let me point to the upshot of operating with this picture of language: in a nutshell, my point is that the inseparability of language and human life makes it possible for language to be a "repository" of objective reason, even despite the fact that language can also be pressed into being an ideological tool of domination. For, by virtue of being inseparable from the human life form, it contains traces of this life form and, thus, of objective reason. Language is not, and cannot be, entirely arbitrary (although it contains arbitrary elements). Indeed, it is not, and cannot be, even merely conventional (although, again, it contains elements arising from conventions). The traces of objective reason inherent in our human life form cannot be eradicated completely from language—even the most ideological conventions cannot, ultimately, change that language harbors opposition to what runs counter to the human life form.

One might be surprised to hear that this is supposed to be Horkheimer and Adorno's view, but I think there is evidence for thinking that it is. One key piece of evidence is a 1941 letter to Adorno. In this statement, prior to *Eclipse of Reason*, Horkheimer writes suggestively:

> Language intends, quite independently of the psychological intention of the speaker, the universality that has been ascribed to reason alone. Interpreting this universality necessarily leads to the idea of a correct society. When it serves the status quo, language must therefore find that it consistently contradicts itself, and this is evident from individual linguistic structures themselves. (1985ff, 17, 171; quoted in Wiggershaus 1994: 505; his translation)

This is a rich passage that would deserve detailed analysis. Three points have to suffice for our purposes here. First, it is noteworthy that—like Wittgenstein—Horkheimer adopts the view that (to use a nowadays common phrase from Putnam) "meaning ain't in the head" of speakers (notably, it is not reducible to their psychological intentions). This fits with the second key tenet of the linguistic turn that I introduced in the Introduction above—that is, the rejection of private language.

Second, one might think that the quotation above sounds rather proto-Habermasian. Talk of universality and how it *necessarily leads to the idea of a correct society* seem to have the ring of Habermas' discourse ethics *avant la lettre*. But, I think, this need not be so. This is not the place to go into the difference between Habermas' communication-theoretical version of the linguistic turn, on the one hand, and the version that I ascribe to Horkheimer and Adorno, on the other. It suffices to note a key feature in the second quotation: whatever Horkheimer means by universality, the implication of his statement

clearly is that there is a mistake to ascribe it to "reason alone." On my reading, what Horkheimer is hinting at here is that we should not primarily locate
the idea of a correct society in something like the subject's reasoning capacities (such as pure practical reason in Kant) or intersubjectivity (such as communicative rationality, as later in Habermas). Instead, there is a connection,
indeed inseparability, between language and objective reason—reason as
manifested in our life form and in the world—and it is thanks to this inseparability that (as Horkheimer puts it in 1956) "[w]hatever is right about human
society is embedded in the language," such that when one uses language, one
commits oneself to this (Horkheimer and Adorno, 2000, 5).

Third, it is the final sentence of the quoted passage that is particularly
important in the context of thinking about the objection I put to myself in the
previous section—namely, that language is not the repository of objective
reason that can be mobilized by and for paupers, but the ideological tool of
the princes. The final sentence of the passage suggests that for Horkheimer
(and, by implication, Adorno) language cannot be purely ideological. Indeed,
its ideological use involves a linguistic mistake, contradicting itself in a way
that "is evident from individual linguistic structures themselves."

At this point, I should add a qualification. The way I read this passage—
Horkheimer and Adorno's work as a whole (see Freyenhagen 2013)—is to
understand it as suggesting a research program, and its ultimate vindication
would require not just the abstract general considerations about possibility
advanced here, but the successful completion of this research program in
relation to actual concrete examples of ideological use of language. In particular, the thesis that such use contradicts itself, just as a matter of grammar
(in the Wittgensteinian sense), would have to be carefully demonstrated by
actual studies of such use. A fuller study would have to engage in detail with
material like speeches or newspaper columns (like Adorno did in relation to
fascist propaganda and popular culture). Also, it would be necessary—perhaps partly by drawing again on Wittgensteinian insights—to investigate the
different kinds of linguistic mistakes that are involved in the ideological use
of language.

For now, it is important that insofar as Habermas and others are even
doubting the very *possibility* of having any resources for Critical Theory, if
Horkheimer and Adorno's theory were true, this qualification is not detrimental to the argumentative aim of this chapter. On its own terms, the common
Habermasian complaint against their theory would be answered, if we can
account for this possibility at a general, abstract level.

Let me be clear about what even a full vindication in relation to concrete
examples would *not* establish. Here, it is helpful to consider something
Garver says about his Wittgensteinian perspective: "human activities involve
norms" reflected in language, some of which are arbitrary, but some of which

are "tightly woven into the fabric of our form of life"; and a perspective which recognizes this "therefore contains the seeds of normativity and of a certain sort of transcendence of the merely empirical and merely factual" (Garver 1994, 278). It is crucial that Garver speaks of "*seeds* of normativity." What he calls such seeds, we might call with Horkheimer and Adorno "traces of objective reason." However called, the key point is that the appeal to language (use) does not yield premises that we can deploy (say in normative ethics or political philosophy) to derive conclusions about what ought to be done (say in relation to suicide or the legalization of same-sex marriage). What is generated is just seeds, not—to stay with the metaphor—full-grown trees with which to build an ethical or political system. (Indeed, the metaphor of seeds is, still, too restrictive, as normally seeds can only become one kind of tree, not different kinds of trees or things other than trees. Perhaps, "ingredients" is a better metaphor—these can be used and combined in a greater variety of ways than what seeds can turn into.)

Translated back to the point about subjective reason's eclipse of objective reason, we can say that, in using subjective reason on its own, we are forgetful of the inseparability of language and our form of life—in Wittgensteinian terms, we are separating meaning and use. Keeping the inseparability in view provides us with resources for Critical Theory, but we have to be careful not to overstate what kind of resources this yields. We get access to traces of objective reason, not full-blown normative premises. It is not that we get access to specific content, such that we could just deduce from this inseparability—for example—whether or not same-sex marriage is morally permissible and should be legalized.

Furthermore, the claim is not that language provides "normative foundations" in the sense that Habermas and others have demanded of Horkheimer and Adorno, but the latter reject as an untenable and problematic justificatory project.[13] (As noted above, we are facing claims here that lie, in Wittgenstein's words quoted earlier, "beyond being justified or unjustified"). Rather, mobilizing the inseparability of language and our life form can help uncover ideological distortions and reveal the inhumane social reality for what it is.

In light of this, the puzzling claims Horkheimer makes in the passage quoted above from *Eclipse of Reason* become more intelligible and compelling. Insofar as he (and Adorno) operates with a picture of language as inseparable from the human form of life, we can understand how he would think that its mission is to "mirror the natural tendencies"—specifically the natural tendencies of the human form of life (such as that, to return to an earlier example, we do not all typically have perfect pitch). In using language what we are doing is agreeing "in form of life" (Wittgenstein 2001, § 241), and this is reflected ("mirrored") in that language use. Specifically, as inseparable from the human life form, language contains traces of "the structure of the reality" (Horkheimer 2013, 6) of this life form, and thus, of (at least part of) objective reason. Insofar as our current social arrangement goes against the grain of the human life form, the traces of this life form in language, and thereby language, do reflect what the oppressed long for, but are denied by this social arrangement. This denial might be buried by ideological distortions, but by becoming "more sensitive to the muted testimonies of language and plumb the layers of experience preserved in it," we can uncover these distortions, and, upon eliminating them, let language fulfill "its mission of mirroring the natural tendencies" (Horkheimer 2013, 117 and 127).

Indeed, it also becomes clear why objective reason can be eclipsed, but never extinguished as long as there are human beings.[14] Language can include arbitrary elements, but it cannot completely become unmoored from the human life form—for then it would not be language anymore—and, hence, it includes—and *cannot but* include—a reservoir of objective reason (albeit possibly only in the negative form of the longings of the oppressed and the plight of nature). Just as our natural impulses can be repressed, but not eliminated (Horkheimer 2013, 80 and 124; Adorno 1973, 92; 1998, 175), objective reason embodied in the human life form cannot be eliminated from language, but only covered over;[15] and attentiveness to language itself can help us to uncover it. This means that Habermas' objection fails.

One could doubt that Adorno and Horkheimer could sign up to what I just ascribed to them because of their trenchant criticisms of appeals to the idea of humanity—and thereby presumably the idea of the human life form. However, as I have demonstrated elsewhere (Freyenhagen 2013; 2017a; 2018b), this would be to conclude too quickly, for they actually are Aristotelian in their ethical outlook: they index evaluative terms to the human form of life, with the important twist that they think we can, in our current wrong social world, only know about what inhumanity is and, hence, what is bad, wrong, and false—not yet what it is to live well, rightly and truly as human beings (beyond avoiding the identifiable evils). Their criticisms of appeals to the human life form turn out, on closer inspection, to be criticisms of appeals to a positive notion of it, not a rejection of any appeal to it whatsoever. (Or these criticisms turn out to be rejections of the justificatory project of discursive grounding, something they—and other Aristotelian ethical naturalists as well as Wittgenstein—reject as unnecessary and misleading.)

Let me end with a brief example of how Horkheimer and Adorno tie the idea of the irrationality of the social world dominated by subjective reason and capitalism to that of the lack of humanity. Already in Horkheimer's seminal 1937 text "Traditional and Critical Theory,"[16] we can see a notion of humanity at play (1972). That notion is a normative one—not a descriptive one about what human beings are like here and now:

Critical thought has a concept of humanity as in conflict with itself [. . .] If activity governed by reason is proper to humanity, then existent social practice, which forms the individual's life down to its least details, is inhuman, this inhumanity affects everything that goes on in society. (Horkheimer 1972, 213; translation amended)

Horkheimer clearly affirms both the antecedent and the consequent—reason is proper to humanity, but the existing society is irrational in forming people in such a way as to deny the full exercise of this capacity (and irrational also insofar as, in many cases, it fails to fulfill many other needs). The actually existing human beings do not yet realize their humanity—such realization lies in a possible future of a differently constituted social world.

This approach seems anthropological not just in referring to a future realization of humanity, but also—albeit possibly relatedly—in holding that this potential realization is already inscribed in human beings, even where—like in our current social world—they do not realize their species being. In the "Postscript" to "Traditional and Critical Theory," Horkheimer writes that "[. . .] the thrust towards a rational society, which admittedly seems to exist today only in the realms of fantasy, is really innate in every human being" (1972, 251; translation amended).

It sounds like Adorno and Horkheimer are making transhistorical claims about human nature and reason. The immediate challenge is that such transhistorical claims would seem inconsistent with their insistence on a thoroughly historical approach and perspective found in the very same texts (such as the "Postscript") as well as in other writings by Horkheimer (see, for example, 1985ff, 3, 132) and Adorno.[17] Some of Horkheimer's successors—notably Habermas—have tried to escape this by way of formal anthropology or universal pragmatics, but Horkheimer (and Adorno) would have rejected this as either empty or insufficiently historical (or both). (Indeed, Amy Allen 2016, her recent critique of Habermas' program of universal pragmatics suggests that his program is anchored in the modern subject, and thus anchored historically, after all.[18])

Elsewhere, I have suggested that a way to meet this challenge is to read Horkheimer's (and Adorno's) claims as postulates about human beings derived from the historical analysis of concrete evils. There are no traditional metaphysical claims about timeless essences, but rather ideal-typical constructions that arise in the context of interpreting and criticizing certain phenomena, such as neurosis and anti-semitism (Freyenhagen 2012; 2013; 2017a; 2018b). In a more Wittgensteinian mode, we might say that they arise out of the conspicuous presentation of our language uses and accompanying practices in our specific historical context.[19]

This way of approaching the matter links up well with the thought that language is a reservoir of objective reason. Specifically, the link would be that concrete evils and the memory of resistance against them have left traces of objective reason in language. Critical Theory's role would then be to mobilize these resources by way of reminders—disclosing concrete evils and how they are interconnected and entwined with a social system that cannot but generate them.

It is here where we can also see the link to the idea of social pathology, already briefly mentioned above. It is helpful to distinguish this idea from a closely related one, the idea of social determinants of health. To say that society is pathological is not just to say that it makes individuals ill, but that it is ill itself. By way of example, let us consider briefly the issue of the human-made climate emergency. There are obvious health and disease implications for individuals—existing and future ones—and in this sense the human-made climate emergency is a clear example of how society can make us ill or be otherwise detrimental to individual well-being (i.e., it is a clear example of the social determinants of health). But the human-made climate emergency *also* suggests the thesis that society itself is ill: arguably, the very idea of human society implies the task of sustaining humanity for the future, and, hence, a society that systematically endangers that future is a pathological society.[20] A humanity-destroying society is in a certain sense a contradiction in terms: it does not fulfill its in-built purpose. To claim that is not to deny that a humanity-destroying society might well exist as a matter of fact. Indeed, we might live in such a society—our capitalist economic system looks like it has us heading for disaster, even extinction. But this does not take anything away from the fact that there is something inherently wrong in a humanity-destroying society—wrong according to the very idea of what a society is, which includes centrally the purpose of sustaining humanity into the future. And, crucially for the purposes of this chapter, it does not take anything away from the fact that this wrongness shows up in language.

While Adorno could not have known about our climate emergency, it is striking that he does reflect on the idea of society along the lines just suggested. Two passages are crucial here. First, Adorno notes:

> The preservation of humanity is inexorably inscribed within the *meaning* of rationality: it has its end in a reasonable organization of society, otherwise it would bring its own movement to an authoritarian standstill. Humanity is organized rationally solely to the extent that it preserves its societalized subjects according to their unfettered potentialities. (Adorno 1998, 272–73; my emphasis; see also 1973ff, 20.1, 147–48)

The inseparability of the human life form and language is here expressed in the claim that there is a *telos* in the very "meaning of rationality" which links any "reasonable organization of society" to one that preserves human beings, both in the minimal sense of securing their survival and the more demanding sense of allowing them to live "according to their unfettered potentialities." Societies that do not secure this are pathological—cases of "irrational societies."

In a second passage, the meaning of something—this time society, not rationality—plays again a crucial role: "Society [. . .] 'means': objectively aiming at reproduction of life consonant with the state of its powers. Otherwise, societal arrangement—even societalization itself—in the simplest cognitive sense is absurd" (Adorno et al. 1976, 62; my emphasis).[21] The appeal to meaning seems, here, more qualified by the quotation marks around "means," and yet this appeal is still pivotal to the passage (which suggests the quotation mark are for emphasis—perhaps to remind us of something we sometimes overlook—not for distancing from what is being said). Insofar as language and the human life form are inseparable for Adorno, it is not surprising that he would display such confidence in appealing to meaning. In virtue of this inseparability, there are traces of objective reason in language, in what we mean.

One might object here that, even if, in a sense, sustainability is built into the very meaning of society, it is unclear why this is important for social critique. In reply, it is important, in a nutshell, because how debates are framed matters enormously to what can be achieved within such debates and within politics more generally. If we present sustainability as something that we should actively adopt as a new aim, then this puts the burden of proof on its defenders to justify why this is, indeed, what we should do. In contrast, if we realize that sustainability as an aim is already woven into the fabric of our language—specifically, into the meaning of society, economy, and even rationality—by virtue of its inseparability from the human life form, then the burden of proof shifts. No particular policy will automatically follow as a consequence of the latter way of approaching the debates about sustainability—this would be to mistake the "seeds of normativity" language contains for more than what they are. Still, such an approach will not simply leave things as they are either, but instead reveal a problematic framing of existing debates about sustainability (especially if further elucidated by exposing the concrete ways powerful groups use their influence to introduce and keep this framing in place). It provides a counter to certain ideological distortions, notably those moves in the public discussion of climate change that present sustainability as an option we might pursue or not, as something that has no default primacy but rather requires justification. And it provides a research program: tracing how language in such public discussions of climate change "consistently contradicts itself" when it "serves the status quo" and how "this is evident from individual linguistic structures themselves" (Horkheimer 1985ff, 17; as quoted in Wiggershaus 1994, 505; his translation).

Fabian Freyenhagen

In this way, we can begin to see how the idea of language as a reservoir of objective reason can have a critical purchase. Specifically, Critical Theory's role would consist in disclosing the way our current society runs counter to the life form we agree in by agreeing in the language we use. Crucially, this way of thinking about Critical Theory inscribes a certain kind of (ethical) naturalism into the heart of its social philosophy, according to which (a) evil is indexed to the inhuman; (b) we can (and perhaps should) think of societies that deviate from the meaning of society as pathological; and (c) the ethical (and, with it, social philosophy and critique) is one of the manifest operations of nature among many others.[22]

NOTES

1. Habermas presents Horkheimer and Adorno's views in terms of total vanishing of (non-instrumental) reason also elsewhere (2001, 141; see also 1984, 372 and 377). His reading of their work has been enormously influential, framing how their work is usually perceived (see, for example, Jay [2016]).

2. I remain agnostic here about the exact relationship of the early to the late work by Wittgenstein, steering clear of resolving whether there was essential continuity or an important break.

3. "Letters from the *Deutsch-Französiche Jahrbücher*," MECW 3, 133–45, in Schiller (2018).

4. See Freyenhagen (2018a).

5. On the same page, he also speaks about how the "collective madness [. . .] was already present in *germ* in primitive objectivization, in the first man's calculating contemplation of the world as prey" (Horkheimer 2013, 125; my emphasis).

6. See also his later essay "On the Concept of Reason" [*"Zum Begriff der Vernunft"*] of 1952 (1985ff, 7, 22–35). My focus in this section will be on Horkheimer, but much of what I will say holds also for Adorno. Indeed, Horkheimer includes an acknowledgment to Adorno in *Eclipse of Reason*, saying that it would be difficult to say which thought in this book originated with him and which one with Adorno. In turn, Adorno picks up the distinction between subjective and objective reason, and the theses associated with it, in a number of his works—perhaps most explicitly in his "Introduction to 'The Positivist Dispute in German Sociology'," in which he refers to *Eclipse of Reason* as elaborating the distinction (Adorno et al. 1979, 5n7).

7. To be precise, what I present in the main text is one side of the characterization of objective reason Horkheimer offers—the other side is "the very ability and effort to reflect such objective order" (*Eclipse*, p. 7). Putting the emphasize on the, so to speak, "objective" side of objective reason is, however, apt for our context here (although it could be said that my reflections in this paper are an instance of the other side). Habermas, in his critique of Horkheimer and Adorno, tends to equate objective reason with metaphysical conceptions of it (see 1984, 346 and 383) and thereby neglects the "objective" side I emphasize. Indeed, the ability to form conceptions of objective reason is, actually, part subjective reason, which—as seen in the main text—itself is

defined in terms of the subject's ability and efforts to reflect. Bringing out what is distinctive about objective reason, thus, means foregrounding the "objective" side.

8. I discuss Horkheimer and Adorno's thesis of a pathological civilization in Freyenhagen 2020.

9. See also Adorno 1951, 135 (aphorism 88 in particular).

10. The parallel to Hegel here is not to imply that these negative instantiations follow a path of progress for Adorno and Horkheimer. In my view, they are rather adopting the Benjaminian line that history has been one single catastrophe in the sense that there has been no progress, and that part of the problem has been the idea of progress itself, with which we should break up.

11. In what follows, I rely on Garver (1994), which I have found helpful in thinking about this material. While his interpretation of (later) Wittgenstein is not without critics, I do not rely on any specifically controversial aspects of it.

12. Adorno would call it "interpretation" [*Deutung*].

13. See Freyenhagen 2017b and 2019. Here is the point where I think one needs to push back against the framing of the problem by Habermas (and others). That very framing hides certain alternatives and also problematic assumptions (see also Freyenhagen 2013, especially Introduction and Ch. 7–8).

14. I am not claiming that Horkheimer and Adorno were fully aware of this implication of the picture of language I propose they were operating with. Sometimes their formulations suggest that they allow for the possibility of a total vanishing of objective reason from language (and, indeed, from the world). This is notably the case in Horkheimer's 1941 essay *The End of Reason*, in which Horkheimer speaks of reasons having "ultimately destroyed itself," its "collapse," and its "revealing itself as unreason" (1978, 27 and 36, 46). However, I think that these formulations should either be understood as exaggerations (for the purposes of disclosing certain tendencies) or as a slip.

15. This does not mean that Horkheimer, Adorno, or Wittgenstein are appealing to a notion of communicative action that is (a) separable from strategic action and (b) which by way of some (purportedly) transcendental or quasi-transcendental argument implies normative constraints for all forms of discourse and action. Rather, the move is one of naturalism in the unrestricted sense mentioned earlier, and one that is thoroughly historical (as I go on to elucidate in the main text)—in two words, the move is one of "natural history" in Adorno's sense (see Whyman 2016 for details). Their stance is neither grounded in universal pragmatics nor requires appeal to an ideal speech situation, but it explicates our language use(s) from within our historical practices. In Wittgensteinian terms, as meaning is use, decoding meaning requires that we always start *in medias res*, from within our historical practices of language use.

16. See also Freyenhagen 2012; 2013 (chapter 9, in particular).

17. See, notably, Adorno's statement in a lecture of his: "criticism ensures that what has evolved loses its appearance as mere existence and stands revealed as the product of history. This is essentially the procedure of Marxist critique [. . .] Marxist critique consists in showing that every social and economic factor that appears to be part of nature is in fact something that has evolved historically" (2006, 135–36).

18. Chapter 2 in particular.

19. One issue in the Wittgenstein scholarship is the historical variability of the human form of life. For a Wittgensteinian view of "our life form" as having a "historical structure," see Williams 2005, 36. A related issue is whether there is one human form of life or many. I will not discuss these issues here, but see Garver 1994 for the claim that there is one uniform (albeit internally "complicated") form of life for Wittgenstein, and Cavell (in Mulhall 1996, chapter 1 in particular) for a view that allows there to be different human forms of life. Another issue is whether Wittgenstein's purported quietism fits with early Frankfurt School Critical Theory. Williams' "Left Wittgensteinianism" demonstrates how a Wittgensteinian approach need not imply a politically conservative or quietist perspective (see also Crary 2018; Lovibond 2004 as well as her contribution to this volume).

20. For detailed discussion, see Raatzsch 2012.

21. See also Adorno 1998, 272–73; 1973, 203–204. In one of Adorno's lectures, he explicates: "By calling this society irrational I mean that if the purpose of society as a whole is taken to be the preservation and the unfettering of the people of which it is composed, then the way in which this society continues to be arranged runs counter to its own purpose, its *raison d'être*, its *ratio* [. . .] While the means used by society are rational, this rationality of the means is really [. . .] only a means-end rationality [. . .] one which obtains between the set ends and the means used to achieve them without having any relation to the real end of purpose of society, which is the preservation of the species as a whole in a way conferring fulfillment and happiness" (2000, 133).

22. For critical comments, I thank colleagues and audiences at Essex, Hamburg, Oxford, Luzern, and Sao Paulo. Special thanks are due to Matteo Falomi, Richard Raatzsch, and Dan Watts. I hereby acknowledge material overlap with my "The Linguistic Turn in the Early Frankfurt School: Horkheimer and Adorno," *Journal of the History of Philosophy*, 61.1 (2023) 127–148.

REFERENCES

Adorno, Theodor W. 1951. *Minima Moralia. Reflections from Damaged Life*. Frankfurt a. M.: Suhrkamp.

Adorno, Theodor W. 1973. *Negative Dialectics*, E.B. Ashton (trans.). London: Routledge.

Adorno, Theodor W. 1973ff. *Gesammelte Schriften*, R. Tiedemann (ed.). Frankfurt a. M.: Suhrkamp.

Adorno, Theodor W. 1998. *Critical Models*, H. Pickford (trans.) New York: Columbia University Press.

Adorno, Theodor W. 2000. *Introduction to Sociology*, C. Gödde (ed.), E. Jephcott (trans.). Stanford: Stanford University Press.

Adorno, Theodor W. 2006. *History and Freedom*, R. Tiedemann (ed.), R. Livingstone (trans.). Cambridge: Polity.

Adorno, Theodor W. et al. 1976. *The Positivist Dispute in German Sociology*, G. Adey, and D. Frisby (eds.). New York: Harper & Row.

Allen, Amy. 2016. *The End of Progress*. New York: Columbia University Press.

Crary, Alice. 2018. "Wittgenstein Goes to Frankfurt (and Finds Something Useful to Say)," *Nordic Wittgenstein Review*, 7: 7–41.

Fink, Hans. 2006. "Three Sorts of Naturalism," *European Journal of Philosophy*, 14 (2): 202–21.

Freyenhagen, Fabian. 2012. "Adorno's Critique of Late Capitalism: Negative, Explanatory, and Practical," in *Conceptions of Critique in Modern and Contemporary Philosophy*, R. Sonderegger, and K. de Boer (eds.). Basingstoke: Palgrave Macmillan.

Freyenhagen, Fabian. 2013. *Adorno's Practical Philosophy*. Cambridge: Cambridge University Press.

Freyenhagen, Fabian. 2017a. "A Whole Lot of Misery: Adorno's Negative Aristotelianism—Replies to Allen, Celikates, and O'Connor," *European Journal of Philosophy*, 25: 861–74.

Freyenhagen, Fabian. 2017b. "Was ist orthodoxe Kritischen Theorie?," *Deutsche Zeitschrift für Philosophie*, 65 (3): 456–69.

Freyenhagen, Fabian. 2018a. "Critical Theory and Social Pathology," in *Routledge Companion to the Frankfurt School*, E. Hammer, A. Honneth, and P. Gordon (eds.). London: Routledge.

Freyenhagen, Fabian. 2018b. "Reply to Pickford: On Social Mediation and Its Substrates," *Critique*, available at: https://virtualcritique.wordpress.com/2018/01/12/reply-to-pickford-on-social-mediation-and-its-substrates/.

Freyenhagen, Fabian. 2019. "Dogmatischer Dogmatismusvorwurf: Eine Replik auf Stefan Müller-Doohm und Roman Yos," *Deutsche Zeitschrift für Philosophie*, 67 (1): 42–58.

Freyenhagen, Fabian. 2020. "Adorno (and Horkheimer) on Anti-Semitism," in *A Companion to Adorno*, E. Hammer, P. Gordon, and M. Pensky (eds.). Oxford: Wiley-Blackwell.

Garver, Newton. 1994. *This Complicated Form of Life*. Chicago/LaSello: Open Court.

Habermas, Jürgen. 1984. *The Theory of Communicative Action*, 1, T. McCarthy (trans.). Boston: Beacon Press.

Habermas, Jürgen. 2001. "Conceptions of Modernity: A Look back at Two Traditions," in *The Postnational Constellation*, 130–56. London: Polity.

Horkheimer, Max. 1972. *Critical Theory: Selected Essays*, M. J. O'Connell (trans.). New York: Herder and Herder.

Horkheimer, Max. 1978. "The End of Reason," in *The Essential Frankfurt School Reader*, A. Arato, and E. Gebhardt (eds.), 26–48. New York: Continuum.

Horkheimer, Max. 1985ff. *Gesammelte Schriften*, A. Schmidt, and G. Schmid Noerr (eds.). Frankfurt a. M.: Suhrkamp.

Horkheimer, Max. 2013. *Eclipse of Reason*. London: Bloomsbury.

Horkheimer, Max, and Adorno, Theodor W. 2000. "Towards a New Manifesto?" *New Left Review*, 1 (65): 33–61.

Horkheimer, Max, and Adorno, Theodor W. 2002. *Dialectic of Enlightenment*, E. Jephcott (trans.). Stanford: Stanford University Press.

Jay, Martin. 2016. *Reason after its Eclipse*. Madison: University of Wisconsin Press.

Lovibond, Sabina. 2004. *Ethical Formation*. Cambridge, MA: Harvard University Press.

Mulhall, Stephen (ed.). 1996. *The Cavell Reader*. Oxford: Blackwell.

Raatzsch, Richard. 2012. "On the Notion of Sustainability," *Inquiry*, 55 (4): 361–85.

Schiller, Hans-Ernst. 2018. "Antagonismus. 12 Thesen zur Vernunft und Unvernunftin gesellschaftskritischer Perspektive," in *Der aufrechte Gang im windschiefen Kapitalismus*, R. Dannemann, H. Pickford, and H.-E. Schiller (eds.): 123–39. Wiesbaden: Springer Vorschlag.

Whyman, Tom. 2016. "Understanding Adorno on Natural-History," *International Journal of Philosophical Studies*, 24 (4): 452–472.

Wiggershaus, Rolf. 1994. *The Frankfurt School*. Cambridge: Polity Press.

Williams, Bernard. 2005. *In the Beginning Was the Deed*, G. Hawthorn (ed.). Princeton/Oxford: Princeton University Press.

Winch, Peter. 1972. "Understanding a Primitive Society," in *Ethics and Action*. London: Routledge.

Wittgenstein, Ludwig. 1969. *On Certainty*, G. E. M. Anscombe, and G. H. von Wright (eds.), D. Paul, and G. E. M. Anscombe (trans.) Oxford: Blackwell.

Wittgenstein, Ludwig. 2001. *Philosophical Investigations*, G. E. M. Anscombe (trans.). Oxford: Blackwell.

Index

About the Editors

Martin Hartmann is professor of philosophy at the University of Lucerne. He focuses on political philosophy, social philosophy, the philosophy of trust, Critical Theory, and the philosophy of emotions. He has published books on trust, John Dewey, the philosophy of emotions, and articles on Critical Theory, pragmatism, trust, David Hume, Adam Smith, and the philosophy of emotions. His next book, *The Feeling of Inequality: On Empathy, Empathy Gulfs, and the Political Psychology of Democracy*, is forthcoming.

Arvi Särkelä is postdoctoral researcher at ETH Zürich, Switzerland. He focuses on social philosophy, the philosophy of culture, the philosophy of nature, and the history of philosophy. He has published many articles on Adorno, Dewey, Hegel, Nietzsche, and Wittgenstein. He is the author of the book *Immanente Kritik und soziales Leben: Selbsttransformative Praxis nach Hegel und Dewey* (2018) and coeditor of John Dewey, *Sozialphilosophie* (with Axel Honneth, 2019), *John Dewey and Social Criticism* (with Federica Gregoratto and Just Serrano, *Journal of Speculative Philosophy*, 2017), and *Pathologies of Recognition* (with Arto Laitinen, *Studies in Social and Political Thought*, 2015). His next book is a metaphorology of disclosing critique of society.